Viewing
New Creations
with Anabaptist Eyes

ETHICS OF BIOTECHNOLOGY

*Published in association with
Eastern Mennonite University and the convenors of the EMU-based
conference "Viewing New Creations with Anabaptist Eyes,"
Harrisonburg, Virginia*

Viewing
New Creations
with Anabaptist Eyes

ETHICS OF BIOTECHNOLOGY

Edited by
Roman J. Miller, Beryl H. Brubaker, and James C. Peterson

Foreword by James F. Childress

Publishing House
the new name of Pandora Press U.S.
Telford, Pennsylvania

copublished with
Herald Press
Scottdale, Pennsylvania

Cascadia Publishing House orders, information, reprint permissions:
contact@CascadiaPublishingHouse.com
1-215-723-9125
126 Klingerman Road, Telford PA 18969
www.CascadiaPublishingHouse.com

Library of Congress Cataloguing-in-Publication Data
Viewing new creations with Anabaptist eyes : ethics of biotechnology / ed-
ited by Roman J. Miller, Beryl H. Brubaker, and James C. Peterson.
    p. ; cm.
"Based on the conference, "Ethics of Biotechnology: Viewing New Cre-
ations with Anabaptist Eyes," held in November 2003 at Eastern Mennonite
University"--Pref.
  Includes bibliographical references and index.
  ISBN-13: 978-1-931038-32-4 (trade pbk. : alk. paper)
  ISBN-10: 1-931038-32-5 (trade pbk. : alk. paper)
 1. Genetic engineering--Moral and ethical aspects--Congresses. 2. Biotech-
nology--Moral and ethical aspects--Congresses. 3. Genetic engineering--
Religious aspects--Christianity. 4. Genetic engineering--Moral and ethical
aspects--Christianity. 5. Bioethics--Religious aspects--Christianity--Con-
gresses. 6. Anabaptists--Congresses.
  [DNLM: 1. Genetic Engineering--ethics--Congresses. 2. Biotechnology--
ethics--Congresses. 3. Protestantism--Congresses. WB 60 V671 2005] I.
Miller, Roman J., 1949- II. Brubaker, Beryl H., 1942- III. Peterson, James C.,
1957 Jan. 10. IV. Title.

QH442.V54 2005
174'.96606--dc22

                                                          2005020124

13 12 11 10 09 08 07 06 05   10 9 8 7 6 5 4 3 2 1

For we are God's workmanship,
created in Christ Jesus to do good works, which God
prepared in advance for us to do.
—Ephesians 2:10 (NIV)

Contents

Foreword

I am honored to write this foreword to *Viewing New Creations with Anabaptist Eyes*. Even though I did not participate in the conference that gave birth to this important book, I felt like a participant while reading the remarkable dialogue that occurs—different chapters address each other directly and indirectly and the book incorporates lively discussions involving give-and-take among the speakers as well as with the audience.

Most volumes growing out of conferences are unsatisfactory, not only because the contributions are frequently uneven in quality but also because the chapters generally stand alone with little connection and interaction with each other. While differing in style—from the scientific and academic to the poetic and homiletical—as well as in content and length, the chapters taken together helpfully elucidate the import of fundamental Anabaptist perspectives and practices for an analysis and assessment of biotechnology. The participants in the conference and contributors to this volume generally identify with the Anabaptist tradition, broadly conceived, or are very conversant and sympathetic with that tradition and its theological-ethical perspectives.

A prospective reader might wonder why it is necessary or even helpful to have another conference and another volume on biotechnology. After all, numerous conferences and volumes—both independent and derived from conferences—have addressed ethical concerns about biotechnology. Not all of them have engaged in secular philosophical or cultural analysis—many have been religiously oriented, attending to comparative religious perspectives or focused on the religious-ethical resources within a single tradition. However, the rich Anabaptist tradition has been largely, though not completely, absent from this discourse.

Blame for this absence can probably find several legitimate targets. One source may be the general perception—sometimes consciously or unconsciously abetted by thinkers within or familiar with the Anabaptist tradition—that it is hostile to modernity, taking what sociologists like to call a sectarian stance or affirming what H. Richard Niebuhr described as "Christ against culture."

Now of course, just as culture has several different meanings and embodiments, so does modernity. As many of the Anabaptist perspectives recorded in this book reveal, it is possible to challenge or reject some aspects of modern culture without totally rejecting it, which, in any event, would be virtually impossible. Modern culture includes, *inter alia*, beliefs, values, and technologies. In this volume and elsewhere, Anabaptist thinkers appealing to Jesus often challenge the beliefs, values, and practices of biotechnology. While distinctive in many ways, their challenges frequently echo themes familiar from other forms of discourse as well—for instance, compassion and justice, which appear in other religious and even secular traditions too.

Several writers stress that technology is not neutral: It is not a mere "fact" or a "tool" to which ethical assessment brings "values." Instead, they probe the values that drive biotechnology, which they assess from the standpoint of Anabaptist tradition. Further, biotechnologies are not all alike, and some pose more serious ethical challenges than do others. Most of the biotechnologies examined in these pages involve some risks that merit careful and thoughtful attention, caution, and even precaution. Some, but not all, of those risks even represent threats to fundamental moral perspectives and practices.

While challenging biotechnologies in various ways, many of the critiques do not entail their total rejection but seek, in some measure, their transformation or at least their restricted use, whether for particular purposes or through particular means. A common theme is that the Anabaptist tradition should show the world a better way by serving as a "contrast community" and embodying "dissenting values." The task is to witness to Jesus and to be his disciples in a community and its practices as well as in individual lives and actions.

Not surprisingly, there is considerable ambivalence in these chapters toward public policy as a context for transforming biotechnologies. While a few authors propose ways to shape public policy in light of such concerns as justice, several chapters stress an evangelical approach of conversion while some extend this to reshaping the broader culture. Nevertheless, the primary emphasis remains on what the Christian community should do.

An examination of particular religious traditions reveals variety in judgments about biotechnologies. This volume is no exception.

Even though these chapters were generally written from within and at least about the Anabaptist tradition, they often come to quite different conclusions. One participant remarked that the conference itself displayed as much variety as a secular conference that does not claim to represent a "common community." Several areas of debate mark this volume, just as they mark moral discourse in the society at large, for instance, the moral status of the developing embryo.

Sounding a theme that reverberates through several chapters, Joseph Kotva stresses that the church is the primary locus for equipping us "with the character, convictions, and relationships that enable us to both navigate through and witness to the world—including the world of biotechnology" (261). Through its various beliefs and practices, the church is—in principle if not always in fact—a community of "discernment," characterized also by other worship-generated and sustained virtues, such as reverence and humility.

Even if the conference did not fully become a discerning community—in part because it was a conference that included worship rather than being a worshiping community—it did achieve genuine dialogue and enhanced understanding, perhaps especially of the kinds of questions that need to be addressed within the Anabaptist tradition as its participants seek to analyze and evaluate modern biotechnologies and determine appropriate responses to them. In addition, the conference produced this volume, which itself makes a significant contribution to the larger societal debate about biotechnologies, in part by so clearly displaying "contrast" and "dissenting" values embodied in a particular tradition.

When I write in bioethics or participate in bioethical debates about culture or policy, I tend to use secular, philosophical categories. Nevertheless, from my Quaker background and convictions, I am very attuned to and sympathetic with many of the themes that mark the Anabaptist tradition. I also learned much from this book, and I look forward to using it in the classroom when I seek to elucidate the views of a range of religious traditions toward biotechnologies. Now we finally have a rich resource for examining the implications of the Anabaptist tradition for bioethics, a resource that can be used alongside works from other religious traditions.

—*James F. Childress*
  The John Allen Hollingsworth Professor of Ethics
  Director, Institute for Practical Ethics and Public Life
  University of Virginia

Preface

*I*n the past decade, the ability to manipulate genetic code directly has provided a new and powerful tool with the potential for revolutionary scientific advances. This tool can potentially lead to cures for presently incurable diseases and to a solution for food supply shortages, with numerous other anticipated and unforeseen breakthroughs as well. The technology raises many ethical concerns, however, such as how to value human life. These challenges cannot be solved through science alone.

This publication is based on the conference, "Ethics of Biotechnology: Viewing New Creations with Anabaptist Eyes," held in November 2003 at Eastern Mennonite University. Although many conferences on biotechnology have attempted to provide a secular framework for these issues, no prior major academic conference has presented Anabaptist perspectives as an important way to understand the world and bring helpful ideas to ethical issues generated by genetic biotechnologies.

This book focuses on the power and use of new understandings in genetic biotechnology by featuring current applications in cloning, stem cell research, gene therapies, and the use of genetically modified plants and animals. The book is organized in three sections: (1) genetic modifications, (2) perspectives, and (3) critique and synthesis.

What do we mean by viewing "with Anabaptist eyes"? Many of the contributors to the book came from an Anabaptist faith tradition or have an appreciation for that theological stream. In American contemporary religious life, Christian church denominations such as the Mennonites, Church of the Brethren, and Mennonite Brethren, are part of this faith tradition. While we consider an Anabaptist perspective to be diverse, this perspective is founded on common principles arising from our heritage and faith, and includes these ideals:

- be life-giving, not death-dealing;
- be concerned with both effectiveness and faithfulness;

- be willing and vulnerable to step outside of societal and cultural influences by obediently following Jesus Christ.

We believe that an Anabaptist perspective can provide refreshing insights into biotechnology.

The conference included presentations from diverse viewpoints and disciplines, with researchers studying genetic biotechnology from both agricultural and medical contexts, ethicists, professors, and community members. This array of perspectives from academic and religious communities provided a unique framework for how to approach biotechnology with excitement and caution both now and in the future.

We hope that this book will raise awareness about biotechnology and its potential influence in the larger community, so that an Anabaptist perspective is considered in the applications and issues that will affect our lives and those of future generations.

—*Roman J. Miller, Beryl H. Brubaker, and James C. Peterson, Editors*
   Timothy H. Shenk and Amy K. Stutzman, Assistant Editors

Acknowledgements

*T*his book represents the proceedings of a conference "Ethics of Biotechnology: Viewing New Creations with Anabaptist Eyes," held on the campus of Eastern Mennonite University on November 13-15, 2003.

We thank Kenneth J. Nafziger, Kristin Shenk Zehr, and Nancy Heisey for their efforts in leading meaningful worship times during the conference. We thank Steve Watson and Ray Gingerich for serving as moderators. In addition, we deeply appreciate Marty King, Mark Zollinhofer, Jerry Holsopple, and the communication students for working with audio/video during the conference. The skilled services of Cheryl Doss, who coordinated the conference details, are gratefully acknowledged. We also thank the following groups and individuals who made financial contributions to the conference. Without them, this conference would not have been possible.

Associate Sponsors

Mennonite Mutual Aid, Lilly Endowment, Anabaptist Center for Health Care Ethics, Mennonite Central Committee, Guesthouse Inn.

Benefactor (Gifts of $5,000 and more)

Mennonite Mutual Aid, Merck Company Foundation

Patron (Gifts of $1,000—$4,999)

Carilion Medical Group, Clarence and Helen A. Rutt, Stanley and Susan E. Godshall, Kurtis and Cindy L. Sauder, Richard and Joy D. Hostetter, Daniel B. Suter Endowment for Biology, Elton and Phyllis A. Lehman, Paul and Carol Yoder Jr., Mennonite Nurses Association, Mennonite Medical Association, and Anonymous

Friend (Gifts of $100–$999)

Kathryn Albright, Robert and Nancy L. Martin, Rhoda Nolt, Diana and Allen Berkshire, Joseph and Nancy L. Mast, Joanne and Wayne Speigle, Jairemy and Pam Drooger, Aimee Miller, Ruth and Sanford Stauffer, Daniel and Elizabeth Dunmore, Fae Miller, Bernice Zehr, Bobby and Ruth Glick, Leon and Lynda B. Miller, Mark and Lois Zollinhofer, Alden and Louise Hostetter, Roman and Elva Miller, Anonymous, Elmer and Marianne A. Kennel, Rodney and Miriam Nafziger.

Contributor (Gifts of $10–$99)

Marian and Bruce Bedford, Darin and Ramona Nissley, Kimberly Hook, Delores and Elwood Reid, June and Larry Kuykendall, Kathyrn Suyes, Janell and William Lederman, Fikir Tilahun, Esther and Darrel F. Mast, Linda and Earl Watson, Susan Miller Ronald and Shirley B. Yoder

Supporter

BioLife Plasma Services, Park View Federal Credit Union, James McHone, Antique Jewelry, Park View Mennonite Church, Layman Diener & Borntrager Insurance Agency Inc., Whitesel Brothers Inc., Music Gallery Inc.

Finally, the editors thank Linda Alley and Patience Kamau for their skilled organizational and clerical services, which enabled the publication of this book. We acknowledge with appreciation the work of Michael A. King of Cascadia Publishing House, the publishing company producing this book.

PART ONE

Genetic Modifications

CHAPTER ONE

The New Genetics: Stem Cell Research and Cloning

John D. Gearhart

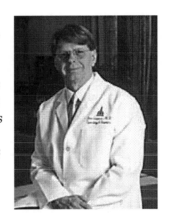

Dr. John D. Gearhart is professor of gynecology and obstetrics, physiology, comparative medicine, biochemistry and molecular biology, and mammalian developmental genetics at Johns Hopkins University. In recent years the major research effort in his laboratory has been the isolation and characterization of human embryonic stem cells. He received his Ph.D. in genetics from Cornell University.

I commend Eastern Mennonite University for hosting a conference on bioethics. There should be many more of them around this country and the world, because society is facing tough decisions. Although we as scientists are here to help members of the general public understand the science and where it is going, we are a part of society and must listen to it.

My task is to talk about current research and also speculate where biotechnology is going. Many people are concerned about the role of biotechnology for the future. Some think biotechnology will go wrong or be abused, but others believe the present can be improved in a safe way with acceptable oversight. I truly believe biotechnology can improve the quality of today's life.

At the nub of the biotechnology controversy is the feeling that science is ignoring and defying God. There is also a feeling that God is permitting us to do these things. As a medical researcher, I am compelled to improve the quality of life with current technologies—while recognizing that they can be abused.

As a result of rapid progress in molecular biology and genetics, scientists are now setting the stage for a real revolution with respect to medicine. Genetics will give humans awesome power. The questions are: "How do we use it? How do we apply it?" Genetics is a double-edged sword. We know that it can do good. We know that each of us is coded. Scientists *will* know who you are; consequently privacy issues are a main concern regarding this technology.

Stem Cell Biology

My research team and I do stem cell biology. We use a special type of cell that comes from early embryonic stages of human development. This cell can do some marvelous things. In cell culture this cell can produce *every* cell type in the human body. We can grow these cells in large numbers. We can transplant them into animal models of various diseases and injuries and demonstrate "proof-of-principle" kinds of experiments. For example, these human cells can function and restore an animal's ability to walk or to produce insulin.

With this potential, stem cell research is going to solve many problems. On the one hand, being a researcher in the field, I am concerned that we may not live up to those expectations. On the other hand, while recognizing that one must be circumspect, I do think humans will benefit from stem cell research. Those opposed to such research are concerned about where the cells come from, who owns them, who owns the technology, and how the benefits of this research will be applied equally among our population. These are all legitimate concerns.

Turning to closer examination of the issues, first I will introduce some basic biology, then I will demonstrate outcomes of our experiments. What are stem cells? Stem cells have two properties that make them very unique. They have a property of self-renewal, which means that in a dish, a single cell will continue to divide and, for example, fill a room with like cells. They also have the ability to form specific cells such as heart muscle, insulin-producing cells, various neurons, and so forth. Some stem cells can produce every cell type that is present in the body. Others can produce only one. For example, there is a certain stem cell in your skin that will produce only a keratinocyte (an outer skin cell).

Where do these cells come from? There are several sources. Some stem cells can be obtained from very early stages of human development. They must be obtained between the time of fertilization of an egg and uterine implantation. This is the stage that is obtained through in vitro fertilization for patients who experience infertility. Another source of stem cells is cadaveric fetal tissue. Fetal tissue has an abundance of stem cells. Only in an early embryo, however, can we find a stem cell that can give rise to every cell type in the body. There is also work in progress on sources of stem cells from the adult.

Figure 1 shows photographs of three embryos in the pre-implantation stage of development. About twenty years ago, it was learned in the mouse that the little center group of cells could be removed from an embryo and cultured in a dish to produce an embryonic stem cell—a cell that will divide indefinitely and that, under appropriate conditions, can form every cell type present in a mouse. James Thompson at the University of Wisconsin in 1998 reported this for human embryos.[1] Subsequently, many laboratories throughout the world have generated cell lines out of human pre-implantation staged embryos for research purposes.

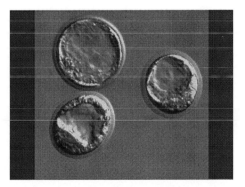

Fig. 1. Photographs of the pre-implantation stage of development

Another source for stem cells is depicted in Figure 2. The identified primordial germ cells will eventually give rise to egg and sperm. If these cells are collected and grown in a laboratory, they will give rise to a cell that is almost identical to the one obtained from the pre-implantation embryo. Figure 3 shows what some of these cells look like. The hundreds of reporters that have come to our laboratory to look at them have been very disappointed. What they expected to see, we could never find out. They are only cells, but their potential mesmerizes the reporters.

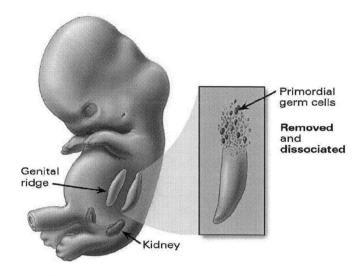

Fig. 2. Germ cells

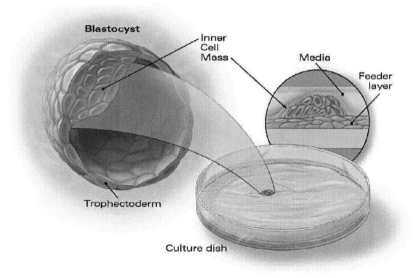

Fig. 3. Stem cells

What do we do with stem cells? How do we take a cell that can form every cell type in the body and instruct it only to form one cell type? We may want liver cells, dopaminergic neurons for Parkinson's patients, or insulin-producing cells. State-of-the-art molecular embryology informs us what genes and growth factors are involved in these processes. Consequently, we manipulate the cells in a dish with these factors and obtain, for example, populations of cells that are eighty-five percent pure heart muscle, skeletal muscle, hair cells of the inner ear, and so forth. It is a difficult task. There are still many cell types that we are struggling to produce in large numbers.

Not only can we grow all the somatic cell types present in the body, but we can also grow eggs and sperm out of these cells. Can we fertilize those eggs with this sperm? Experiments are in progress, which at one point will mean that generating an embryo does not require a parent. We have not yet created an artificial uterus, so the embryo still would need to be placed into a uterus for development to proceed.

I mentioned that our control of these cells in a dish is based upon our knowledge of embryology. The fate of a cell during mammalian development in an embryo is dictated not only by its genetic program but also by the environment in which it is placed. We tried to recapitulate in a laboratory dish the same conditions as in an embryo. We plate these cells out in certain conditions such that eventually we end up with pure cell populations. We then introduce them, as individual populations, into laboratory animals (not humans yet) with different diseases and injuries. Alternatively, we work with biomedical engineers to put the cells together in appropriate combinations to form tissues, blood vessels, and organoids (small pieces of organ). With endocrine glands, for example, one only needs small pieces; these can be grafted into different regions of the body. These grafted pieces function as long as they have access to a blood supply for sensing and distribution. We can also produce cartilage, which can be grafted into animals. We can produce heart muscle in abundance.

How do we know that a cell that we are producing is authentic, equal to the cell that is present normally in the body? We rely on physiology, biochemistry, and many types of markers to assess that cell before attempting to graft it. Grafting is the real test. Will it function? Will it be maintained?

Application of Stem Cells

Figure 4 shows human insulin-producing cells grafted under the kidney capsule of a mouse. These cells are responsive to levels of glucose and can adjust the output of the human insulin appropriately. Normally, blood cells are produced by bone marrow. We have been able to grow all of the components of blood from a dish. Alternate sources of blood cells are desperately needed in many types of treatments.

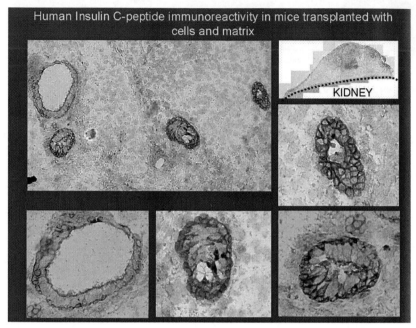

Fig. 4. Human insulin-producing cells
grafted under the kidney capsule of a mouse

One model I worked on dealt with amyotrophic lateral sclerosis (ALS). We destroyed a rat's lower motor neurons, cells responsible for the movement of the hind limbs. Into this paralyzed rat, we grafted human neural cells by infusing them into the spinal cord fluid. The human cells tracked to the site of injury and repopulated the cells within the ventral horns, sending out axons to the muscles in the periphery region. This experiment allowed the rat to almost fully recover and is an example of the ways in which human cells allow recovery in animals. There are examples of stroke animals or animals with cerebral palsy that recover because of human cell grafts into their central nervous system.

Another set of experiments relies on the ability to culture large numbers of dopaminergic neurons, which are the type of cells destroyed in Parkinson's disease. We can grow these cells in abundance from the human stem cells. In the Parkinson diseased animal model, we inject these cultured human dopaminergic neurons into the brain region where the animal's original dopamine neurons were located, but have died. Over time animals injected with such cells recover from the loss of their original dopaminergic neurons. Yet we are having a hard time maintaining these cells longer than three to four months in an animal. The same problem occurs in patients using cells from other sources. This lack is something we must overcome. The experiment is at least a "proof-of-principle" that these cultured cells can be grafted and that animals can recover.

What is the state of this work currently? We at Johns Hopkins School of Medicine are interested in a property called "stemness." In other words the question is this: What happens at the molecular level that gives the cell the capability to specialize into any cell type? We would like to know that because we want to reverse the process. Eventually we want to take any cell from a patient and treat the cell so that it reverts to a stem cell. Then we want to specialize the patient's stem cell into the needed cell type, without the cell being rejected after it is grafted.

We are working on these protocols for producing cell types in abundance. It is crucial to compare and contrast the authenticity among all sources of stem cells, whether they are from the umbilical cord, adults, embryos, or fetuses, to see which work and which do not in cell-based therapies. We are also concerned about possible mutations as the cell divides. We have to monitor the cells constantly to make sure mutation does not occur. It is also important to remember that there is no animal model of any kind that exactly duplicates a human disease process. The Food and Drug Administration (FDA) accepts that, but it is a great concern that we do it right.

What stages of cells do we graft? How do we deliver cells to animals? Safety studies are critical. It is one thing to show that cells work. It is another thing to show that they are safe, particularly when working with rodents and looking at outcomes three to four months in the future. In human patients we want this to be fifteen years.

How do we reach agreement on how much animal work we should do before grafting cells into humans? Will they form tumors? Another major issue is immune response. We can grow cells in the lab, but a patient's body will reject them after grafting if they are someone else's cells. How do we get around this? We are looking at things like tolerance, which is how we trick one's body to think that the cell is part of it. Immunosuppressive drugs are toxic and have many side effects, but the new generation of these drugs will only knock out a specific cell type.

Reproductive and Therapeutic Cloning

The study of stem cells overlaps with cloning. Why is cloning important to us in the field of stem cell biology? Dolly the sheep was the first animal ever produced from the nucleus of an adult cell. Before Dolly many animals were cloned by taking nuclei out of cells, but their nuclei were taken from cells of embryos and fetuses. Since Dolly, there have been hundreds if not thousands of large animals produced via adult-cell reproductive cloning. People are concerned. Will reproductive cloning be tried in humans? Should we be doing it in humans?

I know of no scientist who would approve of such work, because we know that virtually every animal reproductively cloned has genetic problems. Many drop dead as young adults for reasons we do not completely know. Many die in utero; few are born alive, and those that are born alive are abnormal. When the Raelians, for example, promote this experimentation on humans,[2] it is criminal and should not be permitted.

Suppose we *could* make reproductive cloning safe. Should we do it? Some people give compelling reasons why we should be allowed to do it, and they are not just egotistical reasons of trying to produce someone identical to oneself. One must appreciate that a reproductive clone is not identical in every manner to the original source of the cell. If one believes in souls, then every cell in the human body would need to contain part of the soul for a clone is to be absolutely identical. Take identical twins, for example. Every day in this country, thirty clones are born. Identical twins may have similar physical appearance, but they are not identical persons.

The procedure for producing a normal animal through egg and sperm involves fertilization, embryonic development, and implantation. As an alternative, scientists have developed a procedure for producing a cloned mouse. However, many cloned mice are fat; they have heart problems; they drop dead. The bottom of Figure 5 shows that from a cloned embryo, one can generate a stem cell. The intention is not to produce an animal but instead, a stem cell. This type of cloning is called therapeutic cloning.

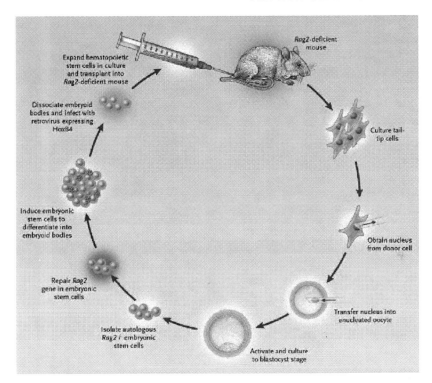

Fig. 5. Procedure for cloning a mouse—therapeutic cloning

Why is therapeutic cloning important to us? As illustrated in Figure 5 with the mouse procedure, we would like to remove an egg's DNA and place a nucleus from a patient into that egg. The nucleus then is reprogrammed to produce a pre-implantation stage embryo from which we can derive stem cells that genetically match the patient's nuclear DNA. We can put derivatives of those cells into the patient and they will not be rejected. Proof-of-principle for this work has been obtained in the mouse. Researchers from MIT experimented on a mouse that had a genetic mutation, rendering it immunocompromised. They extracted tail cells from the mouse, put the nucleus from the tail cell into an enucleated mouse egg, grew an early embryo, and generated stem cells. They then corrected the genetic mutation in the stem cells, grew up blood cells in the lab, and injected them into the mouse, thereby rescuing it.

Many countries are involved in these research areas. Consent forms and ethical considerations take on a cultural flavor regarding what is permitted and what is not. In the experiment in Figure 6, which comes out of China, the investigators—in an attempt to get human stem cells that would be uncontroversial—enucleated a rabbit egg and put a human nucleus in it. With this process they derived an early staged embryo and obtained stem cells that contained human nuclear material. What do you call the interspecies end result? The Chinese investigators called this combination of a human nucleus sitting in a rabbit egg a "unit." It is no doubt an embryo, but what kind of embryo? Would you want to obtain stem cells for your therapy from this type of procedure?

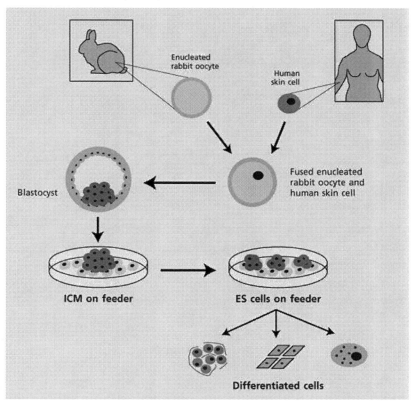

Fig. 6. Chinese experiment with rabbit egg and human nucleus

Future Prospects and Concerns

What does the future hold? I think in the future we will be able to take biopsies from patients, place them in a dish, and treat them to convert them into stem cells. How are we going to do this? The information will come from the study of embryonic stem cells. We will be able to determine the mechanisms of what keeps a cell as a stem cell and what drives that stem cell to specialize into heart muscle, insulin-producing cells, and so forth. "Proof-of-principle" is beginning from experiments in which cell membranes are solubilized and put into extracts and specific growth factors, such that the direction of the cell, which was a differentiated cell, to begin with, is on a different pathway. More recently, a somatic cell of a mouse was put into an amphibian egg, which is very large and has some of the same growth factors as the mouse. In this experiment the amphibian egg will reprogram the mouse nucleus to produce a variety of cell types.

To do such research we must write National Institutes of Health (NIH) grants and talk before Congress. One difficulty is that congressmen tend to have a narrow view of progress and feel that whatever happens must coincide with the tenure of their service. Based on investigators' progress with the human embryonic stem cells to date, I think some of these cell types will be in clinical trials within three to five years.

In the longer term, this work is going to yield a large number of cell lines that can be used clinically, but I think the most significant result of this work will be the information scientists obtain about human cells. What are the mechanisms that make our tissues "us"? With that information, scientists will be able to instruct human cells.

This process gets us into the issue of safety. We currently spend large amounts of money on experiments demonstrating to the Food and Drug Administration (FDA) that when we put 300,000 human cells into a mouse or a monkey, we know where every one of those cells has gone. We are making imagers wealthy with the kinds of technology required to find out where the cells are. The issue here is an important one: will it be safe, or will the cells wander off, form tumors, or specialize in ways that we do not want them to?

To review some of the controversies that have been stirred up: What are the sources of stem cells—embryonic, adult, umbilical cord? How good are the adult sources? Should there be public funding for stem cell research? Should we be able to do cloning? Who owns all these modified cells? How is this work going to be translated into the clinic in an easy and just way, so that everyone has equal access to this technology?

When we consider what the source of stem cells will be, we must ask, "What is an embryo and what is not? Does it matter?" Figure 7 shows the stages to which I will be referring, from unfertilized eggs through the first week of human development. These are the stages that are used to generate stem cells. What value does one put in these structures? When talking about adult sources, one of the frequent arguments is that adult sources will do the job, so why must scientists work on embryonic or fetal sources of stem cells? There certainly are stem cells in adult tissues, but they are very rare, very difficult to grow, and do not have the range of differentiation that the embryonic cells do.

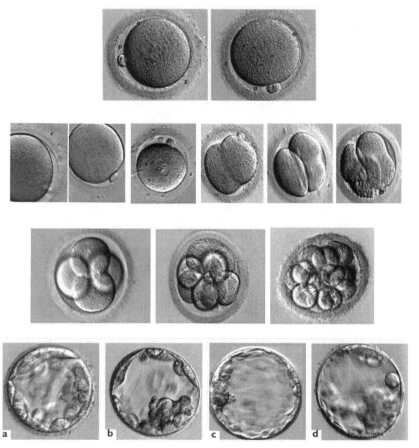

Fig. 7. Stages of embryonic development (fertilization to first week); letters a-d preimplantation blastocyst stages.

The most surprising work to date deals with stem cells from bone marrow. Bone marrow gives rise to blood cells, and we know that bone marrow transplants work. However, bone marrow has the potential to turn into many other cell types as well. Until last year, the adult sources were looking good. For example, one could create a myocardial infarct (heart attack) in an animal. Then when bone marrow cells are injected into that affected animal, the cells track to the site of injury and the heart is improved by a larger output volume. The heart is stronger. It was believed that these cells were forming heart muscle, but this is incorrect. They form blood vessels on the surface of the heart and help restore some of the function of the cells that are dying. That is good, but they are not producing heart muscle cells.

For years, scientists believed that the heart contained no stem cells. We could not find a dividing cell within the heart. Now, excitingly, reports are coming out that demonstrate there are cells within the heart that scientists can recover. The real killer for adult stem cell claims is this: It was recognized that adult stem cells, when placed into various animals, fused with the host's own cells and any marker that was put on the adult stem cell going in was transferred to the host cell. When it was assayed, it was believed to be from the donor, but it turns out it was not. Many examples of adult sources of stem cells introduced into animal models and in humans (e.g. bone marrow transplants) have found the same result. This leads us to conclude that adult sources are not adequate for these procedures.

Clearly the work we are doing with human cells is something that the federal government has taken an active role in with respect to regulating or managing this research. In biomedical research in this country, ninety-five percent of all the federal money that goes into biomedical research comes from the NIH. The importance of federal dollars is enormous. Knowing this, President George W. Bush said that only the specific human cell lines already in place on August 9, 2001 at 9:00 p.m. were eligible for federal funding. This was his first major evening broadcast to the nation. It did open the opportunity for some funding, but only at marginal levels. As an investigator who believes in this work, I see governmental policy and funding as a critical issue.

The United Kingdom, Australia, Japan, China, Singapore, and Sweden are all investing heavily in this work. Not only are they issuing research grants to their investigators, but the commercial part of their governments are doubling and tripling the amount of money sent into those laboratories, because they feel this work is so important and a lot of intellectual property is to be gained. At issue is the destruction of the human embryo balanced against these positive advances. Consequently, investigators certainly are compromised by the United States policy.

Recently, LeRoy Walters and I published two major papers, one on justice,[3] and one on safety.[4] This work came out of an absolutely stellar panel of scientists, ethicists, lawyers, and an international crowd, who said that for the United States to be involved in these advances, we should be developing stem cell banks. We figured out how many cell lines we would need to cover the United States population—Hispanics, Afro-Americans, American Indians, Asian Americans—so that everyone can have access to this technology. We were concerned that the existing lines eligible for federal funding are not safe, and there are various arguments for that.

The take-home point is this: The power humans will soon have will be awesome! We will be able to instruct our cells. I am not talking about genetic enhancement. That is a very different type of manipulation. We can already go on the Internet and get certain types of growth factors, cytokines, and enhance ourselves or our children in many different ways.

We need to begin thinking about who is going to control this. Conferences on bioethics are crucial to begin to talk about these issues. It will take a long time to legislate anything. The science is moving very fast but not out of control. The scientists in the United States (along with many other countries) are bright and industrious. We all have our own ethics and morality, not all of it springing from theology, but we have it nonetheless. What we need is a framework, a backbone, on which to do this kind of work in the United States that will permit it to go forward in a way that is careful and managed.

Notes

1. J. A. Thomson et al., "Embryonic Stem Cell Lines Derived from Human Blastocysts," *Science* 282 (1998):1145-47.

2. http://www.cnn.com/2002/HEALTH/12/27/human.cloning/

3. R. R. Faden et al., "Public Stem Cell Banks: Considerations of Justice in Stem Cell Research and Therapym" *Hastings Cent Rep* 33, no. 6 (Nov.-Dec. 2003): 13-27.

4. L. Dawson et al., "Safety Issues in Cell-Based Intervention Trials," *Fertil Steril* 5 (Nov 2003):1077-85. [Review. Erratum in: *Fertil Steril* 81, no. 1 (Jan. 2004):226.]

CHAPTER TWO

So Who Shall We Be? A Response to John Gearhart

James C. Peterson

Dr. James C. Peterson is the R.A. Hope Professor of Theology and Ethics and a member of the Research Ethics Board at McMaster University, one of Canada's leading research universities. He is an ordained pastor in the Baptist Conventions of Ontario and Quebec, holds a Ph.D. in ethics from the University of Virginia, and has been a research fellow in molecular and clinical genetics at the University of Iowa. His recent publications include Genetic Turning Points: The Ethics of Human Genetic Intervention.

*D*r. Gearhart's presentation exemplified an admirable breadth of concern. As our knowledge increases exponentially, the usual strategy is for each scientist to know more and more about less and less. To make one's work manageable, one focuses on the work on one's own bench. Dr. Gearhart is not only contributing new knowledge to the field. As you have seen, he also takes time to consult with the broader society. He quite rightly calls his coworkers and us to consider not just what is technically possible, but also the formative choices and implications before us.

In this chapter I will highlight three considerations spurred by Dr. Gearhart's presentation. First, ethics is as much about what we should do as it is about what we should not do. I have heard it proposed that if a gathering of geese is a gaggle, of cows a herd, and of lions a pride, maybe we should call a gathering of ethicists "a worry." Ethics discussions often focus on warning of what we should not do, but there is not only a danger in pride. There is also danger in apathy. It is important to raise concerns and limits, but part of Christian ethics is the exhortation to seize opportunities to heal and serve, to love our neighbors (Luke 10:27-28).

The Anabaptist tradition keeps directing our attention to Jesus. Think of how in Matthew chapter 24, Jesus described his future return. That immediately raised a whole series of questions to which he responded in the following chapter. Chapter 25 begins with the story of ten girls who were waiting for a late night wedding party. Some of them did not bring enough batteries so their flashlights were starting to go out. They went to Wal-Mart to buy more batteries and ended up missing the party. Here Jesus reminds us that it might be quite some time before he returns and so we need to be ready to endure. We need to be ready for the long haul. It has already been two thousand years.

That raises the question: "Okay, it might be awhile. We need to carry on. What should we do in the mean time?" The next story in Matthew 25 answers that question. In this story the master gave ten talents (a substantial sum of money) to one servant, five to another, and one to a third. He left for some time. On his return he asked, "What have you done with the resources that I entrusted to you?" The servant with the ten talents had multiplied them for yet another ten, and the master said, "Well done." The master gave the same response to the servant who had multiplied his five talents with another five, but the third servant had simply buried his one talent in the backyard to keep it safe. The master called him a wicked and slothful servant. He could have at least put that resource in the bank to earn interest, but instead he had squandered the opportunity. It might be some time before Jesus returns, but we are to take the resources that we have and use them well, to multiply them, to put them to good use.

What would be a good use of our resources? The answer to this question is the next account in Matthew 25, where Jesus talks about the final day of judgment. When he returns and his angels with him, he will make a great separation between those who are his people from those who are not. His angels will recognize those who are his own by how they have been treating their neighbors. His people are those who have been bringing water to the thirsty, feeding the hungry, visiting those in prison, and healing the sick. These are not actions that get one into God's family, but they are characteristic of one who is in God's family. Some medical technologies can serve our neighbors, such as by delivering them from disease. These technologies are part of our ethical mandate to make a difference, to serve, to help, to love our neighbors.

Second, I have not heard anyone object to using adult tissue stem cells to heal afflictions. The controversy in regard to stem cells arises when they are derived

from the death of embryos. If taking apart an embryo about five days after the sperm first enters the egg is dismembering a fellow human being, it should not be done. We do not take one person apart to save others, even if one person's healthy organs could save the lives of several other people in need of transplants. But if the five-day-old embryo is alive and of a human type but not yet a fellow human being, would it be right to protect tissue in a way that stops research that may eventually save countless lives of people who are suffering from Parkinson's, Alzheimer's, or paralysis? For either reading of the embryo's status, lives are at stake.

Understanding how we should treat embryos is also crucial to how we evaluate prenatal genetic diagnosis and a myriad of other developing and proposed interventions. This question has long been with us and will not be easily dismissed. While there is much else to consider, whether one is dealing with a fellow human being or not is a major consideration.

Third, what we are facing in the use of stem cells and wider biotechnology is not just a series of isolated choices—but the question of who we will become as people. Our genes are formative for our bodies but do not determine them. Identical twins have the same genes but different fingerprints. When one identical twin develops diabetes, the chance that the other twin with the same genes will develop diabetes is higher than the general population, but far from one hundred percent. Although the two have the same genes, one can be afflicted with a disease that never touches the other. Genes are influential for physical form and life, but they do not determine it completely, and physical form is not all there is to being a particular person.

For each of us, however, the physical body is where we make many of the choices in life, and it is in the kind of choices we make that character develops and is revealed. We have the greatest control over what we choose to look at with our eyes, what we touch with our hands, what we say with our mouths, where we go with our feet. Now that we are beginning to make choices about our genes, we have the increasing opportunity to shape and reveal our character by those choices.

What do we value? What should we pursue and how should we pursue it? What is the point of these lives entrusted to us? Some of the most important effects of genetic choices will not be just how they physically shape our bodies and temperaments, but who we become as persons through the choices we make.

CHAPTER THREE

Human Genetic Therapies and Manipulations

Leslie G. Biesecker

Dr. Leslie G. Biesecker works in the genetics research branch of the National Institutes of Health (NIH), where lab research centers on questions pertaining to developmental biology and birth defects. The work in the laboratory includes three main areas: single gene malformation disorders, medical genetics of Anabaptist sects and novel techniques to identify chromosomal aberrations. He received his M.D. from the University of Illinois. While not working in the laboratory, he enjoys taking long-distance bicycle trips with his family.

The task for this chapter is to describe human genetic technologies and manipulations. Genetic technology has found one of its most successful implementations in the field of human genetics. The examples described below are one subset of human genetics—the study and care of children with birth defects. This work is special because it is devoted to some of the most vulnerable humans, children with malformations and mental retardation. Twenty years ago, knowledge of inherited birth defect syndromes was remarkably limited. The tools of molecular genetics research were being developed at that time, and it was clear that these tools had great potential to improve our understanding of these disorders. By improving our knowledge of the disorders, we hope to improve the care of affected children.

Translational Research

The use of basic science research to improve medical care is called translational research, because it translates basic science discoveries into improved care in the clinic. Translational researchers work in both the research laboratory and the clinic studying research patients. The example in this chapter is a translational molecular genetics research project whose purpose is to improve the care of children with birth defects.

In addition to the direct benefit of learning information that improves the diagnosis and care of affected patients, translational research has indirect benefits for general biological knowledge as well. This is a classic medical research paradigm, which is the study of abnormal form and function to understand normal function, such as human fetal development. The hypothesis is that if one discovers mutated genes that cause abnormal development, one can then learn how these genes normally promote healthy development.

At a practical level, translational human genetic research is accomplished by studying a cohort of human subjects with an inherited birth defect to carefully define their phenotype (the clinical manifestations of disease). Then the altered gene that causes that disorder can be isolated and studied. Most diseases are the result of a series of perturbations of normal function, a daisy chain of events that lead from cause to effect. If the scientist can determine the successive biological processes that are abnormal in that patient (Figure 1A), doctors and scientists can devise treatments to ameliorate or correct that disorder (the direct benefit of patient care). The indirect benefit arises because these data also demonstrate that this gene, and the protein it encodes, are necessary for normal development.

Today, much more is known about the form (anatomy) and function (physiology) of the human body than we knew fifty years ago. In the past human disease was studied first by clinical study of patients, followed by research into the abnormal physiologic function, then an understanding of the molecular dysfunction could be learned from the abnormal physiology. This scientific progress works backward, stepwise, from the patient with the disease, through the intermediate steps of pathology, to the root cause of the disorder (Figure 1B).

The most detailed anatomy is the molecular structure of cells. Molecular geneticists study the anatomy of the genome, the DNA, that programs human development. One technique of molecular biology is a set of tools called positional cloning that allow scientists to identify altered genes that cause human disease. This helps other research to understand human molecular form and function. Positional cloning allows scientists to bypass the intermediate step of first having to understand the abnormal physiology to understand the molecular anatomy (Figure 1C).

For many human diseases, we have little or no understanding of the underlying abnormal physiology that causes the disease. It can take years, decades, or longer to dissect the relationship of the phenotype to the abnormal physiology. The tools of molecular biology are nothing more than a shortcut from the disease to understanding the pathophysiology. That shortcut, and the technology of those shortcuts, is the topic of this chapter.

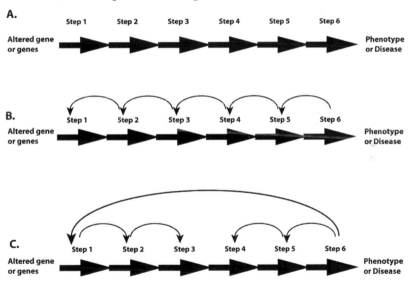

Fig. 1. Pathogenesis. A. Stepwise process in disease development. Successive derangements of normal molecular function lead from the underlying gene abnormality to a disease process. B. Stepwise research to work backwards from the disease to the underlying derangements is time consuming because of the need to work back through many successive steps. C. Human genetics allows skipping directly from the disease to the gene and the steps can be analyzed from both ends, accelerating the entire process.

It should be noted that some diseases are caused by environmental factors, either primarily or entirely. They are an important cause of disease but are not further considered here. Genetics is another important component of many diseases and it causes disease in different ways. For many diseases, the sequence of a single gene in an individual can explain, with a high degree of certainty, the presence or absence of a specific disease. Such disorders are referred to as single gene disorders. Other disorders result from something between single gene disorders and non-genetic disorders that scientists call complex genetic disorders. Complex disorders involve a number of genes, whose alternate forms interact with each other and the environment. The interactions of these alternate forms determine the probability that a person will have a given disease.

McKusick-Kaufman Syndrome

The scientific approach to a single gene disorder can be illustrated by our work in the Amish community in southeastern Pennsylvania. The Amish have a relatively high incidence of a particular birth defect syndrome that includes extra fingers, a uterine malformation, and congenital heart defects. The disorder has variable severity with some patients living long and healthy lives and others dying in infancy or childhood from respiratory or cardiac complications. This disorder, called McKusick-Kaufman syndrome, is named after the doctors who described it nearly forty years ago[1].

McKusick-Kaufman syndrome is categorized as a single gene disorder and is inherited in a simple genetic pattern, which is called autosomal recessive. Geneticists chart family relationships on diagrams called pedigrees (Figure 2). Each parent has two copies of each gene. Each parent is what we call a carrier, so each has one altered form of the gene and one unaltered form of the gene. In autosomal recessive inheritance, the possession of one altered and one unaltered copy of the gene does not cause a disease or disorder, but puts one at risk to have affected children. In this pattern of inheritance each of the children of this couple has a fifty-fifty probability of inheriting either of the altered gene forms from each parent.

The chances of getting an altered or unaltered gene from each of two parents yields four potential outcomes for each pregnancy. The first is that the child inherits unaltered, normal copies of the gene from each parent. The second is that the child inherits an altered copy of the gene from the mother and an unaltered copy from the father.

The third is that the child inherits an altered copy of the gene from the father and an unaltered copy from the mother. The fourth possibility is that the child inherits an altered copy of the gene from both parents (and has no normal copy of the gene). In this pattern of inheritance, the fourth possibility is a child who is affected by the condition, and this pattern of inheritance causes an overall one-in-four chance that each pregnancy will produce an affected offspring.

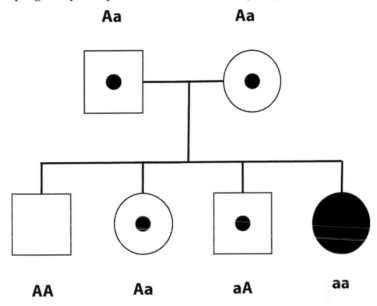

Fig. 2. Simple pedigree. A simple pedigree showing autosomal recessive inheritance. Both parents have one normal copy of the gene ("A") and one altered or abnormal copy of the gene ("a"). Each child inherits one of the two forms of the gene from each parent, leading to four possible combinations. The child who inherits both abnormal copies of the gene ("aa") is affected with the disease.

The probability of two parents being carriers for an altered copy of the same gene is small if one marries a person randomly selected from the population. This is because the carrier rate for common disorders is one out of twenty, lower for less common conditions. However, some cultural groups do not marry people who are randomly selected from the human population but instead marry people who are related to them. This causes their chances of having certain genetic conditions to rise dramatically (note that the overall incidence of disease is not higher, rather some conditions have a higher incidence in these groups and some have a lower incidence). In the Old Order Amish, most people marry another Amish person, and essentially all Amish are descended from a few hundred immigrants in the eighteenth century. Therefore, all Amish are related to each other (consanguineous, or inbred) and they have an increased susceptibility to certain inherited diseases.

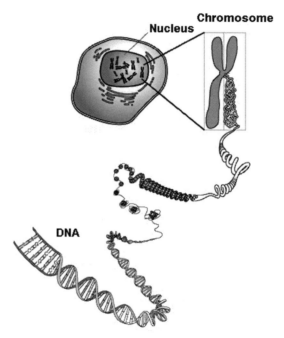

Fig. 3. Cell and genome. The relationship of cells, chromosomes, and DNA. Each cell nucleus contains a complete set of chromosomes, and each chromosome is made up of millions of bases of DNA.

Essentially, no advances were made in our understanding of McKusick-Kaufman syndrome from 1960 to 1997. We did not understand what caused it and could not recognize who was susceptible to effectively treat newborns. One way to approach this problem is to find the gene that is altered in the patients who have that condition. Although the process is conceptually straightforward, it is an intimidating problem. The human genome (or DNA) is made up of three billion nucleotides, or base pairs, the building blocks of DNA that are spread out over twenty-three chromosome pairs which are contained within the nucleus of each cell (Figure 3). It was suspected that McKusick-Kaufman syndrome was caused by an alteration of only *one* of those three billion base pairs. Human molecular genetic tools have been devised to make this search efficient and effective.

This process is called positional cloning, or finding the gene that causes a particular disorder in a human being without knowing the biology of the disease. Scientists know that genes lie on chromosomes and that the twenty-three pairs of chromosome parents each pass down to their children are inherited randomly. Therefore, the genes segregate or sort through families in a random fashion. The research goal is to find a piece of the chromosome that is tracking through the family in the same pattern that the disease is tracking through the family. If this chromosome segment can be identified, the gene for that disease must lie on that chromosome segment. But before one can trace the chromosome segments through the family, the relationship of the families must be accurately characterized.

McKusick-Kaufman syndrome is one disease that is much more common among the Amish than among non-Amish people. Because of this high frequency of disease, my laboratory group sought out members of that community for this research study. It is easier to find the altered genes in affected persons of isolated, consanguineous communities if one knows exactly how each person is related. The Amish of southeastern Pennsylvania (like many Anabaptists) are keenly interested in their genealogy. They record genealogy data in books that are available to the public and can be used to trace lineages back to the likely founder (the term for the ancestor common to all affected families).

To do this, one takes a set of families, all of whom have children with a given genetic condition, and uses the genealogy books to determine how they are related (Figure 4). One can trace back the affected families at the bottom of the picture and try to identify the family's founder, the person who had the original gene alteration. This process is slow and error prone, however, when done by hand. To minimize errors and speed up the process, the genealogy books have been digitized.[2] This allows a computer to analyze sets of families who are affected by certain diseases and, by correcting errors and understanding the relationships between people, find the proper relationships of families to each other. This shortens the time required for such analysis from forty-sixty hours to about half an hour.

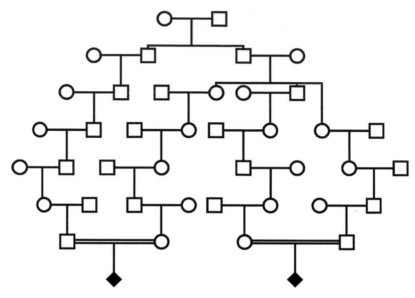

Fig. 4. Consanguineous pedigree. Pedigree showing the relationship of two couples, both of whom had a child with the same rare genetic disorder. The pedigree shows that all four of the parents of the affected children share a common ancestral couple, six generations prior. This figure is reproduced from Agarwala et al.[3]

Once the genetic structure of the families is determined, the next step is to trace the inheritance of the chromosomes in those families. This is done by using genetic markers, identifiable pieces of DNA on the chromosome that can be studied in the laboratory, to see how the chromosomes are segregating through the family. Figure 5 shows an example of what a genetic marker is and how markers are inherited. Genetic markers are normal chromosomal variations that we all have. Markers are not typically in genes, nor are the variants in markers a cause of disease. They are stretches of DNA that commonly have different forms in different people and serve as tags to follow chromosomes. In the example in Figure 5, the marker on a piece of the chromosome is segregating exactly with the disease. Marker form 14 is present in one copy in the father and the mother, and the two affected children have inherited form 14 of the marker from both parents.

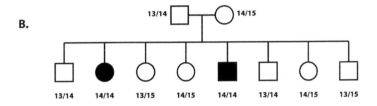

A.

CTTTGACTGAGCCTGCACACACACACACACACACACACACACAATTGCCAGTTGACATAGACAGTGG   13 repeats

CTTTGACTGAGCCTGCACACACACACACACACACACACACACACAATTGCCAGTTGACATAGACAGTGG   14 repeats

CTTTGACTGAGCCTGCACACACACACACACACACACACACACACACAATTGCCAGTTGACATAGACAGTGG   15 repeats

B.

Fig. 5. Genetic markers. Panel A shows a stretch of DNA that includes a short segment where the sequence is a simple repeat, in this case "CA." In this example there are three alternative forms of this stretch of DNA, varying lengths of the repeated DNA. The repetitive DNA is flanked by non-repetitive DNA that is the same in all three alternative forms of the DNA. Panel B shows a family pedigree where two children have a disease inherited in a recessive pattern. Both children with the disease have inherited the 14 repeat DNA from both parents. If the parents were distant cousins, it is possible that they have a common ancestor, from whom they both inherited the 14 repeat DNA. In addition, there is a good chance that the altered gene that causes the disease lies nearby this marker DNA stretch.

If one studies a sufficiently large family where several nearby markers are inherited in the same pattern as the disease within the family, there is a good chance the disease-causing gene is on the chromosome near the position of the markers. We typically do this kind of test with hundreds of markers scattered throughout the genome; usually one or two of them turn out to be close to where the gene lies. We know from the Human Genome Project where particular markers lie on chromosomes, so we can look at the region of a chromosome that has that marker in it and determine the genes that lie in that region (Figure 6A).

The structure of those genes must be determined as genes have segments that are used to make their protein products (exons) and less important DNA between the exons called introns (Figure 6B).

Next, the normal variation in the sequence of each gene among healthy people must be studied. Finally, the entire sequence of the genes in patients with the disease is determined and compared to the sequence among unaffected persons to identify the mutation in the gene that causes the disease (Figure 6C).

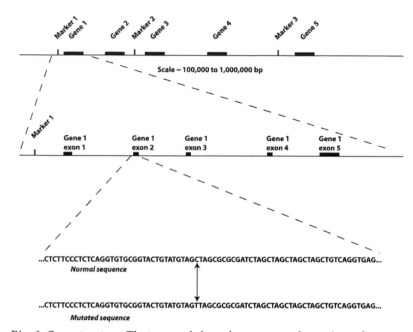

Fig. 6. *Gene structure. The top panel shows how genes and genetic markers are arranged linearly on the DNA strand. In this example there are five genes interspersed among three genetic markers. The middle panel shows a magnified view that demonstrates how the gene lies nearby one of the markers and that the gene is composed of protein encoding segments (exons) that have non-protein coding DNA lying between them. The bottom panel is a further magnified view of one exon of the gene. Here, the two alternative sequences of the gene are shown, with a single nucleotide or base pair that differs when the normal DNA sequence of the gene is compared to that of a person affected by the disease. A single base pair difference in many cases is sufficient to cause a disease.*

This process has been incredibly accelerated by the Human Genome Project. The Human Genome Project is a project to sequence the human genome to learn where all the genes lie. This project has reduced the time required to perform a positional cloning analysis for a human disease from the previous requirement of up to 100 person-years of work to the current requirement of one-half to one person-year. This means discoveries, knowledge, and ultimately treatments will come that much sooner. Figure 7 shows the practical output of the Human Genome Project. These data are freely accessible to the public on multiple websites. Now one can simply click on a gene to determine the location, organization, and sequence of that gene.

In addition, data on the comparative analysis of the human gene to many other species is also presented; this is useful to assess which portions of the gene are likely to vary among healthy persons and which portions of the gene cause disease when altered. Understanding these aspects of a gene now takes five to ten minutes, whereas it would have taken several years of work only five years ago. Once we had localized the gene for McKusick-Kaufman syndrome by using genetic markers, we next had to sequence all of the genes that were in this region. We used DNA sequencers to study the sequence of the patients' DNA and compare that to the normal DNA sequence.

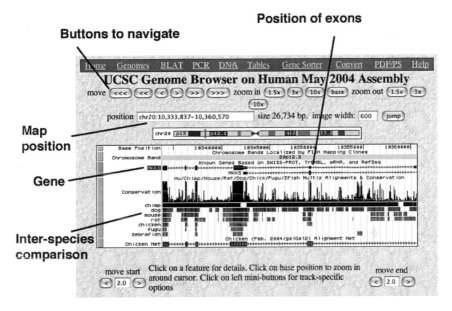

Fig. 7. Genome project. A screen capture of the website of the University of California at Santa Cruz genome browser (www.genome.ucsc.edu). This window shows a view of the MKKS gene. The browser shows the gene structure, position in the genome, and the location of the exons of the gene. They can be navigated using the buttons at the top of the window. An additional powerful feature is that the human gene is compared to that of seven other species. These publicly available data allow a geneticist to acquire data within minutes, whereas only a few years ago it took several years to generate such data.

What we found in McKusick-Kaufman syndrome was an altered gene—we found the exact DNA change among the three billion base pairs of DNA that is different in patients who have this disorder when compared to patients who do not have the disorder.[4] We also learned that the gene that contains the alteration is one that encodes a protein (Figure 8) that was previously not understood to have any role in human health or disease. Surprisingly, it is most similar to a gene in a bacterium that lives in thermal vents on the ocean floor. Therefore, the research has progressed in a few short years from a point where we knew only what the symptoms of the disease were and how it was inherited to the point where we know what gene alteration causes the disease, and we have preliminary data on the kind of gene function that is necessary to normally form these organs.

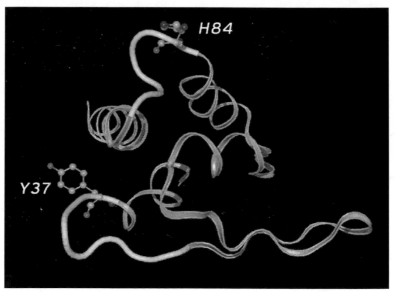

Fig. 8. MKKS protein ribbon. This is a "ribbon" diagram of the protein encoded by the MKKS gene, the gene that when mutated causes the McKusick-Kaufman syndrome. The ribbon is the backbone of the protein, and most of the individual building blocks (amino acids) are not shown. The two amino acid building blocks, shown as Tyrosine 37 (Y37) and Histidine 84 (H84), are mutated in the Amish with McKusick-Kaufman syndrome.

The next step is to ask how such data can be used to improve health. The goal is to use this genetic knowledge to improve the health of those subjects in a way consistent with the cultural values of that community. Not only must the scientific and technical question be addressed, but it has to be done in a way that is consistent with and preserves the values of this community. The Amish highly value medical treatment of newborn infants who have various diseases. The cultural value of caring for children who have serious genetic disorders is as high, if not higher, in this community than it is in the wider population. This group does not value the use of prenatal diagnosis for the purpose of pregnancy termination of affected fetuses, something that might be done outside the Amish community.

One approach that we have developed and hope to test in the future is called a staged screening plan for detecting at-risk pregnancies. Again, the purpose is not to detect pregnancies for the purpose of termination. Instead, the goal is to detect affected pregnancies so that the affected children who are born can have access to optimal medical care to improve their survivability. This is a problem because most Amish babies are delivered in the home by midwives who do not have advanced training or equipment to resuscitate newborns with severe heart or lung disease.

What we propose is a widespread carrier detection program to discover which adults in the population are carriers for this disorder. The people most likely to be carriers are those who are close relatives of affected families. Therefore, we propose to start by screening relatives of those who had an affected child. We will then determine if their spouse is also a carrier of that particular condition. We will offer ultrasound monitoring of the pregnancies to determine which fetuses have the combination of physical anomalies likely to be lethal in the first day of life. If the fetus is affected, the family can be counseled and should consider having the delivery performed in a center that can immediately provide intensive neonatal care and surgical repair. This intervention uses prenatal diagnosis to help generate access to life-saving neonatal care, a highly valued goal in this community.

As noted earlier, a subsidiary goal of this research is to advance basic scientific knowledge of genetic diseases. Science sometimes proceeds in unpredictable ways, both good and bad. In the case of McKusick-Kaufman syndrome, we were pleasantly surprised by other discoveries that followed those described above. Followup research sought to identify non-Amish McKusick-Kaufman syndrome patients to learn more about the function of the disease by studying patients who had other mutations in the gene. It turned out that was impossible to do; we could find no non-Amish children with the disease. We contacted our colleagues who had reported non-Amish patients affected by this condition, and they told us one of three things: either their patient was deceased, they were lost to followup, or their original diagnosis of McKusick-Kaufman syndrome was wrong.

It turned out that as the latter children aged, they developed other medical problems that led the doctors to change their diagnosis. The new diagnosis is called Bardet-Biedl syndrome,[5] which is at least one hundred times more common than McKusick-Kaufman syndrome. Children with Bardet-Biedl syndrome develop blindness caused by retinitis pigmentosa (a degenerative eye disease), severe obesity, diabetes mellitus, and progressive renal disease.

Based on these observations, we predicted that children who have Bardet-Biedl syndrome also might have alterations in the gene that causes McKusick-Kaufman. We tested the prediction in a group of thirty-five patients with Bardet-Biedl syndrome and found that about ten percent of Bardet-Biedl patients have mutations in the same gene as those with McKusick-Kaufman syndrome.[6]

That allowed us to connect two disorders previously thought to be unrelated. We now know that McKusick-Kaufman syndrome in the Amish is a rare subtype or form of the more common disorder Bardet-Biedl syndrome. The two diseases are not the same (McKusick-Kaufman does not cause obesity, blindness, and diabetes). Therefore, our study of a rare disorder in the Amish informed us of a more common disorder in the wider population.

Bardet-Biedl syndrome is a member of a larger class of conditions called degenerative diseases; something about the physiology of these patients causes them to become progressively ill over time. There is no specific treatment for the progressive symptoms of Bardet-Biedl syndrome other than insulin for the diabetes. Knowing the gene that is altered in this disorder, however, may give us a therapeutic target, something we can work on to treat the disorder.

Treatment of Genetic Diseases

There are many approaches to the treatment of genetic disease (Figure 9). The example used here is for diseases that are caused by errors of the breakdown or synthesis of bodily chemicals, but the principles are generally applicable. Unfortunately, one of the more common treatments, which is euphemistically described as supportive, describes non-specific treatment that weakens symptoms but does not cure the disease. Some diseases are caused by the absence of the synthesis of a chemical within the body. For some of these, doctors can package the needed compound in a pill or solution and give it to patients. This is is called product replacement and works extremely well for some diseases. Other diseases are caused by the inability of the body to break down certain chemicals that are toxic to the body, and no medicine can make the body break those chemicals down. The treatment is to reduce the load of those chemicals on the body to ameliorate the disease. One therapeutic approach is to manipulate the diet by altering the amounts of certain proteins or sugars.

For some conditions, specific drugs can correct the abnormality. For others, as for McKusick-Kaufman syndrome, surgery is the treatment of choice. In the case of three or four diseases, doctors can now intravenously inject a form of a missing gene product. This discovery was made possible by two forms of genetic engineering. One advance (as described above) enabled discovering the gene product that is missing in the patients and the second advance made it possible to make that protein for the patients. That protein is made in laboratory bacteria, purified, then infused through the patient's veins.

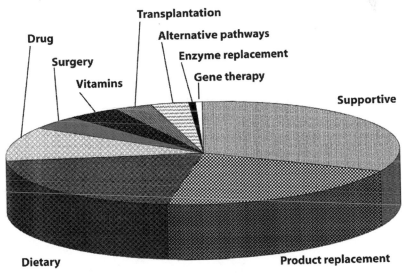

Fig. 9. Treatment of metabolic diseases. Pie chart demonstrating types of treatment that can be used for patients who have disorders of metabolism caused by genetic disease. Note that gene therapy is a very small proportion of the available treatments. Symptomatic care is a common treatment; this is care that helps ameliorate the symptoms of the disease but does not treat or correct the underlying or causative abnormality of the disease. Adapted from: Scriver CR and Treacy EP. Is there "treatment" for genetic disease? Mol Genet Metab 68:93-102.

Out of all the possible treatments for inherited diseases, the small white wedge at the top of the chart in Figure 10 is gene therapy. Although this approach is rarely used, it receives much attention in the media. To use gene therapy, one must meet many difficult criteria. First, one has to know what gene alteration causes the disease, which is the same as the McKusick-Kaufman work described earlier. That gene must be able to be packaged to be small enough to manipulate effectively and efficiently in the laboratory, which often means compressing it into a smaller working copy. The disease itself must create a "substantial burden"—the medical complications for the patient must be severe or fatal. The theoretical risk-benefit ratio of gene therapy must be favorable to the currently available standard treatments to justify its use. There must be good biologic data from the laboratory to suggest that gene therapy would likely correct the defect.

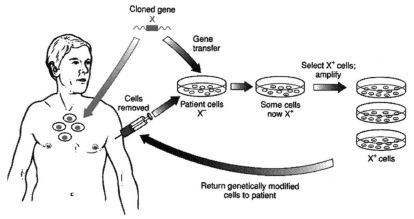

Fig. 10. Gene therapy. Gene therapy is a complex scheme that involves the removal of cells from the patient, manipulation of the genes of those cells to correct the genetic abnormality, selection and expansion of the corrected cells, and the return of those cells to the patient. From: Strachan T and Read AP. Human Molecular Genetics. Third edition, Garland Press, 2003.

The gene then has to be coupled to another set of DNA sequences that will carry the gene into the body and allow it to work; these sequences are called the vector. The vector has to express that gene in the right places at the right times. A target cell that needs the gene product and is likely to correct the disease must be identified. One must have experimental data both from laboratory and animal model work to show that the vector and the target cell work. Then one has to go through an arduous regulatory approval process through institutional review boards and other bodies to gain approval to do this work experimentally.

This process is not only complicated, but scientists have learned that it is high-risk as well. A recent study followed ten patients, all of whom had a disease of immunodeficiency, a disorder that is always lethal in humans. Gene therapy was performed and was successful in eight of those ten patients, essentially curing a previously incurable disease. In two or three of those patients, however, that gene landed in the genome in such a way that it effectively caused them to develop leukemia.[7]

Thankfully, the particular kind of leukemia those children have is a treatable form, and the children are doing well. However, this example underlines the fact that gene therapy is not only expensive and complex but it can have serious side effects. The conclusion is that gene therapy can cure some human diseases that are otherwise incurable. Immunodeficiency disorders are good targets because blood cells are easy to work with, but gene therapy is not without great risk. Gene therapy can cause malignancy, so the disease being treated ought to be as bad or worse than cancer to justify its use. Clearly, there are diseases in relation to which these criteria are readily met. Just as clearly many do not meet the criteria.

A better approach for many diseases is instead to take the defective or absent gene product, figure out what its cell function is, and set up a screening process in the laboratory for drug-like compounds that may correct the cell function deranged by the altered gene. Essentially, this is the use of genetics to speed up the identification of drugs that treat diseases. This approach does not use genes to do gene therapy; instead, it uses gene discoveries as a shortcut to find drugs.

Bardet-Biedl syndrome may be an excellent target for this kind of drug discovery. Bardet-Biedl syndrome causes two kinds of symptoms: birth defects and degenerative disease. It is unlikely that treatments to cure birth defects will be available anytime soon. This is because it is hard and often inappropriate to use fetuses to do the research that would be necessary to develop such treatments. In addition, most birth defects occur during the first few weeks of pregnancy, and it is difficult to imagine how any treatment could be instituted sufficiently rapidly to prevent the malformations from occurring.

However, the degenerative symptoms of Bardet-Biedl syndrome arise slowly after birth and may be good targets for treatment. The eye disease, kidney disease, diabetes, and severe obesity may be targets for drug development that will ameliorate this disorder. This would be an exciting development for thousands of people afflicted by the disease and represents a long and surprising path of discovery from a rare birth defect syndrome in the Amish to a much more common disease that afflicts people throughout the world.

The types of genetic discoveries described here have cured only a few patients with these rare disorders. Yet the stage has been set and the process of discovery markedly accelerated. Our hopes for the future are high, and that is in no small part because of genetic technology.

Despite these exciting advances, however, the field of human genetics troubles many people because it deals with our most individual biomedical attribute, our DNA sequence. Family histories and the inherited genes are major determinants that make persons who they are, in addition to determining which diseases they are likely to develop. The identification of the genes and the diseases is a major challenge and must be done carefully. Gene therapy gives medical researchers the potential to change genes, which is also troubling to some.

Nevertheless, this ability is a wonderful thing if one has an incurable disease. The genetic manipulations described here will revolutionize health care. This is because genetic disease research and gene therapy are extraordinarily powerful ways to understand, treat, and hopefully cure patients who now have incurable diseases. In the future these advances will allow the development of treatment for less severe and more common diseases. Despite troubling aspects of genetics, one can choose to use genetics for useful purposes, while being mindful of the adverse consequences of the misuse of genetics. The goal is for doctors and scientists to harness this tool and improve health care while still preserving the values that we cherish.

The opinions expressed here are that of the author and do not necessarily represent any opinions or policies of the NIH, the Department of Health and Human Services, The Johns Hopkins University or any other institution with which he is affiliated.

Notes

1. V. A. McKusick et al., "Hydrometrocolpos As a Simply Inherited Malformation," *JAMA* 189 (1964): 813-16.

2. R. L. Kaufman, A. F. Hartmann, W. H. McAlister. (1972), "Family Studies in Congenital Heart Disease, II: A Syndrome of Hydrometrocolpos, Postaxial Polydactyly and Congenital Heart Disease," *Birth Defects Original Article Series* (White Plains: March of Dimes), 85-87.

3. R Agarwala, L. G. Biesecker, A. A. Schafferm, "Anabaptist Genealogy Database," *American Journal of Medical Genetics* 121C (2003): 32-37.

4. D. L. Stone et al., "Mutations of a Gene Encoding a Putative Chaperonin Causes McKusick-Kaufman Syndrome," *Nature Genetics* 25 (2000): 79-82.

5. P. Beales et al., "New Criteria for Improved Diagnosis of Bardet-Biedl Syndrome: Results of a Population Survey," *Journal of Medical Genetics* 36 (1999): 437-46.

6. A. M. Slavotinek et al., "Mutations in *MKKS* Cause Bardet-Biedl Syndrome," *Nature Genetics* 26 (2000): 15-16.

7. J. Kaiser, "Gene Therapy: Seeking the Cause of Induced Leukemias in X-SCID Trial," *Science* 299 (2003): 495.

CHAPTER FOUR

Genetically Modified Plants and Organisms

Carole L. Cramer

Dr. Carole L. Cramer was a professor of plant pathology and physiology at Virginia Polytechnic Institute and State University (Virginia Tech) and co-founded CropTech Corporation and Biodefense Technologies, Inc. Currently she is Director of the Biosciences Institute at Arkansas State University in Jonesboro and also serves on the Biotechnology Industry Organization (BIO) subcommittee on plant-based biologics. She was recently appointed to the USDA Advisory Committee on Biotechnology and twenty-first Century Agriculture. Dr. Cramer received her Ph.D. in molecular biology and biochemistry at the University of California, Irvine, in 1982.

*M*y task is to discuss agricultural biotechnology. Most likely, people have been aware of agricultural biotechnology's relationship to genetically modified (GM) foods. GM foods have implications for what people eat everyday, feeding the world globally, and enhancing the overall health and nutrition of our human population. Below I initially discuss those more global areas, then I describe my own research, which is actually an interesting combination of agriculture and medicine.

People may not realize how much GM plants and organisms affect their lives. Many of the products we consume already have significant biotechnology components. One can define agriculture as nothing more than the exploitation of plants and animals for human nutrition and clothing. Scientists have been modifying plants throughout the millennium to enhance their ability to serve as good food or clothing sources. What is different about GM or transgenic crops is the concept that scientists are actually manipulating them directly by insertion of a gene.

Genetically Modified Plants

Scientists define a gene as having two components. They have a promoter, which is the on/off switch or the dimmer switch, and a coding region, which actually provides the information to tell the cell how to make a protein. The gene is DNA, but the gene product is a protein. In most cases scientists study the impact of the protein on a particular phenotype or characteristic of a plant or animal. In this way transgenics involves taking a gene from one organism (which could be an organism completely unrelated to the one receiving the removed gene) and introducing that gene into the actual genetic material of another organism.

Fig. 1. Tobacco seedling with a beta glucuronidase-encoded enzyme

The example shown in Figure 1 is a tobacco seedling with a bacterial gene which encodes the enzyme beta glucuronidase. By introducing that gene with a plant promoter into plants, we at the Fralin Biotechnology Center at Virginia Tech were able to show where that gene was expressed and detect it by giving the plant a chemical.

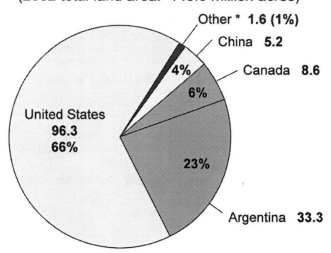

PERCENT OF GLOBAL LAND AREA PLANTED
IN BIOTECHNOLOGY VARIETIES BY COUNTRY
(2002 total land area: 145.0 million acres)

Other * 1.6 (1%)

China 5.2

Canada 8.6

4%

6%

United States
96.3
66%

23%

Argentina 33.3

Fig. 2. Percentage of global land area planted in biotechnology varieties by coun-
try. Acreage in millions. The planting of genetically modified crops in the
following countries totaled one percent of global GM crop production:
South Africa, Australia, Mexico, Romania, Bulgaria, Spain, Germany,
France, Uruguay, Indonesia, India, Columbia and Honduras.
Source: International Service for the Acquisition of Agri-biotech Applications
(ISAAA) Global Review of transgenic crops

Genetic modification for enhancing agricultural outcomes has
greatly increased in recent years. Figure 2 shows the global acreage
of transgenic or genetically engineered crops, which involved about
150 million acres. This may seem a large amount, but it involved a
relatively few number of crops and specific gene alterations. Currently the United States is the greatest producer of transgenic crops,
although both China and South America are expected to exceed that
acreage amount within a decade. Presently corn, soybeans, and cotton are the predominant plants used in this technology. Unless one
lives on a farm and grows all of his own food, I can guarantee that
one has eaten GM foods, because corn meal, corn oil, and soybean
meal are components of almost every processed food one eats.

Genetic modification has primarily targeted insects, disease resistance, and concepts of herbicide resistance so that weed control is
enhanced. All of these events have been targeted to enhance the effi-

ciency of production for the farmer. Through the results of genetic modification, a farmer has the capability to reduce the amount of insecticide usage and to produce a significantly greater yield per acre.

Genetic modification also has key environmental benefits. One type of virus-resistant squash significantly reduces the insecticide needed. In some cases, genetic modification also allows the use of chemicals that are much more environmentally friendly. For example, one can buy Roundup at Wal-Mart. Roundup-ready soybean is a weed-control herbicide used while the crop is growing; otherwise one would have to use multiple herbicides before planting to kill the weeds and then use significantly less effective herbicides while the crop was growing. Roundup is an amino acid analog, so it involves a glitch on amino acids, which are part of every one of a person's proteins. Anything not used goes into the soil, and the microbes use it for nitrogen. Essentially, there are no long-term residues or toxic effects, so Roundup is environmentally friendly, allowing growers to forgo other harmful chemicals currently used. Roundup is integrated fully into the food supply and is a demonstrated safe technology.

Interestingly (and probably problematic for overall acceptance of this technology), the first sets of crops farmers grew using genetic modification had no clear benefit to the consumer. A new technology is a tough sell when that technology does not directly benefit one completely. Enhanced productivity has significant potential where parts of a population are malnutritioned or starving. Therefore, enhanced efficiency of food production has very real global implications.

Fig. 3. Pest and disease-resistant crops

To give two examples, "Bt-corn" involves the introduction of a bacterial gene that is in a microbe, *Bacillus thuringiensis*, which is actually used in organic farming as a spray on the surface of leaves because it contains a toxin. The toxin binds to a specific receptor in the intestines of particular insects. By binding to the receptor, it blocks uptake of certain nutrients, so it is lethal to those insects. The advantage of transgenics, as one can see in Figure 3, is that the bug does its damage inside the corn. One can put a lot of spray on the outside and never get the chemicals inside to destroy a harmful insect. However, if one has a plant that is expressing this toxin through its genes, this is very effective and has a significant impact in reducing pesticide use. Fungi use insects to get inside the plant. One of the biggest problems in corn production is the potential of fungi on the ears that deliver a toxin called aflatoxin. Scientists are finding that the Bt-corn has significantly lower fungal-based toxins because of the way it deals with insects.

The second crop is not one of the most popular ones on the market, but it gave me a perspective for potential risk/benefit analysis of this technology. Figure 3 also shows an example of the yellow, crook-necked squash. When people go into the grocery store, they will only buy the gorgeous, completely yellow, crook-necked squash. They would not buy the virus-infected squash on the far-right side of Figure 3. As the virus propagates, it blocks the progression of those cells to turn nice and yellow. To bring yellow squash to market, most growers will grow three acres to bring one acre to market. The virus that causes the disease is vectored, or carried by insects. To prevent that, for the last two to three weeks before they harvest the growers will add insecticides on a daily basis to control the virus-carrying bugs. The growers are able to have the squash genetically engineered so no insecticides are required. As a result, growers only have to plant one acre to bring one acre to market.

The examples I just gave demonstrate the first generation of applying genetic modification, now widely used in the food supply. However, other international issues involve trade, interactions, and acceptance. The second generation of applications involves a series of changes targeted to consumer benefits. Examples of the second generation include enhanced vitamins. I will also include lettuce, because one researcher at Virginia Tech has engineered the pathway of lettuce by sticking a rat gene in the lettuce that makes vitamin C. Therefore, this lettuce now has between two and five times as much vitamin C on a per leaf basis.

I also include French fries, mainly because I have a thirteen-year-old son who eats many French fries. Both Monsanto and DuPont developed a high-density potato. This potato, with extra amounts of starch, was targeted for French fries and potato chips. When one puts GM potatoes into oil to fry, they absorb only thirty percent of the oil that a regular potato absorbs. Unfortunately, because of the challenges of consumer acceptance, both these companies have dropped this project, so this will never come to market in the current consumer arena. McDonalds, the biggest French fry supplier in the world, has said they will offer no transgenic foods.

Golden rice is probably the best example of where the second generation really targets nutritional aspects. It addresses deficiencies in vitamin A and iron use. These two deficiencies are significant health problems in areas where rice is the major staple. Scientists took three plant genes from daffodils and one bacterial gene, introduced them into rice, and recreated the pathway for making carotenoids. Carotenoids are not only products of the carotinoid pathway but are also pro-vitamin A. If we can produce the carotenoids in golden rice, it has the ability to make pro-vitamin A. Once people ingest it, they make vitamin A from pro-vitamin A.

The second objective was to target iron deficiency. Scientists took three different genes: *ferritin*, which grasps the iron; *phytase*, which is an enzyme that breaks the molecule to which iron binds so it is released and useful; and *metallothionein*, which takes the iron and transports it across one's gastrointestinal tract so the body can use it. Through genetic modification, scientists are able to enhance the iron availability in golden rice by ten-fold. Iron is a huge cause of anemia, which is not always lethal but compromises people's ability to work and participate in life to their full potential.

These examples have significant global implications if scientists can bring them to fruition. These traits are now being crossed into the major rice strains used in Malaysia, the Philippines, and parts of China and India. There is reluctance to eat yellow rice, because many of these cultures have shown that the richest people get the whitest rice. Thus cultural implications are present.

Non-Traditional Products
from Genetically Modified Plants

The third generation of applications uses biotechnology for agricultural outputs that are completely non-traditional. These include using plants to produce vaccines, pharmaceutical proteins, industrial enzymes, and compounds not traditionally linked to agriculture. I will use two examples from my own research. One is the bioproduction of a human therapeutic protein made in transgenic tobacco. The second is the use of plants to produce vaccines.

I chose to become a scientist during the heat of the environmental era in the 1970s. When I saw the genetic modification technology emerge, I realized that there was huge potential to enhance the ability of agriculture in the production of the food supply to make it sustainable and more compatible with the environment. As I developed expertise in this area, I saw the greater potential to tackle some of the real issues and limitations in human health and medicine, which shifted my focus. I am also based in Virginia, where until recently tobacco was the largest cash crop in the state. If we at the Fralin Center can come up with a new high-value, health-positive use of tobacco that allows growers to move economically from traditional uses into those that support human health, we will have achieved a worthy goal.

One potential biotechnology holds is use of information developed through the human genome project to understand and identify disease genes, translating that information directly into producing a product to address diseases. A challenge of biotechnology is that humans are complex organisms, and many human proteins are equally complex. One cannot make a protein in a test tube, or at least not at large scale. Thus one needs a biological system to make proteins, which traditionally can be made in bacteria. Insulin is a bacterially produced for diabetics, but many of these more complex proteins and the next generation of these molecular medicines are or will be made in mammalian cell cultures in biofermenters.

Scientists call these biofermenters "Great Big Round Things" (GBRTs). There are issues with GBRTs. For instance, it is quite expensive to build the facilities and run them. However, an animal cell culture with Chinese hamster ovary (CHO) cell, an immortalized line developed a long time ago, is a very effective, easy-to-grow cell line. Since CHOs are mammalian cell lines, there may be issues of whether or not viruses or prions like mad cow disease can be propagated through them. Many steps are built into these processes to ensure that there is no contamination, which adds to the cost as well. At the Fralin Center we believe transgenic plants have a potential to deal with some of these issues. Essentially, think of what one pays for a head of lettuce, and imagine that as the cost for which one is producing biomass. It is quite cost-effective.

This technology has definite limitations. For example, if one needs a large amount of something to tackle a problem on a global scale, one cannot grow enough. Finally, there are issues of fidelity, which means that with every recombinant system, one needs to ensure that the finished product is effective and similar to what the human body produces.

Plants are sufficiently different from humans and animals in that they cannot host the disease agents about which people worry. Surprisingly, one can give tobacco a human gene, and the tobacco will make that protein. However, the tobacco will not just make it; it will actually assemble it by putting subunits together, putting sugars on, shaping it, and adding the right amount of bonds. It is surprising how perfectly tobacco can make some proteins, with a few exceptions. Tobacco is the easiest crop to genetically engineer. Tobacco, a tremendous biomass producer, is a big six-by-four-foot plant. At the Fralin Center, we grow it to about three feet at very high density. We mow it, harvest the leaves, and remove its proteins. The tobacco plant grows back, and we harvest it again. Using this system, we harvest kilograms of human protein from tobacco on a per-acre basis.

Tobacco is also a prolific seed producer, which means that scientists can start with one genetic engineered plant and propagate to a very large scale quite quickly. Tobacco is a non-food plant, so using this system, scientists never have to worry about whether pollen could escape and move into the food supply. In Virginia, the seeds used to grow tobacco are produced in a greenhouse in the Midwest. Finally, there is public support for finding new, high-value, health-positive uses for tobacco.

Scientists also have instituted some interesting molecular strategies. They have developed an expression system called MeGA-PHarM™ (Mechanical Gene Activation). At the Fralin Center, we use a wound promoter; wounding the plant activates the gene. PHarM stands for Post-Harvest Manufacture, so one can grow the transgenic plant that now has a human gene using this mega promoter. One then harvests the leaves, brings them back, and puts them through the equivalent of a coleslaw maker. After slicing the tobacco in the machine, one leaves it alone for twenty-four hours. Over those hours, every cell that received the wound makes the transgenic product. Then the transgenic product, a protein, can be extracted.

This technology has some interesting advantages from the pharmaceutical point of view. Every protein harvested using the MeGA-PHarM™ system has been made within the last twenty-four hours, so it is all very fresh. It is not going to start decaying. This gives one complete control of the protein's expression. One does not have to worry that the protein products are going to be at high levels in the field. The technology allows protein manufacturing at levels that might be detrimental to growth by separating biomass production from protein production.

The first protein I tried to produce in tobacco was an enzyme called glucocerebrosidase, a therapeutic replacement for people with a genetic defect called Gaucher Disease. This is a single-gene defect for an enzyme that functions to break down products in the cells. In every human cell, there is a lysosome, the recycling bin of the cell. The lysosome takes big macromolecules, breaks them up, and sends them back out to be used as building blocks. If the cell lacks enzymes to do this, the body has no way to get rid of the macromolecules.

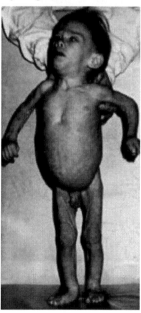

Fig. 4. Four-month-old child with characteristic gaucher disease symptoms.
Figs. 4 and 5 provided to the author by Gregory A. Grabowski, M.D. (Director of Human Genetics, Children's Hospital Medical Center, Cincinnati, Oh., as part of a Gaucher "Lecture."). From Verderese CO, et al. Gaucher's disease: A Pilot Study of the Symptomatic Responsed to Enzyme Replacement Therapy. *J. Neuroscience Nursing*, 1993. 25(5): 296-301.

Figure 4 shows a child who, without treatment, would probably be dead by six months of age. He is probably four months old in the picture, and because he cannot get rid of a single lipid that is commonly made and has to be broken down, it is building up to toxic levels in his liver and will eventually mineralize his bones.

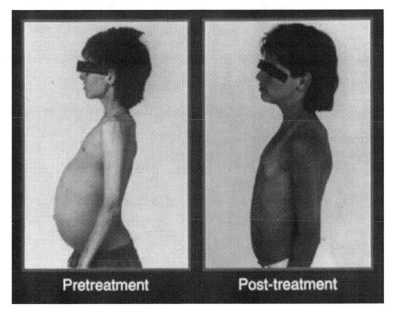

Fig. 5. Fourteen-year-old child at pre- and post-treatment stages

This was the first prototype for a demonstration of replacement therapeutics as an effective therapy. Figure 5 shows a girl who was eleven in the pre-treatment picture and who had the juvenile form of Gaucher's Disease. At the Fralin Center, we have a Gaucher patient who visits us from Illinois. By the time he was four, before he went on a drug, he had already had forty bone fractures. He was not allowed to go to school or play with his brother, because if he stubbed his toe it would break in two places. In the post-treatment picture, the girl has been on the treatment for thirteen months. For treatment, one receives the human protein intravenously every two weeks, because the protein does not last long. However, it reverses the symptoms of the disease very effectively. When we started this therapy, this was the most expensive drug in the world. Currently, the Cincinnati patient's average cost for the drug is $210,000 a year. Part of the reason is that it is difficult to make the drug.

The first glucocerebrosidase was marketed under the name Ceredase and was actually purified from human placenta. For a time, forty percent of the placentas in France and twenty-five percent of those collected from hospitals in the United States were used to try to collect this protein. Sometimes it would take up to 2,000 placentas to get a single dose of Ceredase. Genzyme, the company that has marketed this drug, recognized the limitation of pulling the protein out of placenta and established a CHO-based system. Doing so has dealt with safety and supply issues but has not lowered the cost.

At Croptech Corporation we introduced this gene in tobacco and found that we could get one tobacco plant to yield a single dose of enzyme. To do this, we take the wound-inducible promoter and fuse it to the human coding sequence for glucocerebrosidase, making a transgenic tobacco. This is interesting when thinking about human cells, stem cells, and totipotency, because everything hard to do with animals is easy to do in many plants.

Literally, we start the process with our "high-tech piece of equipment," otherwise known as a hole-puncher! We take a piece of leaf and create a wound site. We use the bacterial vector system, a bacterium called *Agrobacterium tumefaciens* that normally interacts with the plant. When the bacterium recognizes a wounded host plant cell, the bacterium copies a piece of its DNA, covers the DNA with protein, and ships it into the plant cell. We take the tobacco disc and soak it on Agrobacterium that has been engineered to have a little vector with a human gene. We perform a vacuum infiltration and let it sit together for twenty-four hours. We put it on selective media, which selects for plants with Agrobacterium. The antibiotic kills Agrobacterium and tobacco cells unless they have a piece of DNA that we use as a marker next to our human gene.

The tobacco leaf cell has the potential to dedifferentiate and then create an entire new plant from a single cell. People use this technology all the time with houseplants. At the Fralin Center, we cut the tobacco stem with leaves off, stick it in rooting media, and in a week get a nice flush of roots. With tobacco, we can go from a new piece of DNA to plants in a greenhouse in about eight to ten weeks.

We produced tobacco plants that were carrying the gene for glucocerebrosidase, which we call hGC. We could show that the protein was actually synthesized and accumulated in response to the wound that turned on our promoter. We could also show that it was enzymatically active. Glucocerebrosidase chops a sugar molecule off a complex substrate, so we could show that it functioned as a glucosidase. We could purify it and show that if it looks like a duck it quacks like a duck, so it could function on the human substrate. One could employ the exact same protocols used to pull it out of human placenta to pull it out of tobacco, so it behaved more or less identically.

In our best plant, it was the second most abundant protein in the entire tobacco cell.

However, this has not gone into patients yet. Most complex proteins have many more modifications that occur, and in the case of glucocerebrosidase, a number of sugars need to be placed on it for it to be functional. Because we had enzyme activity, we knew the sugars were placed in the right place. The tobacco read those clues and put on sugars. The problem is that a very specific terminal sugar needs to be on that molecule before it will be taken up correctly in the patient. However, we now have a tobacco strain that will be able to produce the appropriate sugar. Our next step will be to take the sugar-modified tobacco strain, cross it with our glucocerebrosidase strain to see if we can create a molecule appropriate for human trials.

We demonstrated that tobacco could make it in fully active form. We also showed that we can get very high levels of production, but we still need to deal with the glycan before we can see whether it will be effective with patients. It is clear that if one is working with 2,000 placentas versus one tobacco plant, the cost of materials will decrease significantly.

The last area to discuss concerns work the Fralin Center has been doing in collaboration with others to develop tobacco as a "mean, green, vaccine-making machine." Vaccines have been incredibly effective in a number of diseases. They are used as a preventative measure. Vaccinations have helped eliminate polio from much of the world. They also have eliminated smallpox and reduced the amount of mortalities and sickness from the flu. Vaccines have truly revolutionized the approach to infectious disease.

The problem is that there are still more than four million children who die every year of diseases for which there are effective vaccines. They die, of course, because bringing those vaccines to that population is currently too expensive. The other reason we will never have a success like smallpox of eliminating a disease using traditional technology is because the world population now exceeds six billion. Distributing these technologies on such a wide scale becomes a significantly larger burden. The cost of vaccinations includes the production of the vaccine and the cost of needles. With diseases such as AIDS and hepatitis, one must ensure that the needle used for the vaccine is sterile for each patient. The cost for vaccination also includes refrigeration for the vaccine and time spent training personnel to administer the vaccine. Society cannot afford to completely vaccinate the population if one is looking at the major killers of children.

Two major categories of infectious killers are acute respiratory disease and digestive tract diseases. I will discuss mucosal vaccines that relate to these infectious diseases. An individual makes antibodies in two different areas. A person produces antibodies that circulate in the blood. A person also makes antibodies at mucosal surfaces. These are the same surfaces where one is most susceptible to infection, including the respiratory tract, digestive tract, and reproductive tract. If scientists can find more effective ways to get vaccines to these areas, it will be a critical step toward tackling the globally infectious diseases.

As a reminder, when a person receives a vaccination, that individual is exposed to either an attenuated or a killed pathogen, training the body how to recognize that pathogen. The body then sends antibodies to prevent the pathogen from getting access to its cells. If the pathogen enters cells, the body sends cells and antibodies that will actually kill those cells that have the pathogen. The body has excellent defenses. In a good vaccine, what one would like to do is have surveillance antibodies in one's blood and one's mucosal surfaces. One also wants immune memory.

Traditionally, vaccines have dealt with viruses. The most common type of vaccine involves a killed or weakened virus, which has implications with respect to potential safety, especially in immune-compromised patients. However, viruses are big, and one's body is trained to keep surveillance up for big molecules like bacteria and viruses. Recombinant DNA allows scientists to use only the protein as a way to train the body, relieving issues such as growing too much of one virus or having potential side effects because one is bringing toxins and other components into the body. However, these recombinant proteins are small, and the body is not that activated to look for them, so they are usually bad immunogens.

At the Fralin Center, we have been looking for ways that we can use our plant biotechnology to target the development of subunit mucosal vaccines, which would not be injected into the body. We are researching the potential of whether a person could be vaccinated by a nose spray. We also are researching whether one could have oral or even dermal vaccinations. Dermal vaccinations would involve a Band-Aid-like patch that one would put on an arm or the inside of the cheek as a way to deliver antigens and provide protection. The advantage to mucosal vaccinations is that they are considered safer than traditional vaccines. If one vaccinated a mucosal surface, he gets much stronger mucosal protection. However, one needs an adjuvant, which is a compound or a protein that notifies one's immune system of the protein.

Presently, there are no protein adjuvants approved for human use. Therefore, this is a real need as far as the ability to take this technology to the developing world. At the Fralin Center, we have been looking at whether plants could be an interesting model to develop edible vaccines. As I have learned more immunology, I am less excited about the oral approach and have become more dedicated to trying transdermal or nasal vaccines. Some researchers have made transgenic potatoes, fed them to mice, and demonstrated that they could get a good mucosal response. The antigens also showed that they would protect the mouse from the pathogen's toxin, and in some cases, the antigens also demonstrated immune memory. However, it was hard to get enough because the potatoes did not have an adjuvant, so in some cases with the first generation of transgenic potato, the mouse had to eat five times its body weight in raw potato to be vaccinated. Hopefully, if one used adjuvants to enhance that ability, this technology could be developed.

In recent years, I have participated in a National Institutes of Health project that involved collaboration between the University of Virginia, Virginia Tech, and TECHLAB, a company in Blacksburg, Virginia. Our main job has been to develop a mucosal vaccine for the tropical disease amebiasis, or amoebic dysentery. This disease is caused by protozoa, so it is very challenging. One cannot simply grow it up and inject it, because the protozoon is such a complex organism. Amoebic dysentery is a water-borne disease, so it occurs in areas with poor sanitation. The disease causes chronic diarrhea. The disease can cause the protozoon to leave the digestive tract and end up in the liver, creating lethal abscesses. Presently, 40,000,000 to 50,000,000 cases of the disease occur worldwide, causing more than 100,000 deaths a year.

Amoebic dysentery begins when the amoeba is ingested. The amoeba travels in the environment in a cyst. When the cyst gets into one's stomach, which has a low pH, the amoeba starts emerging from its cyst and dividing. Once it gets into the large intestine, the amoeba has proteins that bind it to the epithelial cells. An amoeba causes extreme inflammation in the intestines. In response, the body brings white blood cells to fight the amoeba. However, the amoeba feeds on red and white blood cells. It can occasionally eat its way through the intestines, eventually ending up in the brain, liver, or lungs and causing extremely severe diseases.

As mentioned before, the project was a collaboration. Bill Petri is the program director and has been involved in Bangladesh in the epidemiology of amoebic dysentery for many years. TECHLAB is into diagnostics, so they have been identifying the proteins of the amoeba that would be the best protective antigens in order for us to make a vaccine. My job was to identify a mucosal adjuvant as well as to see if we could use plants to produce these vaccines in a cost-effective way.

Meanwhile Bill Petri works with Rashidul Haque in Dhaka, Bangladesh, in what was a refugee camp with incredibly high incidences of these diseases. Petri and Haque established a health clinic and have a relationship with 235 children. Every time children get sick they can go to the clinic for free health care. They not only are diagnosed but also give fecal samples and blood samples, so Petri and Haque can establish why the children are really getting sick. They have found that as the children become more resistant to dysentery, the antibodies in their blood do not seem to have any correlation with protection. If, however, they take stool samples and find mucosal antibodies, the children are protected. Thus the team realized that we needed a way to get mucosal vaccines specifically for this disease.

My job was to find ways to make vaccines and to enhance immunogenicity. An adjuvant triggers immunogenicity, and the gold standard when we do mouse trials is cholera toxin, which is very effective but can never be used in humans. The same amount of cholera toxin I use in a mouse would actually cause severe diarrhea in a human, so we looked at the concept that plant lectins may be effective adjuvants. A lectin is a protein that binds to a sugar. A number of plant lectins have been effective at binding to the sugar on mammalian cell surfaces, especially those involved in mucosal systems.

The lectin that we targeted was ricin. Ricin is among the nastiest toxins around. It is made by a castor bean plant and is at very high levels in the castor bean. Ricin is a defense mechanism for the bean; it is a ribosome-inactivating factor; when that toxin enters an animal cell, it destroys the ribosomes, which are the machinery that makes proteins. Ricin is a nasty toxin because it also has the B-subunit. The B-subunit takes the toxin and drags it into mammalian cells so that it can be dumped where the ribosomes are located. Our team knew that the molecule is very good at getting into human cells. If one inhales ricin, it can be lethal; if one rubs it on skin, it can be lethal; if one ingests it, it can be lethal. However, we get rid of subunit-A, through recombinant DNA, and only use the B-subunit. The B-subunit itself has no toxicity; it is only a carrier.

Our team thinks that ricin is particularly interesting because of the types of cells it likes to target. The concept is that one actually makes a fusion protein by fusing the two genes where one puts the ricin B toxin or RTB. One fuses the genes with a vaccine antigen, and the B toxin will then take it and deliver it to the key cells. Those cells in the intestine or nasal passages sample and present to the immune system. Because ricin has high affinity for both epithelial cells, specifically these cells that are called M cells—cells that take molecules from the intestine and present them to all of the antibody-making cells—they are important immune modulators. They also have ways to take proteins into the dendritic cells. These cells are the mobile cells of the immune system, so the dendritic cells will take the protein from the nose, for example, and take it to the lymph nodes. In this way, it activates the whole body so that if one vaccinates at the nose, one actually receives antibodies in the intestine.

To test this, we took the green fluorescent protein (GFP) from jellyfish, because it is a very nice model, and we fused it to ricin B. We took a plant viral promoter and a small piece of potato gene that would direct our protein. We also took the ricin B gene and a jellyfish gene and put them in bacteria. We introduced them into tobacco, purified the protein, and stuck it in mice to test for vaccines in humans. So, ricin B:GFP was introduced into transgenic tobacco. We can also do hairy root cultures with tobacco. We introduce Agrobacterium rhizogenes into the midrib of the transgenic tobacco plant that expresses this vaccine. By doing this, we can produce roots, and we take those roots' tips and put them into liquid culture. After this process, they express GFP. Through these procedures, we produce a vaccine, which is ricin B fused to GFP. We nasally apply the vaccine into mice. We then collect blood, which will contain serum antibodies. We also collect fecal pellets from the mice to determine whether they have activated an immune response against GFP.

The different agents have varying degrees of effectiveness. GFP alone is a lousy immunogen; it only produces about ten antibodies in a microliter of blood. Cholera toxin in two different concentrations produces more than 100,000 antibody molecules. Tobacco extract alone from a none-transgenic plant does not help, but if we add ricin B and GFP, it is very effective. When we look at the fecal pellets and extract the protein, we find that the tobacco, ricin B, and GFP together work as well as cholera toxin for inducing immunity.

How far have we progressed? We have reached an exciting point, because we have adjuvancy in mice equivalent to mucosal adjuvantcy, triggered by the "standard," cholera toxin. Ricin B appears to be very effective, yet there are no toxicity issues. Presently, we have transgenic plants that are fusing ricin B with a protective antigen from the surface of the amoeba. We are purifying this protein and characterizing it, but we hope to initiate mouse trials sometime soon so we can show whether the tobacco and ricin B functions as a protective agent.

Will vaccination be as simple as eating a banana? The idea has been pushed by some people, but I think it needs to be done with caution. Many vaccines require very effective dosing. We need to ensure that if we are using an oral route, we use a contained and specially used crop that will not enter the general food supply. One does not want to have an antigen over a long period; one wants to get a big vaccine. I have moved more strongly toward using tobacco as an effective way to produce the biomass through two simple steps of purification. If one chooses to develop transdermal vaccines, one can still get very cost effective purification sufficient for the vaccines that should make them accessible to the developing world market.

In summary, biotechnology has brought significant benefits to agriculture and has tremendous potential for positive impacts on human health, the environment, and society's ability to feed the world population. However, in the future, issues of anti-GM food sentiment, labeling trade, and lack of regulatory harmonization have potential to block the ability of these technologies to be taken to their future capability for helping humanity.

CHAPTER FIVE

Shaping Creation: A Response to Leslie Biesecker and Carole Cramer

James C. Peterson

Dr. James C. Peterson is the R.A. Hope Professor of Theology and Ethics and a Member of teh Research Ethics Board at McMaster University, one of Canada's leading research universities.

*P*ediatrician Leslie Biesecker describes entering the field of genetic research to better care for his patients. Carole Cramer speaks of seeking to develop genetic research and genetic modifications to lessen the use of pesticides or to improve vaccines and nutrition. These are fitting goals for someone who wants to work within the Christian tradition. Of course, we still need to address concerns such as those of equity, safety, the attitudes that intervention engenders, social momentum, how we treat animals, nonviolence, and who makes the decisions concerning biotechnology; however, the stated intent of care for our world and one another is admirable.

At this point it might serve us well to focus on an underlying conviction about how we look at attempts to modify our physical world. It is important to remember that to intervene in God-given nature is part of our God-given nature. For example, what did Jesus spend much of his waking earthly life doing? He did not begin his active public ministry until about age thirty. We read in Mark 6:3 that up to that point, the friends and neighbors of his small town remembered him as a carpenter/builder, transforming trees into useful implements like plows and frames for doors—actively changing his environment to better serve God and people. That Jesus was a carpenter for much of his life does not mean that we should also take up tools to work with wood, but Anabaptists have long seen what Jesus did to be as instructive as what he said.

Or think back to Genesis 1. There God gives creation over to human dominion and places humans not in a wilderness but in a garden. A garden needs to be tended. One cannot encourage the roses without driving back the aphids. The humans are directed to care for the garden and how to care for it. God tells them not to eat fruit from certain trees[1] nor to eat meat.[2] It is still God's world. It is not their world, one with which they can do anything they want. Nature is entrusted to humans to care for it as stewards. They are responsible to God for what they do with God's world, a place given to them in which to exercise stewardship. That includes making choices to shape and develop that which God has entrusted to them.

Few of us live in a place where we could survive because the temperature is always right, with no need for clothing or shelter, or where we could catch our food with our bare hands and eat it raw. As soon as we use a hook to catch a fish or fire to cook it, we use technology. This is part of who we are designed to be. We are designed to shape, modify, and work with our environment and ourselves.

Nature is something God has created and declared good. Humans are to enjoy and use it to serve God and neighbor. Should nature then be left as it is? Should we have left smallpox alone? No. Is it the wisdom of evolution over time that as people age they have poorer eyesight? Do individuals contravene evolution or God-designed nature when they accept glasses or laser surgery? The physical world can be improved, and it is our human nature and call to do so.

Saint Augustine argued in the fourth century that the world is not perfect and should be restored to what it was like before sin corrupted it.[3] That requires shaping the nature we have received. Further, there is a long tradition in church history that humans should not just restore the Earth. Instead, part of our calling is to improve it.

For example, Saint Irenaeus, who wrote before Augustine, argued that when God created the world, the Genesis account describes God declaring the creation good each day, yet returning the next day to develop it further. Irenaeus argued that there is a pattern of God creating and doing that which is good, coming back and improving upon it, developing it, growing it, making it even better.[4]

Is our calling in God's image to shape creation as stewards limited to the environment? Does it include intervention in our own physical form? Think of how God developed the people of Israel, then assigned them a sign to show they were indeed God's people. That sign was circumcision, the intentional cutting off of a normal part of the male human body. Here God's people were specifically directed to shape the human body, not just the general physical world.

We are to sustain the whole of creation including ourselves, to restore it where it has fallen, to develop it as best we can. For example, think of our teeth. If we ignore them, they will go away. We brush them to sustain them. When we have cavities, we restore our teeth by filling the cavities. It is also appropriate to improve our teeth beyond what they naturally were by using the fluoride in toothpaste or water to resist cavities We are to sustain, restore, and improve what has been entrusted to us. To sustain our health, it is good to get enough sleep and eat a proper diet, but if we do become ill, it is appropriate to take an antibiotic to restore health. If we get a vaccination, we have actually improved our immune system beyond received capability, so that we do not become ill with a given disease in the first place. To sustain, restore, and improve is good stewardship.

Our responsibility is not just to avoid harm. We also are responsible to do what good we can. Previously, in chapter 2, I discussed Matthew 24 and 25, where three stories tell us what to do until our Lord returns. Each group of people in Matthew 25 that falls short fails by *not doing* something. Among the ten maidens, the ones who did not bring enough batteries for their flashlights missed the celebration. Among those who received the talents, the one who is rebuked is the one who did not bring an improvement to the resources he had. At the final day of judgment it is those who did not care for their neighbors who are left outside. In each case omission was taken as seriously as commission. We are responsible to do the best we can with what we have.

Any calling, including to use well what we have, can be corrupted. There is a lengthy list of concerns that we need to take into account about how we intervene and to what end, but intervening in God-given nature is appropriate. To better serve God and people, sharing what we have, including our physical world and selves, is part of our design and calling as God's people.

Notes

1. Gen. 2:16-17.
2. Gen. 1:29-30, 9:1-3.
3. As stated in his multiple commentaries on Genesis.
4. Irenaeus, any edition of *Against Heresies*, Book 4, Chapters 37-38.

CHAPTER SIX

Audience Questions: Genetic Modification

Are you concerned that there is the potential, as with nuclear science, for misuse of biotechnology in ways that would or could be very destructive to human kind and to the future of life on this planet? What is being done in the scientific community as a safeguard both ecologically and for the human species?

Carole Cramer: There is no question that any of these technologies can be misused. All technologies need to be used under appropriate scrutiny. In order for me to do a field trial and grow transgenetic tobacco in Virginia, I must go through a number of regulatory steps, which includes disclosing all pieces of recombinant DNA that have gone in and justifying why they are there. There is a fear that the transgenic crops could escape into the wild population, but we harvest the tobacco before it ever goes to seed. It also is a self-pollinator, so there is no issue; it is relatively easy to contain.

Certainly if we look at the consequences, for example, of plant-made pharmaceuticals, we do not want these elements to become part of food and feed. As we have looked at issues of pollen flow, from corn for example, that is a real concern. The regulatory constraint now for human pharmaceuticals is such that it will never become commercialized and freely available. It will always be done under full regulatory scrutiny.

With corn regulators we have instituted at least five constraints that would prevent out-crossing for pharmaceuticals. Currently pharmaceutical corn cannot be grown within a mile of any other corn crop. There has been discussion as to whether for pharmaceuticals that should be increased to five miles, which would take pharmaceutical production out of most of the corn-growing states. There is temporal distribution as well, where researchers plant pharmaceutical corn differently, so it does not come to sexual maturity at the same time as any neighboring corn. Researchers detassle corn so the plants are not sexually active for their pollen to transfer. They tend to use cultivars that are not identical to the others.

79

In my opinion there are risks and benefits with any technology; all should be looked at from a risk-benefit point of view. The best thing we should be doing is insisting that our regulatory oversight committees have very high standards and that the enforcement and the participation of the regulatory agents be quite strong in this area. High standards are one reason biotechnology, or genetically modified (GM) foods, has been more accepted in the United States than Europe. There is significant respect for the United States Department of Agriculture (USDA) and the Food and Drug Administration (FDA) in ensuring that these products are safe. Those released for widespread use have had very high levels of scrutiny before being commercialized. The types of things I do are monitored multiple times every time and done under extremely contained situations. Yes, there are risks, but I believe that appropriate regulatory oversight will be able to manage most such risks.

Leslie Biesecker: My related comment has to do with the human genetic applications. It is my general belief that the more powerful the technology is to do good, the more powerful the technology is to do bad. Whenever you hear someone arguing about the incredibly great things you can do, I think that you need to be thinking carefully about the adverse problems that can occur. This was recognized early in human genetics and is part of the Human Genome Project (HGP). The genome project prospectively set aside—in a decision by James Watson, the founder of that program—five percent of the research budget for the Ethical, Legal, and Social Implications Research Project. That is the first time to my knowledge in human history that money was prospectively set aside in a large-scale research project to study side-by-side, even as the science developed, the ethical, legal, and social implications. The goal then has been to anticipate the risks and to ameliorate or regulate the use of genetic technology to maximize the benefits and minimize the harms.

When GM seed crops are introduced into rural farms in Africa and other developing areas, does it not undermine the many generations of natural seed selection that have produced crops and that are more drought resistant or resistant to diseases particular to that area?

Carole Cramer: It is clear that local varieties have been optimized for that local region. I think ultimately what will happen with these biotechnological applications is they will be crossed into local varieties such that the diversity and the value of those local varieties will be maintained, but the biotech component that is advantageous for growth will be delivered or brought in. Ultimately, rather than one strain being grown everywhere—which actually will not be successful—we want to give the developing countries the ability to introduce these traits into their own cultivars. That will give them both the benefits of their years of selective breeding as well as the benefits that biotechnology can bring.

How will genetically engineered seeds affect food security among the world's poor if the farmer needs to buy seeds from Monsanto because he can no longer use his own seeds collected from the previous year's crop?

Carole Cramer: I do not think the farmer in Kenya will be buying his seeds from Monsanto at all. Monsanto is not going to be putting its effort into developing cultivars that will be successful in very diverse growing regions. What Monsanto has agreed to do in many cases is to allow the intellectual property to be widely available that would allow people in Kenya or Zimbabwe to take these traits and move them into their cultivars. There is no economic benefit for Monsanto to try to control the local varieties, and I do not see that happening.

Has Leslie Biesecker explored genetic screening to help Amish couples declare whether it is a good idea for them to marry? Is this level of prevention viewed as positive?

Leslie Biesecker: Genetic screening has actually been implemented in the Dor Yeshorim community, a conservative orthodox religious community in New York where genetic screening is performed. The results are transmitted to the rabbi, not to the individual—individuals do not learn the results of the genetic screening—and the rabbi, who arranges marriages, uses genetic data as one of the factors in determining who should marry. The culture in this particular community is entirely distinct from that of the Old Order Amish, where arranged marriages are essentially not part of the cultural fabric. I have never given it a moment's consideration, because what I try to do is implement things that are consistent with the community as it exists. I have no interest in trying to implement new cultural practices in that or any other community.

Carole Cramer said that it was too expensive for us to vaccinate the world. Why then can we get Coca-Cola or weapons of major destruction anywhere in the world?

Carole Cramer: We make many choices, and our government makes many choices. Most people have made choices that are linked with what we hope is improving the good for mankind. We choose what we spend our money on, what we consider all right for our children to do, where we send our sons and daughters in the world, and the risks in which we put them. Our society has an incredible amount of waste, and our government and society make many decisions with which we do not individually agree. The fact that people put their money into weapons before they put money into vaccines is a bad choice, and I would love to see that change.

PART TWO

Perspectives

CHAPTER SEVEN

Viewing Bioethics Through Anabaptist Eyes

Roman J. Miller

Dr. Roman J. Miller is the Daniel B. Suter Endowed Professor of Biology at Eastern Mennonite University, where he teaches courses in physiology, developmental biology, philosophy of science, and bioethics. His diverse research interests include the role of phytoestrogens in the development of mammalian reproductive tissues and the interaction of Anabaptist thought in bioethics. He is also the editor of Perspectives on Science and Christian Faith, *the quarterly journal of the American Scientific Affiliation, and serves the church as an overseer for a cluster of five Mennonite congregations.*

*I*n this chapter I describe an evangelical Anabaptist, bioethical perspective as a distinctive way of thinking, being, and doing that contrasts with other Christian bioethical systems. Among such contrasting systems are the obedient love covenantal ethic portrayed by Paul Ramsey;[1] the foundational principled perspective built on general revelation, dominion mandate, and common grace espoused by Scott Rae and Paul Cox;[2] or the ethic of noetic theology rooted in Christian mysticism of the first millennium described by H. Tristram Engelhardt.[3] The approach of this paper blends scriptural insights, historical/theological Anabaptist understandings, and contemporary Mennonite expressions to describe evangelical Anabaptism as a way of responding to bioethical issues.

We live in a world that is both post-Christian and neo-pagan. An Anabaptist theology, which centralizes the unique claims and life of Jesus Christ—the God-Man—as normative ethics, diverges from the ideals of secular culture. Thus not only the theological presuppositions but also the practical lifestyle applications of Anabaptist Christian bioethics often counter the decision-making consequences of secular bioethics.

Emerging technologies have brought new issues and questions to our society. Choices and opportunities abound to originate life, to end life, or to change the quality of our human lives by genetically altering our bodies. Foundational questions abound. What leads us to make specific bioethical decisions? What is the source of our motivation? What kind of persons ought we to be? Are we abusing or caring for creation when we genetically alter animals and plants?

The adjectives *Christian* and *Anabaptist* describe the theology that underlies the bioethics described here. For a Christian bioethic, the transcendence of a triune God revealed in Scripture and in human experience is a foundation upon which the ethical system is built. Secular bioethical systems miss this dimension, which skews their bioethical building. This bioethic is also Anabaptist in its orientation, making it differ from a wide diversity of Christian theologies, such as Catholic, Reformed, Protestant, Eastern Orthodox, Fundamentalist, Evangelical, Liberal, and so forth. Contemporary evangelical Anabaptism, rather than being generically Christian, uniquely values the insights and ideals of sixteenth-century Anabaptism while attempting to contextualize many of those insights into the bioethical issues of the twenty-first century.

Few ethicists have had greater impact on the development of bioethics in the contemporary American culture than Tom Beauchamp and James Childress, with their strong advocacy for a secular bioethical system based on principlism. Their system uses a framework of four principles derived from considered judgments in the common morality and medical traditions.[4] Their seminal work, *Principles of Biomedical Ethics,* now in the fifth edition, has become the prominent textbook for many health care workers, physicians, ethicists, and hospital ethics boards.

Beauchamp and Childress espouse four primary principles: (1) respect for autonomy, (2) nonmaleficence, (3) beneficence, and (4) justice.[5] Traditional medical ethics has emphasized nonmaleficence (not causing harm) and beneficence (providing a benefit). Modern democracy, humanism, and the emphasis on the individual have led to the importance of autonomy (respecting the decision-making right of the individual) and justice (fair distribution of benefits, risks, and costs). Specification, the process of providing action-guiding content to abstract norms, creates derivative rules that have application to specific moral dilemmas. Moral reasoning, involving a reflective equilibrium or justification, provides a balancing of conflicting rules in reaching some pragmatic judgment or resolution in specific bioethical dilemmas.

Inherent in the Beauchamp/Childress secular bioethical model are two fundamental problems.[6] First, a universal standard is lacking, resulting in a relativistic outcome. Their scheme is not subject to rational or empirical justification, but rather the reasoned outcome is a product of an arbitrary acceptance of one value versus another value. Two contradictory conceptions of moral principles may well result in two extremely different outcomes. For example, on the basis of beneficence, one physician may prescribe expensive medical interventions to prolong the life of a terminally ill patient; another physician may withdraw the same interventions to provide for a peaceful death. Second, ethical specialists, rather than embodying the ethics of care and compassion, have apparently reduced the practice of medicine or health care to the application of specific principles and their derivative rules.

Secular bioethics that does not incorporate a transcendent God into its realm of activity will always be lacking. Our reasoning and motivations are typically self-serving and protective of our own interests rather than the interests of others. Christian bioethics, which responds to the motivation and presence of God, will always be countercultural in a secular society, and in many cases its outcomes will vie with popular opinion and thinking.

A Three-Fold Vision of Anabaptist Thought in Bioethics

The core emphasis of any authentic Anabaptist perspective is the centrality of Jesus. Character virtues, interpretation of Scripture, righteous living, communal responsibilities, establishment of right relationships, and motivation of action all are based on the teaching and example of Jesus and the personal transformation brought on by one's encounter with Jesus. As disciples of Jesus, early Anabaptists advocated the transforming and enabling experience of grace, the essentiality of the voluntary Christian community committed to discipleship, and the capacity of suffering love to transform human relationships. In bioethics, these values of Anabaptism may be encapsulated as the ethics of being, ethics of relationship, and ethics of action.

The centrality of Christ is the foundation of an Anabaptist perspective both theologically and ethically. A thematic biblical passage frequently cited by the early Dutch Anabaptist leader, Menno Simons (1496-1561), expresses this conviction: "For no one can lay any foundation other than the one that has been laid, that foundation is Jesus Christ."[7] With this understanding, we interpret Scripture, culture, science, and behavior through the teachings and experiences of Jesus Christ. Thus Jesus Christ is the ultimate representation of godly behavior. Faithful discipleship is following the example of Jesus and obeying his teachings. The community of transformed Christian believers provides the best environment for the discernment of difficult bioethical issues. The character of Christ—his love, compassion, and humble service—becomes the model for human relationships and ultimately determines how we should value life and resolve bioethical dilemmas.

Typically Anabaptists have defined themselves by the action of "following Jesus" rather than by emphasizing the role of "personal faith." Consequently, theology is a means, not an end.[8] Obedience within discipleship is the fruit of grace; it is not the means by which grace is won.[9] This ontological (composition of its essential reality) change in the life of the believer comes from the transforming power of the grace of Christ and is consequentially evidenced by a complete life renovation and Christlike discipleship.[10] Within the Anabaptist framework, it is impossible for one to truly be a Christian without a lifestyle transformation that displays Jesus' character through discipleship[11] that impacts both personal and community ethics.

Many contemporary bioethical systems guide resolutions to dilemmas following a methodological application of rules derived from foundational principles. Yoder, however, proposed that "the Christian moral life is simply too complex to be fully captured by any attempt to codify it at the level of method or theory."[12] The belief that theology consists primarily in the analysis of theoretical questions promotes a decisive shift away from embodied practices that constitute the body of Christ.[13] In contrast, ethics within true Christian discipleship moves away from theorizing and deriving specific rules and focuses on obeying Christ within the context of the community.

Ethics of being: Creation and existential grace

Our conception of "who we are" as human persons directly impacts our bioethical understandings. Our definition of personhood ultimately represents the value we place on human life. The importance of creation in the ordering of Anabaptist understanding of human personhood is illustrated in an early statement of faith, the *Dordrecht Confession of Faith*, adopted by Dutch Mennonites in 1632[14] and by Alsatian Mennonites in 1660.[15] This confession was used by early American Mennonites from the seventeenth century through much of the twentieth century.[16] The text of the first article, "Concerning God and the Creation of the All Things," described the character of the triune God as Creator of humankind:

> One eternal, almighty, and incomprehensible God, the Father, Son, and Holy Ghost . . . we confess as the Creator of all things, visible and invisible. . . . [God] created the first man, Adam, the father of all of us, gave him a body formed "of the dust of the ground, and breathed into his nostrils the breath of life," so that he "became a living soul, created by God in His own image and likeness." . . . [God] gave [Adam] a place above all other creatures and endowed him with many high and excellent gifts.[17]

Two ideas from this Anabaptist confession deserve emphasis. One, the character and activity of God involves a trinitarian mutuality interacting with creation, while remaining distinct from creation. Secondly, humankind is given life by God, created in God's image (*imago Dei*), and endowed with gifting.

Since humans are created in God's image, human life is sacred. The creation account makes it clear that the *imago Dei* is not something humans attain but rather something they are given.[18] Thus, God's gift to humanity, *imago Dei*, is a divine/human relationship that was originated and given by God through the act of creation. Scripture describes the early ontological roots of this relationship, which encompasses embryonic and fetal development in the uterus.[19] God's image is part of our essential character, which places our existence within the realm that provides species membership, metaphysical connection, and life protection by the community.[20] A contemporary Mennonite theological statement emphasizes that humans created in the image of God are "made for relationship with God, to live in peace with each other, and to take care of the rest of creation."[21] This God-given relationship identity is the primary innate part of our created being or essence and not a capacity that we can attain or lose.

Normal human biological development unfolds the primary aspect of God's image in humans as secondarily visible human characteristics that reflect God's expressive nature. Among the most distinctive of these are the abilities to communicate in abstract symbols, to have a reflective self-concept, to relate within a community exhibiting moral autonomy and responsibility, and to "love your neighbor as yourself."[22] While these attributes do not need to be functional for us to consider someone a person, they are unique to potential human experiences and deeply connected to each person's maturing relationship with God.

Our ultimate human nature is both a consequence of God's original creation and of God's re-creation through existential grace. The biblical story in Genesis and the expressions of sin and pain in contemporary society remind us all is not well in the world—we are broken and need re-creation to be whole. The Anabaptists used a German word, *Bekehrung,* which defines God's re-creation as a "turning around."[23] This re-creation, illustrated by a dramatic change of inner nature—becoming as a child—is based on the directive of Jesus, "Truly I tell you, unless you change and become like children, you will never enter the kingdom of heaven."[24] The term *turning* described renouncing sin and refocusing with a new attitude.

What is the mechanism of this re-creation? For the Anabaptists it was the grace of God that empowered and endowed the yielded person who surrendered to Jesus Christ. This grace was an existential (containing substance in time and space) element with transformative power. Alvin Beachy succinctly described this concept of grace for the Radical Reformation (Anabaptists):

> Grace is God's act whereby He renews the divine image in man through the Holy Spirit and makes the believer a participant in the divine nature. The Radicals did not think that this grace could be earned through any meritorious work. It came as a sheer gift from God. . . . [G]race is . . . an act of God, which brings about an ontological change within the believer himself rather than a forensic change in status before God.[25]

Similarly, Pilgram Marpeck, a sixteenth-century Anabaptist leader in South Germany, described God's grace as the inpouring of the Spirit through faith:

> While the law breaks the human and points out sin, the yielded heart (*gelasen*) through faith experiences the transfer of the Spirit of God who reaches and secures the human spirit. By receiving

the divine Spirit, the human participates in the very nature of God and experiences a heart renewal so that the human and divine may exist together.[26]

In the 1995 *Confession of Faith in a Mennonite Perspective*, contemporary Anabaptists describe this same understanding:

> We believe that Jesus Christ calls us to take up our cross and follow him. *Through the gift of God's saving grace, we are empowered to be disciples of Jesus*, filled with his Spirit, following his teachings and his path through suffering to new life. As by faith we walk in Christ's way, we are being transformed into his image.[27]

Re-creation is the transforming work of Jesus. No one can simply elect to follow Jesus in any faithful way. Rather, the grace of God transforms our character and will so that we can actually *do* the will of God! The actions and works that emerge are not a testimony to our innate strength or goodness but spring from the grace of God enabling us to do God's will. Consequently, it is from this status that a virtuous ethic of being emerges and enables Christlike relationships and actions.

Ethics of relationship:
Nature, family, church, and contemporary society

Our relational ethic expresses, both individually and corporately, what we are. A Christlike being directs righteous living. How is righteous living discerned? Traditionally, Anabaptists have understood righteousness by balancing three authoritative voices: the revealed written word of God (Scripture), the redeemed people of God, and the Spirit of God. Through understanding of the revelation of God in Scripture, Anabaptists judge and critique the voices of the people of God and individual perceptions of the Spirit of God. A key to this perspective is a true immersion in Scripture. In the words of Sara Wenger Shenk, a contemporary Mennonite seminary professor:

> [I]mmersion in Scripture grew out of desire to live faithful lives of discipleship. The desire to know the Scriptures so well that one's life is conformed to the language, metaphors, practices and vision of Scripture was an all-consuming passion for the Anabaptists. Becoming a disciple of Christ meant "indwelling" the story and the reality of Christ to such an extent that one would come to know Christ and become like Christ.[28]

Importantly for Anabaptists, this was not a solo individual effort or experience. Rather, the congregation of believers became the interpreting community of the Scriptures, validating life as faithful disciples of Jesus.[29]

Sixteenth-century Anabaptists struggling with issues of martyrdom and survival did not develop a theology of nature or articulate how the followers of Jesus should relate to the environment. However, they lived in and related as friends with their natural environment. Sheltered by caves and forests, they found places of refugee and sanctuaries of worship that protected them from the hunters of Anabaptists, who wanted to annihilate them. Initially, many of the early Anabaptists and Mennonites were urban dwellers and artisans, especially those in the Low Countries and Northwest Germany. By the mid- and late 1500s, however, agriculture became a primary way of life, as Mennonites became effective farmers.[30] In the following centuries, as Mennonites migrated to North America from Europe and Russia, they settled on farms and rural areas, a practice that promoted their relationship to the land.[31] Farming provided them with sustenance, a place of security, and a safe environment to raise their children.

Consequently, during the subsequent generations (until the past few decades), most North American Mennonites worked in agriculture and lived on family farms. Taking care of the land, planting and harvesting, and managing livestock on the farm were activities that connected them to the heavenly father who created the world and continues to sustain it. Agricultural practices were based on the concept of Christian stewardship, the belief that God entrusted humans with these gifts that are to be used responsibly, carefully, and respectfully.

Resting contentedly in the care of Christ's Lordship over creation and participating as a steward of Christ's gifts is a persistent Anabaptist-Mennonite ideal[32] that contrasts with the "subdue and dominate" theme advanced by some Christian traditions. An early Anabaptist prayer book dating back to the 1700's contains an evening prayer with these words translated from the original German: " . . . and help us be gentle with your creatures and handiwork so that we may abide in your eternal salvation and continue to be held in the hollow of your hand."

That prayer embodies the Anabaptist theology of nature—to live *with* God's land rather than simply residing *in* the land.[33] Believing that the "earth is the Lord's" calls earth's residents to care for and respect God's creation, because life depends on and is affected by that caretaking. Anabaptists and Mennonites have traditionally valued their relationship to the land and the cycles of nature and have seen them as God's creation and gifts for human welfare. The influence of nature guided practices such as the seasonal selection of specific Scriptures and hymns, spring and fall communion church services, prayer for summer rain during dry periods, and autumn thanksgiving offerings for world relief effort. These responses reflect a theology of living that links faith to the environment.[34]

Thomas Finger, a contemporary theologian, has described an Anabaptist-Mennonite theology of creation.[35] For Finger the beginning of such a theology is not the story of creation in Genesis nor the "creational mandate" given to Adam and Eve in the garden, but rather discerning how Jesus' life and teachings reflected an appropriate Christian response to creation. Jesus' reverence for nature's intricacy and beauty was expressed through the natural illustrations and stories that he told.[36] Jesus taught that the universality of God's rule was expressed in the rhythms of nature and that God was concerned about seemingly inconsequential and weak creational members such as grasses, lilies, sparrows, and lambs. As an extension of this compassionate relationship with nonhuman creatures, Jesus focused attention and care toward the weak and victimized human creatures.

Furthermore, the New Testament Scriptures express the truth that the creation event was not a solo project by God the Father; rather the Word (Jesus Christ) was a maker of everything that exists and has entered as well into the essence of creation through the incarnation.[37] The New Testament writers describe an "incarnational theology" where Christ, the Agent of Creation, takes on a human natural body and becomes one with created human beings.[38]

Two implications can be drawn from this theology: first, the paradox of an infinite God becoming limited in time and place by entering created order; and second, the capacity of created material to mediate the presence of the divine. Since Christ is the Lord of creation, as created mortals we need to relate to other created elements giving the respect and care that is due. Having experienced the effects of sin and destruction, humans along with the rest of creation await with anticipation the restoration promised when the Lordship of Christ is fully realized in nature.[39]

Human initiative in nature is bounded. Abusing and destroying nature trivializes God's activity and work. Appropriate involvements in nature include the following: harvesting and replenishing nature's resources, respecting the integrity of created kinds, and accepting our mortal place in the natural order by freely participating in natural cycles such as birth, life stage, and death experiences. It matters if the rain forests are destroyed, if living species are extinguished from existence, if the soil is eroded, or if the rivers are poisoned with pollutants.

We must also remember that material things, including biotechnologies that we discover and use, are not the essence of life. Consequently, we ought to expend our efforts to narrow the gulfs that separate the rich and poor, privileged and underprivileged and minister to the natural and spiritual needs of individuals.[40] Such efforts reflect the activity of Jesus.

As a further development of an Anabaptist theology of nature, Calvin Redekop, a Mennonite sociologist, proposed a "third way," neither Catholic nor Protestant, which presents a God who has always been concerned about forming a people who would fulfill God's plans *on* earth.[41] Anabaptists interpret this concept as "the rule of God in society"—the kingdom of Christ. Fundamental to this understanding is that the "rule" includes wholistic relational living with the natural environment. We must consider this important question: Do our genetic modifications and biotechnologies enhance or hinder this wholistic relational pattern?

The Anabaptist concept of family is based on a mutual commitment of heart and mind to Christ.[42] Consequently, marriage partners are optimally chosen from the community of faith. Courtship is a time for potential partners to discern their mutual commitment to the same ideals. The principle of unity is the essential factor in marriage, when the "twain shall be one flesh."[43] The covenant of marriage establishes the Christian home led by life-long committed companions, who as husband and wife create a nurturing environment in which to raise children. For many traditional Mennonites, the family farm was the primary location of this activity.

The period of pregnancy can deepen the relationship of marriage partners, bringing them closer together than at any time in their marriage.[44] While embryonic/fetal development is an exciting biological process in itself, a committed Christian couple can experience tremendous excitement as they joyously anticipate the birth of their child and the subsequent responsibilities of parenthood. Conception and embryonic/fetal development of the unborn link human life and eternity. When a human ovum and sperm are joined, resulting in a developing embryo, a unique human individual is formed having the potentiality of eternal existence.

Whether the joining occurs through natural human sexual intercourse or through the manipulation of human gametes in a Petri dish does not fundamentally change the potentiality and value of the developing embryo. Within the developmental process the human individual unfolds, matures, and progressively forms interdependence, relationships, and status. Consequently, conception and development of the unborn is an awesome and sacred time that requires the best efforts of parents to be loving and compassionate caretakers. The period after birth is the unfurling of what has already been germinated in the soul.[45]

Identification with the unborn embryo or with a needy child through adoption establishes the basis of a trans-generation relationship with moral responsibilities. To discard either an unwanted embryo or an unwanted neonate abuses *imago Dei*, God's gift. Consequently parents, who bring children into their world either as their genetic offspring or through adoption of others' genetic offspring, have an awesome responsibility to form a relationship and to nurture and train children in the home. Consistent religious instruction, moral discipline, and developing a work ethic within a harmonious, loving home atmosphere provide the foundations for quality child-training and characterize the attractiveness of an Anabaptist family ideal.[46] Traditionally, Mennonites have valued and gratefully nurtured large families, believing that the Bible commended such practices.[47] An old German proverb reflects this view: "Many children make many prayers, and many prayers bring much blessing."[48]

Anabaptists did not baptize their infants or children but believed that they were in a state of spiritual innocence. Only as children matured into youth, in a "coming of age" experience could a person say, "I believe and choose to follow Jesus," with any meaningful understanding of the consequence of baptism.[49] As baptized members of the church, Anabaptist youth had a new primary relationship and responsibility to others in their Christian community that transcended their home responsibilities. When youth mature and leave their familial home as young adults, they become responsible to carry on these qualities and ideals to the next generation. In this manner, the Christian home becomes a foundational constituent of the on-going Christian church.

The Anabaptist concept of church is experienced within a community in which discipleship is matured through relationships. The interactions resulting from these relationships provide teaching, accountability, and new understandings of the true nature of Christ.

Within this community, "there is an insistence on the practice of true brotherhood and love among the members of the church, and 'within this love is the fullness of the Christian life ideal.'"[50]

The Christian community provides a context for understanding the complex relationship each member has with God, other members of the community, and the surrounding world. These relationships offer insight, encourage accountability, and require humility and love. Within a Christian community, discernment occurs through the Holy Spirit's leading within a gathering of believers, who corporately seek for solutions to difficult issues. Equally valued members have different roles, which contribute to the ultimate goal of the Christian community: to support each other toward living in ways that keep Christ at the core of our lives.[51] Christian discernment, diversely enriched by the complementary strengths and weaknesses of its members, provides creative and imaginative alternatives in bioethical dilemmas.

When viewing difficult issues within the context of a Christ-centered community, relational meanings offer new perspectives. The important bioethical questions a community should be asking shift from definitional answers for what is to be valued and protected to questions such as, "What kind of community must we be to welcome a new life as a gift from God, especially when tragic and complex circumstances surround it?"[52] This paradigm shift in approaching bioethics uses the discernment of the community to shape its Christ-reflecting character into a body that emulates the compassion of Jesus. In turn, the ethos created within the community will be the foundation for approaching complicated issues that involve members of the community.

Peter Rideman (Riedemann), the influential Hutterian theologian of the sixteenth century, originated the metaphor of a "lantern of righteousness" as a functional description of the mission of the Christian community in society. Rideman used this term in a Confession of Faith that was written "in the dry summer of the year 1540, as he lay a prisoner in Hesse."[53] One section of this Confession of Faith which describes the church contains the following words:

> The Church of Christ is the basis and ground of truth, *a lantern of righteousness, in which the light of grace is borne and held before the whole world,* that its darkness, unbelief and blindness be thereby seen and made light, and that men may also learn to see and know the way of life. There is the Church of Christ in the first place completely filled with the light of Christ as a lantern is illu-

minated and made bright by the light: that his light might shine through her to others. And as the lantern of Christ hath been made light, bright, and clear, enlightened by the light of the knowledge of God, its brightness and light shineth out into the distance to give light to others still walking in darkness, even as Christ himself hath commanded, "Let your light shine before men, that they may see your good works, and praise God, the Father in heaven."[54]

The Anabaptist approach to the evils and ills in contemporary society was to model a welcoming Christian community that invites the societal hurt and wounded to come and find healing and health through the power of Christ's grace.

The early Anabaptists had two primary convictions regarding the world. First, they accepted the fundamental dualism they saw in Scripture between Christian values and values of a corrupt world.[55] This dualism is often expressed as a two-kingdom theology—the kingdom of Christ and the kingdom of this world. Thus the third article of the *Schleitheim Confession of Faith*,[56] written in 1527, says that

All those who have fellowship with the dead works of darkness have no part in the light. All who follow the devil and the world have no part with those who are called unto God out of the world. All who lie in evil have no part in the good.

An excerpt from the fourth article of the same document reads,

For truly, all creatures are in but two classes, good and bad, believing and unbelieving, darkness and light, the world and those who have come out of the world, God's temple and idols, Christ and Belial, and none can have part with the other.

In response to this two-kingdom understanding, the early Anabaptists did not withdraw or become isolated from the world. They went boldly into the world as "messengers" of the gospel of Christ.

Early Anabaptists, fleeing persecution, were unable to become involved with political affairs in the ways many contemporary Christians can in a democratic society. Some present-day Anabaptists believe Christians should have a prophetic voice in government issues. Democratic governments that value freedom of religion provide a setting in which Christians have the opportunity to humbly express their values within the political system.

True Christian discipleship involves citizenship in the kingdom of God.[57] Donald B. Kraybill says that this kingdom "permeates all of Jesus' ministry, giving it unusual coherence and clarity. It is the core, the very essence, of his ministry."[58] Accountability and teaching within this kingdom occur in the setting of a church community. Scripture presents the church as a "holy nation,"[59] calling believers to give full allegiance to Christ as the ultimate authority by following the examples of his teachings. The church is called to be a "city on a hill,"[60] witnessing the way of Christ throughout its surrounding political structures. We are to be ambassadors[61] for Christ, calling all persons and institutions to move toward justice, peace, and compassion for all people.[62] A virtuous ethic of being, matured by Christian relationships, energizes the ethics of action.

Ethics of action: Compassionate care and suffering love

Our virtue enables our action. From an Anabaptist perspective, virtue stems from the ontological work of God's grace transforming one's character into the image of Christ. As followers of Jesus, we are concerned with both effectiveness and faithfulness. Belief and practice, as well as means and ends, are all woven out of the same life-giving fabric. The quality of our life work is shaped in the context of the Christian communities in which we participate. Within historic Anabaptism, this ethic of discipleship is rooted both in the teachings and example of Jesus. The entire life and ministry of Jesus reflected the active application of his love, care, and compassion to a needy and hurting humanity. Furthermore, we demonstrate willingness and vulnerability to step outside of societal and cultural influences in obediently following Jesus as "lanterns of righteousness" in the world. In historic Anabaptism, this vulnerability was referred to as the freedom and courage to "bear one's cross."

In our time the acronym WWJD (*What Would Jesus Do?*) is frequently used by Christians as a quick fix to a tough ethical problem or situation. Imitating Jesus has legitimacy if we live our life, as Jesus did, in renouncing personal power, prestige, and honor in obedience to his Father. Our culture values the autonomy and power of the individual along with his/her rights of self-determination. Too often in our positions of pride and power, we pretend to respond as we think Jesus would respond in a specific situation, while being careful to protect our personal interests of power and pride. Such an imitation of Jesus is a sham. The predominant theme of the "doing of Jesus" in the Gospels stems from Christ's humble yieldedness to God. "Servanthood replaces dominion, forgiveness absorbs hostility. Thus— and only thus—are we bound by New Testament thought to 'be like Jesus.'"[63]

One of the "hard" sayings of Jesus that illustrates the cost of discipleship is found in the gospel of Luke: "Whoever does not carry the cross and follow me cannot be my disciple."[64] In response to this call, the apostle Paul described his commitment to share in the sufferings of the Savior when he wrote, "I want to know Christ and the power of his resurrection, and the [koinonia] sharing of his sufferings, by becoming like him in his death, if somehow, I may attain the resurrection from the dead."[65] In this passage the Greek word for "sharing" or koinonia is translated in the German to gemeinschaft. The Anabaptists used gemeinschaft frequently in their writings. The Anabaptists held communion with Christ much higher than family, security, or comfort. They were willing to suffer physically as Jesus suffered to do the will of God. Gemeinschaft, the glory of communion with Christ through cross-bearing, led the early Anabaptists even to martyrdom.

An ethic of suffering love, care, and compassion is a fundamental aspect of Anabaptist thought, and is ultimately expressed by persons *within* the community of believers and *by* the community of believers to the broader society. The life of Jesus demonstrates compassion to all of humanity, especially to the "least of these," the weak, vulnerable, and marginalized members of society.[66] Compassion is both a matter of feeling and a form of reason, and its extension is the true realization of Christ's character.

The original meanings of the biblical words representing compassion provide insight on the intent of this divine virtue. The Hebrew word raham indicates either the love of a father for his children, or of a mother who is nursing her child. Another form of this word, rehem, literally means "womb": communicating the deep connection associated with the compassion of raising a child. These meanings offer wisdom in the process of understanding God's intent for true compassion.[67]

Compassion is rooted in the kenosis of Christ, the act of emptying one's self in a way that deflects love toward others. Paul writes in Philippians that we should have the same attitude as that of Jesus, imitating Christ's infinite humility toward all possible relationships.[68] The visible expression of Christ's humility was his sacrificial servanthood and his call that his followers should "take up their cross and follow Him." The early Anabaptists described this kenosis, or emptying of self, as yieldedness, which was described with a German word, gelassenheit, literally meaning "a letting loose." Hans Haffner from Moravia wrote a tract in the 1530s in which he said:

> True surrender [gelassenheit] is to put to death the flesh and be born another time. . . . Whoever wants to have Christ must have him also in the way of suffering. It is foolish to say: "We believe that Christ has redeemed us, but we do not want to live like he lived." True surrender [gelassenheit] to Jesus involves two things: enduring persecution and overcoming ourselves.[69]

Some Christians interpret sicknesses or natural calamities as the "crosses" they bear for Christ. Yet such difficulties are not the consequences of our choosing, rather they are the normal fabric of living in a sin-cursed world. The cross bearing described by Jesus, the apostle Paul, and the early Anabaptists, was the difficulty that came on the individual as a consequence of a choice to follow in the footsteps of Jesus. Yoder describes this essential difference in the *Politics of Jesus*:

> The believer's cross is no longer any and every kind of suffering, sickness, or tension, the bearing of which is demanded. The believer's cross must be, like his Lord's, the price of his social nonconformity. It is not, like sickness or catastrophe, an inexplicable, unpredictable suffering; it is the end of a path freely chosen after counting the cost. It is not . . . an inward wrestling of the sensitive soul with self and sin; it is the social reality of representing in an unwilling world the Order to come.[70]

This personal humble acceptance of "cross-bearing" decenters selfish love and focuses care in a way that transforms and deepens the compassionate dimension of our relationships.

Genuine compassion can be expressed through a Christlike relationship. We express our love and compassion to Christ as we interact lovingly and compassionately with others. Jesus said, "Truly I tell you, just as you did it to one of the least of these who are members of my family, you did it to me."[71] Compassion characterizes an aspect of the relationship of God with his children, and it is further expressed within human relationships that reflect the kenosis of Christ.

Love is an attribute that has meaning only in action. That God intended for this attribute to be characteristic of his children is illustrated in the response of Jesus to the query, "which commandment in the law is the greatest?"[72] Furthermore, the apostle John in his epistles frequently repeats the admonition to love.[73] Many of the doctrines of the Christian church, our lifestyle directives, and our personal devotion are prompted by God's love either directly or indirectly.

In the command of Jesus to "love your enemies," the Greek word *agape* is used to describe love. Agape is having a genuine concern for someone, irrespective of his or her attractiveness or the possibility of any reciprocative response.[74] It is an active love or suffering love that gives for the benefit of another at a cost to the donor. The early Anabaptist *Dordrecht Confession of Faith*, written in 1632 in Holland, describes this suffering love as a response that one should have toward an enemy:

> We believe and confess that the Lord Christ has forbidden and set aside to His disciples and followers all revenge and retaliation, and commanded them to render to no one evil for evil, or cursing for cursing, but to put the sword into the sheath . . . we must not inflict pain, harm, or sorrow upon any one, but seek the highest welfare and salvation of all men . . . we must not harm any one, and when we are smitten, rather turn the other cheek also, than take revenge or retaliate.[75]

The underlying concept that motivates suffering love rather than a destructive vengeance is the realization that life is a precious gift from God. God is the giver and sustainer of life. Life matters to God. While God is not oblivious even to the death of a bird, Jesus makes it clear that human life is far more consequential and important.[76] Responding with demonstrative love to the most needy and vulnerable—"the least of these"—becomes a high obligation for the followers of Jesus.[77]

Myron Augsburger, a contemporary Mennonite theologian, highlights three consequences of suffering love (agape) by saying that love personalizes, energizes, and immortalizes relationships rather than institutionalizing, legalizing, or temporalizing them.[78] The consequences of such demonstrations of love are that persons are valued, compassion touches our justice, and we look beyond the temporal with eternity in view. Thus, love is fundamentally a practice, not simply an emotion or an attitude.

Conclusions

Anabaptist theological perspectives may helpfully inform bioethical approaches for the broader public. Early Anabaptists based their theology and praxis on the teaching and example of Jesus Christ and thereby advocated the transforming and enabling dynamic of existential grace, the authority and power of the voluntary Christian community committed to discipleship, and the capacity of agape love to transform human relationships. In bioethics these values of Anabaptism may be capsulated as the ethics of being, relationship, and action.

An Anabaptist ethic of being recognizes the act of God in creating human life in the very image of God, thus forming a sacred relationship. Having experienced the detrimental erosion of sin, humanity becomes broken. God's further act of re-creation is an exercise of grace in which the human creature is restored to wholeness by a renewed relationship with God. Just as a quality physician is formed by her training and experience, so is a quality ethicist formed by his encounter with Christ and the subsequent appropriation of Christ's grace into his life and conduct. Virtue of the individual precedes authentic Christlike action, which is needed in difficult bioethical dilemmas.

An Anabaptist ethic of relationship reveals that we are not in isolation but are part of larger communities—living with nature, growing within family structures, participating primarily as voluntary members of a community of faith, and sharing light to contemporary society. As such, we live humbly and give place to others, so their welfare is enhanced. Such a commitment must go beyond mere accommodation to a grateful self-sacrifice. We humbly serve God and others as we realize we have been recipients of life-giving and formative relationships from both divine and human sources.

An Anabaptist ethic of action resists our cultural tendency to live in private isolation, expending most of our energies for personal gratification and satisfaction. This Anabaptist ethic moves us from such a self-centered approach to a life-giving praxis that ministers to the needy. Love is meaningful as it practically touches the life of another and meets individual needs. Compassion is experienced when the donor and recipient in a relationship both are touched in their spirits and intuit a common intent and purpose.

Evangelical Anabaptist Christians, who live in a postmodern, post-Christian society, are counter-culture. Our presuppositions, values, and goals do not mesh with those of secular society. Yet as "lanterns of righteousness," we can, with humility and grace, show the world a better way, one that faithfully lifts up the ethics of Jesus. That is our commission and call as we work in bioethics.

Notes

1. Paul Ramsey, *Basic Christian Ethics* (Louisville: Westminster John Knox Press, 1950), xxxi.

2. Scott B. Rae and Paul M. Cox, *Bioethics: A Christian Approach in a Pluralistic Age* (Grand Rapids: Eerdmans Publishing Company, 1999), 3.

3. H. Tristram Engelhardt, *The Foundations of Christian Bioethics* (Lisse:

Swets & Zeitlinger, 2000), xiii.

4. Tom L. Beauchamp and James F. Childress, *Principles of Biomedical Ethics,* 5th ed. (New York: Oxford University Press, 2001), 23.

5. Ibid., 12-13.

6. Scott B. Rae and Paul M. Cox, *Bioethics: A Christian Approach in a Pluralistic Age* (Grand Rapids: Eerdmans Publishing Company, 1999), 74-8.

7. 1 Cor. 3:11.

8. Harold S. Bender, *The Anabaptist Vision* (Scottdale, Pa.: Herald Press, 1944), 21.

9. Alvin Beachy, *The Concept of Grace in the Radical Reformation* (Nieuwkoop: B. De Graaf, 1977), 175.

10. Robert Friedmann, *The Theology of Anabaptism* (Scottdale, Pa.: Herald Press, 1973), 93.

11. Harold S. Bender, *The Anabaptist Vision* (Scottdale, Pa.: Herald Press, 1944), 33.

12. Chris K. Huebner, "Can a Gift Be Commanded? Theological Ethics without Theory by Way of Barth, Milbank, and Yoder," *Scottish Journal of Theology* 53, no. 4 (2000): 486.

13. Ibid., 489.

14. John S. Coffman and John F. Funk, compilers, *Confession of Faith and Minister's Manual* (Scottdale, Pa.: Mennonite Publishing House, 1958), 33-4.

15. Ibid., 35.

16. Ibid., 2-3.

17. Ibid., 5-6.

18. Gen. 1:26-27.

19. Ps. 139:13-16.

20. Scott B. Rae and Paul M. Cox, *Bioethics: A Christian Approach in a Pluralistic Age,* 132.

21. *Confession of Faith in a Mennonite Perspective* (Scottdale, Pa.: Herald Press, 1995), 28-9.

22. Conrad Brunk, "In the Image of God," in *Medical Ethics, Human Choices,* ed. John Rogers (Scottdale, Pa.: Herald Press, 1988), 30-33.

23. Peter Hoover, *The Secret of the Strength: What Would the Anabaptists Tell This Generation?* (Shippensburg: Benchmark Press, 1998), 90.

24. Matt. 18:3.

25. Alvin J. Beachy, *The Concept of Grace in the Radical Reformation* (Nieuwkoop: B. De Graaf, 1977), 4-5

26. Stephen B. Boyd, *Pilgram Marpeck: His Life and Social Theology* (Durham: Duke University Press, 1992), 78.

27. *Confession of Faith in a Mennonite Perspective* (Scottdale, Pa.: Herald Press, 1995), 65. Emphasis added.

28. Sara Wenger Shenk, *Anabaptist Ways of Knowing* (Telford, Pa.: Cascadia Publishing House, 2003), 46.

29. Ibid., 48.

30. Harold S. Bender, "Farming and Settlement," in *The Mennonite Encyclopedia*, vol. 2, ed. Cornelius Krahn (Scottdale, Pa.: Mennonite Publishing House, 1956), 303-6.

31. Calvin Redekop, *Mennonite Society* (Baltimore: Johns Hopkins University Press, 1989), 13-29.

32. *Confession of Faith in a Mennonite Perspective* (Scottdale, Pa.: Herald Press, 1995), 28-30.

33. David Kline, "God's Spirit and a Theology for Living," in *Creation & the Environment: An Anabaptist Perspective on a Sustainable World*, ed. Calvin Redekop (Baltimore: John Hopkins University Press, 2000), 61-9.

34. Ibid., 61-69.

35. Thomas Finger, "An Anabaptist/Mennonite Theology of Creation," in *Creation & the Environment: An Anabaptist Perspective on a Sustainable World*, ed. Calvin Redekop (Baltimore: Johns Hopkins University Press, 2000), 154-69.

36. For example see, Matt. 6:28-29.

37. John 1: 1-14; Col. 1:15-17.

38. Dorothy Jean Weaver, "The New Testament and the Environment," in *Creation & the Environment: An Anabaptist Perspective on a Sustainable World*, ed. Calvin Redekop (Baltimore: Johns Hopkins University Press, 2000), 122-38.

39. Rom. 8:18-25.

40. Kenton R. Brubaker, "Science, Technology, and Creation" in *Creation & the Environment: An Anabaptist Perspective on a Sustainable World*, ed. Calvin Redekop (Baltimore: Johns Hopkins University Press, 2000), 27-38.

41. Calvin Redekop, "The Environmental Challenge before Us," in *Creation & the Environment: An Anabaptist Perspective on a Sustainable World*, ed. Calvin Redekop (Baltimore: Johns Hopkins University Press, 2000), 206-14.

42. Cornelius Krahn, "Family," in *The Mennonite Encyclopedia*, Vol. 2, ed. Cornelius Krahn (Scottdale, Pa.: Mennonite Publishing House, 1956), 293-5.

43. John R. Mumaw, *Marriage, Marital Relations and the Home* (Scottdale, Pa.: Herald Press, 1941), 3.

44. Johann Christoph Arnold, *A Little Child Shall Lead Them: Hopeful Parenting in a Confused World* (Farmington, N.M.: Plough Publishing House, 1996), 9.

45. Ibid., 11.

46. John R. Mumaw, *Marriage, Marital Relations and the Home* (Scottdale, Pa.: Herald Press, 1941), 22-7.

47. Ps. 127:3-5.

48. John R. Mumaw, *Marriage, Marital Relations and the Home* (Scottdale, Pa.: Herald Press, 1941), 12.

49. Hillel Schwartz, "Early Anabaptist Ideas About the Nature of Children," *Mennonite Quarterly Review* 47 (April 1973): 102-14

50. Harold S. Bender, *The Anabaptist Vision* (Scottdale, Pa.: Herald Press, 1976, c1944), 29, 34.

51. 1 Cor. 12:12-27.

52. L. Gregory Jones, "Christian Communities and Biomedical Technologies" in *Bioethics and the Beginning of Life,* ed. Roman J. Miller and Beryl Brubaker (Scottdale, Pa.: Herald Press, 1990), 118.

53. From a marginal note in the Hutterian *Greater Church Chronicle* by Dr. Rudolf Wolkan, Vienna, 1923, p. 167 quoted in Peter Rideman, *Confession of*

Faith: Account of Our Religion, Doctrine, and Faith (Rifton: Plough Publishing House, 1970), 267.

54. Peter Rideman, *Confession of Faith: Account of Our Religion, Doctrine, and Faith* (Rifton: Plough Publishing House, 1970), 39-40. Emphasis added.

55. Robert Friedmann, *The Theology of Anabaptism* (Scottdale, Pa.: Herald Press, 1973), 38.

56. Quoted in Robert Friedmann, *The Theology of Anabaptism* (Scottdale, Pa.: Herald Press, 1973), 39.

57. Philippians 3:20, Ephesians 2:19.

58. Donald B. Kraybill, *The Upside-Down Kingdom* (Scottdale, Pa.: Herald Press, 1990), 19.

59. 1 Peter 2:9.

60. Matt. 5:14-16, Isa. 49:6.

61. 2 Cor. 5:20.

62. *Confession of Faith in a Mennonite Perspective* (Scottdale, Pa.: Herald Press, 1995), 86.

63. John H. Yoder, *The Politics of Jesus* (Grand Rapids: William B. Eerdmans Publishing Company, 1972), 134.

64. Luke 14:27.

65. Phil. 3: 10-11.

66. Matt. 25:40.

67. Oliver Davies. *A Theology of Compassion: Metaphysics of Difference and the Renewal of Tradition* (Grand Rapids: William B. Eerdmans Publishing Company, 2001), 244.

68. Phil. 2:1-11.

69. Hans Haffner, "About the True Soldier of Jesus Christ," quoted in Peter Hoover, *The Secret of the Strength: What Would the Anabaptists Tell This Generation?* (Shippensburg: Benchmark Press, 1998), 35.

70. John H. Yoder, *The Politics of Jesus* (Grand Rapids: William B. Eerdmans Publishing Company, 1972), 97.

71. Matt. 25:40.

72. Matt. 22:35-40.

73. 1 John 4:7-19.

74. Walter L. Liefeld, "Luke," in *The Expositors Bible Commentary,* vol. 8, ed. Frank E. Gaebelein (Grand Rapids: Zondervan Publishing House, 1984), 893.

75. "Dordrecht Confession of Faith, 1632" quoted in John C. Wenger, *Introduction to Theology: A Brief Introduction to the Doctrinal Content of Scripture Written in the Anabaptist-Mennonite Tradition* (Scottdale, Pa.: Herald Press, 1954), 382.

76. Matt. 10:29-31; Luke 12:6-7.

77. Matt. 26:31-46.

78. Myron S. Augsburger, *The Robe of God: Reconciliation, the Believers Church Essential* (Scottdale, Pa.: Herald Press, 2000), 227.

CHAPTER EIGHT

The Biotechnology Vision: Insight from Anabaptist Values

Conrad G. Brunk

Dr. Conrad G. Brunk is professor of philosophy and director of the Center for Studies in Religion and Society at the University of Victoria in British Columbia, Canada. His areas of research and teaching include ethics, philosophy of religion, environmental and health risk management, conflict resolution, and philosophy of law. Dr. Brunk served on the Canadian Biotechnology Advisory Committee, which advises the government of Canada on matters of biotechnology regulation and development, and served as co-chair of the Royal Society of Canada Expert Panel on the Future of Food Biotechnology. He holds a Ph.D. in philosophy from Northwestern University.

*T*he experience I bring to discussion of a biotechnology vision in Anabaptist perspective has come from working in the Canadian context in public policy development in biotechnology. I have become involved in recent years with technology policy, looking at the ways people regulate risks associated with new technologies, particularly biotechnology.

I am an ethicist, not a scientist, theologian, or church historian. My assignment is to address Anabaptist values. I do that from the perspective not of a theologian who is an expert in Anabaptist values but through reflection on the values I have brought to the debate as someone raised in the Anabaptist Mennonite tradition and deeply influenced by its values.

I want to discuss first what values I see as driving biotechnology. I raise some troubling issues posed by new technologies in general which are also intensely present in new biotechnologies. Then I discuss how one thinks ethically about the risks of biotechnology in society. I conclude with reflections on what insights may be gained from the Anabaptist tradition.

What Are The Values Driving Biotechnology?

Although I will address both agricultural and medical biotechnology, my focus will tend to be on the agricultural side. Agricultural biotechnology provides tremendous economic gain for farmers and the farming industry. Many promoters argue that agricultural biotechnology will provide more food, better nutrition, and better health for humanity. Agricultural biotechnology also promises environmental amelioration with fewer pesticides and plants that place less burden on the ecosystems around them. Biotechnology can provide new energy and industrial resources that will allow increased consumption as well as a response to depleting natural resources in the world. Improvement of human health with "farmaceuticals," nutraceuticals, xenotransplants from genetically modified animals, and so forth, through biotechnology can contribute greatly to the promotion of health and the alleviation of disease and illness in society.

One primary moral value that underlies these goals of biotechnology is beneficence, that is, the promotion of human good. Of course, in many societies today, one defines human good in terms of the maximization of one's desires and the minimization of the things one does not like.

What values drive biomedical biotechnology? Again, the dominant value is the alleviation of human suffering through genetic therapies for gene-based illnesses. Scientists also want to alleviate suffering through reduction or elimination of genetic diseases. This is the therapeutic, ameliorative goal of biotechnology. However, also in the background is the larger idea of the promotion of human well-being and happiness, which James Peterson introduced earlier. With this value, one deals with the desire of many for a prolonged life as well as an enhanced quality of life. This also includes the ability to enhance human performance athletically, intellectually, artistically, and in other ways, as well as the potential to enhance human emotional life through psychic alteration or elimination of qualities of appearance and performance that lead to emotional distress in our society. Many people are talking about the promise of these new technologies to improve the human condition in these ways.

However, there are other drivers of biotechnology development besides those often mentioned as the moral reasons for pursuing this technology. The first of these is science and the quest for knowledge itself. Science leads technology, and technology makes new science possible. The sheer attraction of power over nature, which is essentially the ability to control the conditions of one's life, is a tremendous driver. For the scientist there is the "lure of the technically sweet," as Robert Oppenheimer called it in the context of the development of nuclear technology. When he was asked the question, "What was it that made you so devoted to the development of the atomic bomb?" which he eventually regarded as a terrible technology, he responded, "It was for all of us scientists working on the project the lure of the technically sweet."[1] One can hear the excitement about "the lure of the technically sweet" whenever one hears scientists talk about the potentials of this leading-edge knowledge.

There are also the imperatives within technology itself that authors such as Jacques Ellul and Langdon Winner speak about eloquently. These authors talk about the imperatives within technology itself that tend to drive it and its development in certain directions.[2] Although space must limit significant discussion of this agenda, discernment of constraints upon what becomes ethically possible in a society is essential.

Another driver of biotechnology development is a need to be competitive in the globalized economy. I sit on the Canadian Biotechnology Advisory Committee, which advises the Canadian federal government on biotechnology policy, particularly regulatory policy. One of the things that has impressed me during this experience is that what drives Canadian biotechnology policy is the concern that if Canada does not keep pace, the country will lose out on the intellectual property and the patents, and profits to be gained. Then the economy and health care system will lag behind world standards. Therefore the major focus of government policy regarding biotechnology is on how Canada can promote development of this technology through support for research and streamlining of the regulatory system to remove all significant barriers to innovation and commercialization.

For example, in medical biotechnology in both the United States and Canada, governments face the problem of how their respective regulatory systems are going to work in the context of custom-tailored medical therapies. Each person has a different genome, which means that everyone responds differently to vaccines, antibiotics, and various therapies depending upon this genetic inheritance. The great hope is that we will be able soon to tailor therapies to individualized genomes. What happens to a regulatory testing regime for such technologies? Will it have to test every individualized, customized therapy? Obviously not. One could never get them to the market. Therefore, each country will have to change the stringent regulatory system that it has in place now. In the case of biomedical technology, the regulatory system may have to be altered in ways that will be less careful in assessing the risks and other implications of these technologies.

I want to discuss the unprecedented power of biotechnology to redesign nature. Several speakers have already referred to biotechnology as a new, highly powerful technology to achieve human good. That power also has implications that may not always serve our best interests. Those in favor of biotechnology often argue, "Have not people always been redesigning nature, since the land was first plowed and seeds first planted?" However, the claim by many biotechnology promoters that there is nothing fundamentally different about plants engineered with human DNA is, in my view, profoundly misleading. The technology *does* allow scientists to create the combination of gene sequences that would not occur in nature or by traditional hybridization techniques, and this is precisely what makes the technology so significant. Biotechnology represents the power to do things that could not otherwise be done, and in that way intrudes into nature in a way that in a sense is "unnatural." I am not using the term *unnatural* in any philosophical or moral sense, but simply in the ordinary sense that scientists are now able to do things that would not have happened in nature. In that important difference lies a tremendous new power.

Biotechnology has the power to redesign humans. The physical, psychological, moral, and spiritual characteristics of people all have a genetic component, although surely they are not genetically determined, as some have argued or assumed. The ability to manipulate human genes confers upon one an unprecedented power to change one's children and grandchildren into beings who could be morally and spiritually unrecognizable to us today. This power has profound moral, metaphysical, and theological implications. How will we be capable of thinking about the world as a creation of God and about ourselves as moral creatures, or as a creation of God rather than a creation of our parents and their genetic therapists?

In plants and animal germ cells, new engineered gene sequences can be passed on to an unlimited future and environment by reproductive processes that are not controlled by their designers. Scientists are not yet performing germ cell therapy in biomedicine, but it will surely come. However, scientists are regularly performing germ cell therapy in the products of agricultural biotechnology, so that they reproduce themselves with the engineered genetic trait. Thus, genetic intervention implies possible impacts upon the future of the environment and the human that are unforeseeable, potentially uncontrollable and even irreversible.

Troubling Issues Posed By the New Technologies

What moral framework is sufficient to guide the technology that has these unprecedented implications? What kind of moral framework will help us think about this technology in terms of a long-term future where the effects will be highly significant? I will begin the discussion of this problem by looking at some issues related to technology itself. New technologies push the frontiers of scientific knowledge. Sometimes the technology is actually out in front of the science. It is often said that the new technologies are advancing far ahead of the ethical thinking about the issues they pose. I am interested in the fact that technology also tends to be out in front of the science. That might be an odd thing to say; let me explain. The technology often comes before the full science in biotechnology, especially agricultural biotechnology, because of the way in which agricultural biotechnology has moved to the product level much more quickly and with a different kind of regulatory system than biomedical biotechnology, which usually requires more careful testing and scrutiny.

It is important to understand the difference between theoretical and applied science. This distinction, which most scientists and philosophers of science theoretically understand, is becoming increasingly erased in the context of biotechnology. Theoretical science seeks understanding of the complete physical or biological system and is able to achieve high levels of certainty, because it can wait until the requisite levels of data are available to achieve the confidence levels needed for reliable conclusions.

Applied science, science enlisted in the development of technology, needs to understand only how to produce a wanted consequence within a system. Applied science does not need to understand the larger system in its entirety. Therefore, it is relatively easy to discover how to engineer a corn plant resistant to European corn borer. One need not understand the total biological or ecological system in which that plant will be cultivated to get the wanted technological effect. One can produce the corn plant that successfully expresses the wanted trait, and if something unexpected or adverse happens later on say, "Oh, I wonder how that happened?"

Carole Cramer earlier presented an example of this phenomenon when she discussed the case of a corn engineered to produce a specific advantageous toxin. The corn also unexpectedly produced resistance to fungi. Why? No one knew for sure, nor was the effect anticipated. In that case, the unexpected consequence was benign, but what if it had been an adverse consequence? The unanticipated effects were not built into the design of the technology. That is what I mean by saying that the engineering of the intended consequence is the easy part of the technology. It can be accomplished without full scientific understanding of the underlying systems.

Technology is an applied science; it is interested in solving a particular problem. The science that supports new technology just because it is leading-edge technology will usually have particularly high levels of uncertainty about the underlying system in which these effects can be produced. For example, there can be uncertainty about the peripheral impacts within the system. Scientists talk about pleiotropy, for example, in the context of biotechnology. When one inserts a gene sequence into a genome, one may achieve the trait that has been found to be associated with that sequence. But one may not know what other things may also result as a consequence of the location of that sequence in the genome or its interactions with other genes in the genome. There is uncertainty about the unintended— and often highly undesirable—consequences.

Leslie Biesecker gave an example of the possibility of unknown consequences in biomedics in the case of McKusick-Kaufman syndrome that occurs among the Old Order Amish. The development of the genetic therapy, which appears to arrest the usual disorder associated with a gene sequence, also increases the risk of leukemia or other cancers. Why does this unanticipated effect happen? It is part of the conundrum of uncertainty that surrounds applied science. Therefore, designing a technology to produce certain immediate benefits is the easy part of the task. Scientific understanding of the physical, biological, and social aspects of the system and ecosystem is the more difficult part and often follows years after the technology is first developed.

What are some of the most significant underlying uncertainties in genomic science? The early reductionistic models of genetics are turning out to be quite inaccurate. Take, for example, the notion that DNA, through the messenger RNA, codes for a protein, which then produces certain metabolites leading to the development of cell structures and thereby produces a certain phenotype or trait. Most scientists now agree that this linear causal model is inaccurate. The causal pathway seems to go both ways, producing a complex synergism between gene, cell, organism, and environment. In other words, the pathway can move both directions in complex ways. Therefore, it is not surprising that many of the early promises of the immediate benefits from biotechnological therapies have proven to be far more difficult to achieve than scientists anticipated. The linear causal model of genetic structure has turned out to be much more complicated than scientists first thought. The bottom line is that at this point a powerful technology is pushing rapidly forward, while many uncertainties remain in the underlying science.

Has this always been the case with technology? Of course. However, older, low-tech technologies do not have the power to extend their consequences so far in space and time, particularly into the future. That gives biotechnology a critical importance.

I suggest the general rule that the simpler the technology, the more its impacts remain spatially and temporarily immediate, and the easier it is to observe and repair the negative impacts of that technology. The converse of this rule is that the more complex and sophisticated, and even immediately beneficial, a technology, the more it tends to displace the negative consequences upon others who are remote in space and time–and the more difficult it is to foresee and estimate these negative consequences, or even to see their causal relation to the technology. This is critical to understanding how one should think about the development of biotechnology and its regulation.

The regulation of this technology involves critical ethical issues. We have a basic obligation to deploy such technologies cautiously. Traditional moral theories and methods are not adequate to provide this precautionary stance. Two approaches are common in society. The first is consequentialist; it seeks to maximize human welfare and minimize the harmful consequences. Even though this approach has dominated economic and ethical approaches to public policy regarding technology development in the last century, it is becoming increasingly questionable as a moral algorithm for dealing with the issues posed by complex technologies, because we are in a situation where determining consequences over a long period is increasingly difficult. Thus, one cannot get clear calculations of the balance of good over harm.

Both our predominant ethics and our technologies are biased in favor of immediate benefits and against concern about long-term risk. Many people have pointed out that technologies are designed to produce the wanted benefits. The concerns about the unintended risks tend not to get the same research interest. One of my deep concerns is that the new system we have now in both Canada and the United States of promoting scientific research that can be commercialized immediately has increasingly oriented the agenda of science in these countries toward the production of immediate benefits, which are tremendous and promising. However, that has an impact. It means less money and concern can be generated to research unwanted consequences. Therefore, the technology and the science become less motivated to investigate the risks. So do our consequentialist moral algorithms, because the benefits are immediate and easily weigh in the balance, while the unwanted consequences are long-term and difficult to assess. So our economic analyses will tend to overemphasize the benefits and underemphasize the risks. This is a built-in bias in the way we think about the ethics of these issues.

On the other side, the traditional "duty" ethics are inadequate, because their focus is on the meaning of actions and the immediate moral context as well. "Do not harm;" "Do not lie;" "Be truthful." These refer to issues of relationships between existing persons. Somehow, when one deals with what kind of human future one will produce for one's children, grandchildren, and great-grandchildren, this ethic is too short-sighted.

In his powerful book, *The Imperative of Responsibility*, Hans Jonas argues that we need a new way of thinking ethically about the future—one based on what he calls the "heuristics of fear."[3] That is, we should concentrate on those absolutely unacceptable things that could go irreversibly wrong as a result of our technologies and design these technologies in ways that guarantee that they do not lead to these consequences. The "heuristics of fear" is best understood as what we now are calling "precaution."

How Should We Think Ethically About the Risks of Biotechnology?

Here let me simply summarize some of the risks involved. There are environmental risks of genetically modified crops, including potential impacts upon natural ecosystems and biodiversity. Transgenes have the ability in some plant species to "outcross" into related wild and domesticated species, thus conferring their associated traits similarly or in unexpected ways upon those species. This raises concerns about the development of more aggressive weeds ("super-weeds"), new invasive species, and loss of biodiversity in natural ecosystems.

Carole Cramer presented the potentially tremendous advancements that may be achieved through agricultural biotechnology. However great these achievements, it is important to recognize their potential downsides as well. When one uses genes to produce various toxins or antigens and therapeutic medicine in plants, these genes can theoretically not only cross over into other plants but also into the food chain. What happens if the genes designed to produce new substances for purely therapeutic or industrial uses get into the human or animal food chain? What plants should we be using to produce these new products? Sunflowers and corn are attractive candidates, but because these are food plants the risks of transfer of human toxins into the food chain is significant. Plants like tobacco are probably a better choice. We want to be sure that the plants we choose do not have close relatives into which the transgenes could cross.

Such issues must be thought through carefully. We must consider the impact not only on natural ecosystems but also on agricultural ecosystems. We must also think, for example, about the impact on humans of unintended allergens in genetically modified foods as well as unintended effects of other genetic interventions.

There are also moral risks. That is, risks to the structure of the moral community and ways we interact with it. What impact does biotechnology have on people's relationship with nature? How do we view an environment that is our own creation? How long can our children continue to think about nature as a divine creation when it is increasingly an artifact of our technologies? There are risks of biotechnology's impact upon our relationships with each other, because our children and grandchildren will view themselves differently; it will be harder for them to view themselves as creations of God rather than creations of their parents or of a technological intervention.

I want to give a glimpse of what I am concerned about when I discuss how Anabaptist ethics applies to biotechnology. Of course, there are unintended effects of cloning. They were mentioned in John Gearhart's presentation. Many unexpected things are happening in the first generations of cloned animals that should tell scientists they have a long way to go before they can clone human beings. If this is happening in reproductive cloning, could it also be happening in therapeutic cloning? Society must proceed very carefully with this technology. Do we have reliable enough knowledge of the risks from stem cells derived from embryos and chimera embryos like the recent Chinese "Humabit"?

There are also unintended effects of genetic intervention with *in vitro* fertilization embryos. Potential unintended harms of reproductive genetic manipulation cannot be consented to by the future person involved, and if the genetic change is germ-line, then affected successive generations will not have consented to the risks or even to their "improvement" if there are no real harms. The gap between the animal and the human model in science has always been a problem in bioethics. This problem is now magnified in the context of biotechnology because of how easily the barriers between animal and human genomes are crossed.

Biomedical technology also poses moral risks. A major one involves personal privacy. Population health promotion requires gene data banks. Who has access to the genetic information? How can it be used? How can it be protected? The same computers required to do the mapping and sorting of prodigious amounts of genetic data, which make genomic technology possible, are also the computers that can take "anonymous" information and put it together in profiles that make it identifiable.

There is also a risk to the future of the human moral community posed by the use of human zygotes, embryos, or fetuses for tissue harvesting. At issue is not just the status of the embryo itself but also the impact of this technology upon the way one thinks about oneself as a human being.

There is a moral risk to using genetic engineering and screening techniques to improve human nature. New genetic technologies increasingly erode the distinction between therapeutic and eugenic interventions. Ethicists, theologians, and social critics are hotly debating this issue, and the answer to the question about how to draw this distinction is not clear. Is it really possible to use new genetic interventions therapeutically without sliding down the slippery slope to eugenics? Where does the elimination of "undesirable" human traits or curing of 'diseases' end and the improvement of human nature (i.e., the building of the ideal human and the devaluation of the less than ideal human) begin. The answers are not at all clear.

What Values Should We Protect?

I have summarized above not only some of the most significant values that drive the new biotechnologies but also some of the most significant values they place at risk. So a central moral question we need to face is that of what values we should be most concerned to protect. In a liberal, pluralist society like ours, this is a hard question to answer, because the answer is relative to the dominant set of desires and fears within a society at any given time. Liberalism is about the freedom to maximize preferences, whatever those preferences are. So we hire economists and pollsters to tell us what preferences people have at a given time. We assume these will be the preferences of the redesigned future generations who live in the environment we have also redesigned. This all affects the policies that the government presently adopts in deploying and regulating the technologies. I see this happening all the time in the Canadian context—that is, government technology promotion and regulation policy dictated by public opinion polls, a process by which we take the dominant preferences expressed today and make them into policy that will bind many future generations.

In modern democratic societies like ours, there is a set of what I call the "liberal consensus values." These are the values that currently dominate the discussion of biotechnology ethics. I summarize them only briefly:

- the value of maximizing individual autonomy;
- the freedom to pursue goods;
- the freedom to pursue knowledge;
- the value of personal privacy;
- the duty to minimize harms and maximize goods;
- respect for equal human dignity (although society has no consensus about what constitutes dignity);
- being just (although society has no consensus about what justice, fairness, and equality mean).

There are also some contested values brought into the debate by religious and other value communities:

- concern about "respect for life," which produces the debate about when human life begins or becomes deserving of full respect, and whether non-human lives, such as endangered animal species, should be included in this respect;
- concern to protect the integrity of "nature" or "human nature."

I have placed certain words in quotation marks to highlight that these are contested concepts. These contested issues are behind the concerns many people have when they say one should not be "playing God"—meaning that one should not be tampering with certain sacred things. Concerns about human nature or nature itself are both "essentialist" assumptions, that is, assumptions that these things have certain God-given essences that are very much challenged or undermined by the evolutionary biology intrinsic to biotechnology.

Mainstream Christian moral thinkers in the United States, and to a certain extent in Canada, largely share what I call the "consensus values." Many would argue that maximizing human good has been a distinctive Christian value. In fact, many commentators say that the whole notion of the improvement of humanity as a moral imperative is an idea Christianity has contributed to modern society, and this idea is the moral driver behind technology. However, the uniquely Christian ethical debate about biotechnology, particularly in North America, has centered on the two contested values I mentioned earlier. Christian concern about embryonic cell research and therapeutic cloning has focused upon the value of "respect for life," which is the source of many debates.

The irony is that the very values placed at risk by biotechnology are also the values driving it forward. This irony has been pointed out eloquently by the President's Bioethics Counsel in their recently issued report.[4] For example, the right of autonomy gives free reign to the very technology that may undermine the possibility of autonomous choice in future generations. Also, how can one maintain the value of equality when engineered humans are more equal than un-engineered humans? Humanitarianism, understood as the maximization of human welfare, may lead to the "abolition of the human" in any morally recognizable sense.

What Insights Can the Anabaptist Tradition Provide?

I have been asked to address the question of what unique insights into these issues can be gleaned from the Anabaptist-Mennonite theological tradition. The first difficulty anyone faces when answering this question is that there is hardly a consensus on what "the Anabaptist perspective" is on any issue. There is no normative view of early sixteenth-century Anabaptism, since the movement took many forms and its leaders disagreed widely on many theological issues.[5] Neither has there been uniformity of thought and practice among Anabaptist or Mennonite communities since the sixteenth century. Only the late twentieth century has seen attempts to provide systematic Anabaptist theologies and ethics.[6] Thus the best I can do is simply to identify some of the dominant themes that emerge in both Anabaptist practice and in developing Anabaptist theologies, as I understand them. The deepest values of a culture are reflected in its practice, and Anabaptist ethics have been molded much more by the practices of communities in various social contexts than by systematic theological reflection. Therefore, I do not claim to offer a systematic Anabaptist ethic of biotechnology.

The significant factors that shape the Anabaptist understanding include most importantly its various communities' experiences as persecuted minorities in majority cultures throughout its history. A second factor is the central emphasis of discipleship to Christ in Anabaptist theology and ethics. Discipleship is understood as involving nonconformity with dominant values in a majority culture, which is the world. In this respect, Anabaptist ethics is an "ethics of dissent," a theme well developed in the writings of John Howard Yoder, Stanley Hauerwas, and others.[7]

The worldly virtues Anabaptists often view as vices include a reliance on power and violence for social and environmental control, which is seen as lack of trust in divine sovereignty over human affairs in history. In the Anabaptist tradition this is seen as a sin of faithlessness. A second vice is arrogance about the capacity of human reason to know the truth and achieve it infallibly, which is seen as the sin of pride. Other vices include the unconstrained maximization of human desire and disregard for the poor, the weak, and the humble. The dissenting virtues deal with humility in respect to social or environmental control, and a deep suspicion of power, which is at the heart of Anabaptist commitments to nonresistance. This has a direct bearing on Anabaptists' understanding of the importance of precaution.

Other dissenting Anabaptist virtues include humility with respect to human knowledge, frugality, or constraint on consumption, and love of neighbor, or giving the cup of cold water. In the Anabaptist tradition, this virtue has been understood as commitment to the amelioration of suffering, not as a global improvement of the human condition. The importance of loving one's neighbor is central to this dissenting stance. Loving one's neighbor involves the acceptance of everyone, regardless of undesirable characteristics, whether moral, physiological, or psychological. Another dissenting Anabaptist virtue is the priority of the moral community, which is the church.

From the perspective of these "dissenting values," biotechnological development should be guided by sober humility about our ability to know or control the impacts of the technology. In other words, we should be committed to a principle of precaution. Using this principle, we should show a bias for protecting human and environmental safety. There should also be a demand for high scientific confidence in the avoidance of unacceptable and irreversible outcomes in the long-term future, as well as a burden of proof on developers and beneficiaries of the technology to provide the scientific assurance that these outcomes will not materialize. We should be especially precautionary with respect to the risks of irremediable consequences.

The virtue of frugality should sensitize us to the way biotechnology is driven forward by the promise of the satiation of unlimited human wants, which include the desires for longer life, immortality, and enhanced physical and intellectual capacities. Many people sincerely believe more food through more production is the essential technological solution to growing world population. In other words, they believe that producing new genetically modified foods, designed to increase food productivity in marginal soils and in adverse climates will alleviate the situation of widespread malnutrition and starvation in Africa.

However, we need to recognize that we currently live in a world where there is already enough food to feed the world's hungry. What we face now is not a situation of food scarcity but rather a moral problem concerning the distribution of that food. The great temptation of technological advanced and affluent societies is to avoid the question of unjust distribution of food and other goods in the world by seeking the "technological fix." Technology is the preferred instrument for solving what are really social and moral problems. Our mortality, morbidity, weakness, and imperfection are part of what keeps us recognizably human. Perhaps reduced consumption and more equitable distribution to meet human needs is the morally preferable solution, from an Anabaptist perspective.

The mainstream Christian understanding of neighbor love has been largely a utilitarian one, which strives to maximize the good—

to make life better, even if we must do evil to accomplish it. This ethic says that any risk of harm is acceptable, as long as there is enough good achieved to outweigh the harm. Thus, loving one's neighbor is taken as an imperative to remake the world for maximum human benefit, and biotechnology promises to fulfill this imperative.

I believe the virtue of neighbor love in Anabaptist thought is interpreted as an imperative to love one's neighbor in a different way, and that is as a limit on how one treats one's neighbor nonviolently and with equal regard, as well as an injunction to relieve suffering, which is not the same thing as maximizing good. In other words, the primary responsibility to one's neighbor is in terms of harm prevention, not good maximization. This ethos of neighbor love, in contrast to utilitarian maximization of human wants, is exemplified by organizations like the Mennonite Central Committee, which demonstrate the meaning of the "cup of cold water in the name of Christ" to which I previously referred.

Medical biotechnologies always raise the ghost of eugenics—the aim to improve the human species according to some vision of the ideal human being. These visions are almost always discriminatory against those humans who do not fit the ideal. The eugenic movements of the early twentieth century, not limited only to the genocidal eugenics of fascism, are a grim testament to this moral danger. Most contemporary ethical analyses maintain that there is no way to draw a clear conceptual line between genetic therapy (sometimes called "negative eugenics") and genetic improvement ("positive eugenics"), yet the eugenic use of biotechnology is recognized as one of its greatest moral risks. A solution must be found for this moral risk before we proceed so far down the road that we lose the ability to even perceive the moral loss. The Anabaptist sensitivity to the distinction between remediation of suffering and the complete amelioration of the human condition is a much-needed perspective in this debate. Anabaptists have drawn several implications from the priority of the moral community, including the subordination of the individual autonomy to the discipline of the community.

Another implication Anabaptists have drawn from the moral community includes the idea that truth is found in the Spirit-led discernment of the community, with the criterion of truth being the edification of the community. Thus, Anabaptists have always been suspicious of the enlightenment faith in individual rationality, as well as the medieval faith in natural theology, with the idea that if one had a good theology of nature, one would understand how to treat it.

The focus of the Anabaptist perspective has not been as much on the nature or "essence" of humanness or of the natural environment as it has been upon the nature of the moral *community*. Biotechnology poses a uniquely new ethical conundrum: If one has the power to re-design human beings, where does one find the template?

I see two options here. One is a naturalistic or essentialist conception of human nature, which has been the preoccupation of classical Christian theology but not the focus of most Anabaptists. The second is a normative concept of what it is to be a human moral community and what it should look like in the future. This is more consistent with the Anabaptist tradition, as I understand it. Anabaptist thought has been generally suspicious of natural theology. It has been criticized by other Christians as ignoring a doctrine of creation in favor of an exclusive preoccupation with the doctrine of redemption.

In the context of biotechnology, this may turn out to be a great strength of an Anabaptist perspective. This alternative approach concerns itself with the question of how to maintain a faithful moral community in the future. This has been the typical Anabaptist argument from the very beginning. The fundamental question one must ask about biotechnology is this: How can we use biotechnology in ways that will not undermine the fundamental values that make a human moral community possible?

Notes

1. Robert Jungk, *Brighter Than a Thousand Suns* (New York: Harcourt Brace 1958).

2. Jacques Ellul, *The Technological Society* (New York: Knopf, 1964); Langdon Winner, *The Whale and the Reactor: A Search for Limits in an Age of High Technology,* (Chicago: University of Chicago Press, 1986).

3. Hans Jonas, *The Imperative of Responsibility: In Search of an Ethics for the Technological* Age (Chicago: University of Chicago Press, 1984).

4. The President's Council on Bioethics, *Beyond Therapy: Biotechnology and the Pursuit of Happiness* (Washington, D.C., 2003).

5. Arnold C. Snyder, *Anabaptist History and Theology: An Introduction* (Kitchener, Ont.: Pandora Press, 1999).

6. These include James A. Reimer, *The Dogmatic Imagination* (Scottdale, Pa.: Herald Press, 2003); J. Denny Weaver, *Anabaptist Theology in Face of Postmodernity* (Telford, Pa.: Pandora Press U.S., 2000); Thomas N. Finger, *A Contemporary Anabaptist Theology* (Downer's Grove, Ill.: InterVarsity).

7. John Howard Yoder, *The Politics Of Jesus: Vicit Agnus Noster* (Grand Rapids: William B. Eerdmans Publishing Company, 1972); Stanley Hauerwas, *A Community of Character: Toward a Constructive Christian Social Ethic* (Notre Dame: University of Notre Dame Press, 1981).

CHAPTER NINE

Ethical Issues in Biotechnology: Human Embryonic Stem Cell Research and the Anabaptist Vision

LeRoy B. Walters

Dr. LeRoy B. Walters is the Joseph P. Kennedy Senior Professor of Christian Ethics at the Kennedy Institute of Ethics, Georgetown University, where he is also a Professor of Philosophy. He has studied at Messah College; Associated Mennonite Biblical Seminary; University of Heidelberg; Free University of Berlin; and at Yale University, where in 1971 he earned his Ph.D. in Christian ethic. His interests include human genetics, human embryonic stem cell research, ethics and the Holocaust.

My focus is on ethical issues in human embryonic stem cell research. I will also aim to relate that field of research to the Anabaptist vision. I begin by describing the science of human embryonic stem cell research, showing several graphics. Second, I outline five policy options on human embryonic stem cell research. To do so, I will take a trip around the world, figuratively speaking, to explore how different cultures and countries have wrestled with this problem and what conclusions they have reached. Third, I examine a central ethical question involving this research: What is the moral status of a five-day-old human embryo? Again I take a comparative perspective and look at several religious and philosophical traditions. Finally, I go out on a limb and talk about the relevance of the Anabaptist tradition to this topic. We certainly have to extrapolate from the thinking of the sixteenth- and seventeenth-century leaders of the Anabaptist movement. I seek to argue that this type of research is compatible with the Anabaptist vision.

Every industrialized country in the world has had to wrestle with the human embryonic stem cell research. My first presupposition is that this is an important field. In other words, we are not simply hearing the hype of scientists who want research funding. This field does have the potential, in the short term, to have a major impact on basic science. In the long term, it may provide new approaches to therapy for serious diseases. I also think it is too early to know whether adult stem cells will have all the desirable properties of embryonic stem cells. Thus, the most prudent policy, in my view, is to pursue both lines of research simultaneously, not to wait for five years to see whether adult stem cell research is successful.

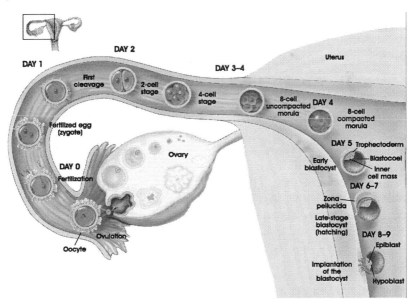

Fig. 1. Development of the pre-implantation blastocyst in humans[1]

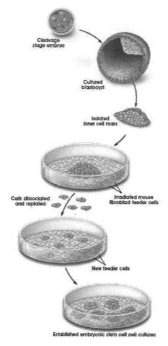

Fig. 2. Techniques for generating embryonic stem cell cultures[2]

The Science of
Human Embryonic Stem Cell Research

I turn now to the scientific background for human embryonic stem cell research. Figure 1 depicts fertilization and early embryonic development inside the body of a woman. On the left a single egg is being ovulated; if there are sperm at the far end of the Fallopian tube, fertilization may occur on what is called day zero. During the first five days after fertilization, the early embryo floats down the Fallopian tube. Notice day five at the right hand side. That is the key day for human embryonic stem cell research. It is the day on which the early blastocyst stage is usually reached. The inner cell mass is the key component of the five-day old blastocyst. Stem cells are produced by removing the inner cell mass, which kills the embryo, and by placing the cells from the inner cell mass (perhaps 25 or 30 cells) in a Petri dish.

In Figure 2 the cells have been placed on a layer of mouse feeder cells. Since this report from which I took the illustration was published, techniques have been developed for using human cells as the feeder layer in the Petri dish to avoid contamination by mouse viruses.

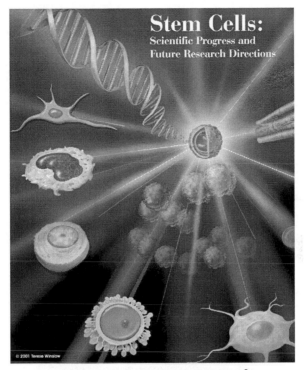

Fig. 3. *National Institutes of Health stem cell report cover*[3]

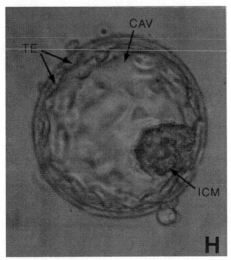

Fig. 4. *Five-day-old blastocyst*[4]

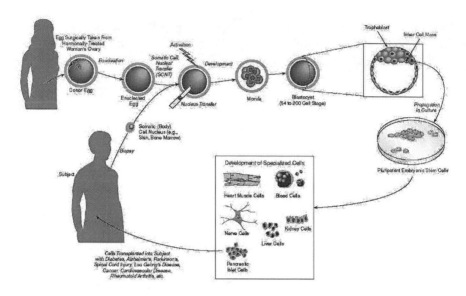

Fig. 5. Nuclear transplantation to produce stem cells

Figure 3 shows the cover of the July 2002 National Institutes of Health (NIH) report on this topic. It has a Star Wars quality; the stem cells appear to have almost cosmic properties. The reality of a five-day old blastocyst is more prosaic, less colorful. Figure 4 shows a photo of a five-day-old blastocyst; at the lower right (near the four o'clock position) is the inner cell mass. One can also see (at the 5:30 position) that the blastocyst is just beginning to hatch out of its shell.

Figure 5 is from a 2002 report by the National Research Council on *Scientific and Medical Aspects of Human Reproductive Cloning.*[5] This very detailed figure shows that an egg cell is removed from a woman and the nucleus of the egg is removed. A somatic cell, perhaps a skin cell, is removed from a man, and the nucleus of that cell is removed and fused with the enucleated egg cell. A gentle shock is administered to this combination to induce cell division. If all goes well, the combination of the woman's egg cell and the man's nucleus begins to divide like an early embryo. At the blastocyst stage of embryonic development the inner cell mass is removed and placed in a Petri dish. If the procedure is successful, embryonic stem cells begin to grow. The final stage in this figure reflects a hope for the future rather than a current reality. It shows stem cells being transplanted into the man from whom the somatic cell had been removed. These cells would be genetically matched to the donor's other somatic cells.

Five Policy Options for
Human Embryonic Stem Cell Research

What ethical positions can one take on human embryonic stem cell research? What policy options have countries around the world adopted? The first option is to say, "No. We will neither derive embryonic stem cells, nor will we use stem cells that have already been derived that others have derived (that is, produced)." This policy would be the adult-stem-cell-only option. People who hold that human embryos should be protected from the time of fertilization forward are almost compelled to adopt Option 1 as their preferred option.

They are not alone in the world. Austria, France, Germany (until July 2002), Ireland, Italy, Norway, Poland, and Portugal have adopted Option 1. Several of these countries are predominantly Catholic, but Norway is predominantly Lutheran; Germany is about evenly divided between Catholics and Protestants. There are also eleven states in the United States that have adopted Option 1, as Figure 6 indicates.

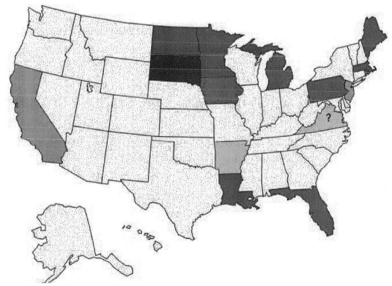

Fig. 6. States with laws on human embryos

The eleven darkly shaded states all prohibit human embryo research. South Dakota even prohibits the importation of human embryonic stem cells from outside the state. You may notice the question mark on Virginia; I will come back to Virginia a bit later. It has an anti-cloning law, but I cannot figure out exactly what kinds of cloning are prohibited by the Virginia statute. All the unshaded or lightly shaded states have adopted some other option than Option 1.

Policy Option 2 says it is permissible to use existing stem cells but not to derive any additional embryonic stem cells. A rationale for this view would be that there is nothing that can be done to rescue the embryos that have already been sacrificed to produce the stem cells that exist now, so scientists should use them. Further, those who support this option do not want to provide incentives for infertility clinics to try to produce surplus embryos.

Two countries in the world have adopted Option 2. The U.S., during the later years of the Clinton administration and in the Bush administration, has limited NIH funding for research on human embryonic stem cells to research that uses existing stem cells. After the U.S. had adopted this policy, President Bush added the time limit of August 9, 2001; federal funding for human embryonic stem cell research is restricted to stem cells derived by August 9, 2001. Germany has accepted Option 2, as well, but with a later deadline date.

A third option says, "It is acceptable to derive new embryonic stem cells, but the only permissible source is remaining (or unneeded) embryos from infertility clinics." Given the fact that there are about 400,000 frozen embryos in the United States in infertility clinics around the country, it would seem as if that *should* be an ample supply. This is just one country in the world. On the other hand, only 11,000 or so of those frozen embryos have been donated for research, and there remain questions about how many of those will be viable for producing stem cells.[6] Here is the rationale for Option 3: Is it not preferable to use embryos for research rather than to discard them? For example, some couples have completed their reproduction and may wish to donate remaining embryos for research—in the hope that scientists will be able to develop new knowledge and perhaps, in the long run, new therapies. Of course, the informed consent of the genetic parents is an important part of the donation process.

Option 3 is, in fact, the mainstream position in most of the world. In Europe, it has been possible almost to hear an ice jam breaking within recent years, as several countries that formerly rejected human embryonic stem cell research or human embryonic research, have begun to affirm it. The following European countries accept Option 3: Belgium, the Czech Republic, Denmark, Finland, Greece, Hungary, the Netherlands, Russia (de facto), Sweden, and the United Kingdom. Spain and Switzerland are also moving in this direction. In the Middle East, Iranian scientists have recently derived human embryonic stem cells, causing the Supreme Leader of the Islamic Republic to receive the scientists into his office and congratulate them on their great achievement. It is ironic to think that Iran is slightly to the left of the U.S. federal government in terms of its policy on the public funding of stem cell research. Israel also accepts Option 3. Asian countries such as China, India, Japan, and Singapore are moving ahead rapidly. Australia has a new law that is also more liberal than the U.S. federal government policy. Canada has guidelines in place that permit Option 3, and the Canadian Parliament may endorse this option soon.

Thirty-nine states in the United States permit Option 3. These states include all the unshaded states, which have no laws in this area, as illustrated by Figure 6. Two other states (Arkansas and Virginia) also permit Option 3. As best I can determine, both states prohibit any form of cloning, including research cloning. California and New Jersey also accept Option 3, as well as allowing research cloning.

One now crosses an ethical threshold. With Options 4 and 5, embryos will be created specifically for research purposes, so it is no longer a matter of remaining embryos frozen in infertility clinics. It is a matter of making new embryos for research purposes. The fourth option says that one can use *in vitro* fertilization for creating new embryos but must stay away from cloning or nuclear transfer. The argument for this position is that the remaining embryos may not be sufficient in terms of quality, quantity, or genetic diversity to allow the research to go forward as it could, and perhaps should.

A survey conducted in 2002 and published in *Fertility and Sterility* suggests that from the 11,000 frozen embryos that have been donated for research in the United States, only about 275 useful stem-cell lines would be produced.[7] Most of those embryos would probably come from rather well-to-do couples, perhaps primarily couples of European descent, so it would not be a diverse cross-section if one would ever consider developing a stem cell bank.

Europeans have a special issue with creating embryos for research purposes. Any country that has ratified the 1997 Convention on Human Rights and Biomedicine has agreed, in advance, that the creation of embryos for research purposes should be prohibited.

Several countries have adopted Option 4. Belgium has a new permissive law. The United Kingdom has had this option in place since 1991. In thirty-nine states of the United States, it is not illegal to create embryos for research purposes through in vitro fertilization.

Sweden and Singapore also seem to be moving toward accepting Option 4. China has the most permissive stem cell research policies in the world, in my view.

The fifth and most radical of the policy options would be to create embryos through nuclear transfer, which is also referred to as cloning. I will studiously avoid the phrase "therapeutic cloning." I think that phrase over-promises. In my view, scientists made a major mistake by using that phrase early on. Research cloning (or somatic cell nuclear transfer for research purposes) would be a much more descriptive and neutral phrase.

Why would anyone ever propose something that sounds so frightening? As John Gearhart mentioned, cloning may be the only way to produce genetically matched cells for transplantation if this technology ever works, to provide, for example, neural stem cells for spinal cord injuries or stem cells for people afflicted with juvenile-onset diabetes. This technique may also allow scientists to study what goes wrong in the cells of someone who is afflicted with a particular genetic disorder—for example, amyotropic lateral sclerosis (also called "Lou Gehrig's disease"). In addition, Option 5 may provide the only way to create a stem cell bank (assuming that the technique works) that is sufficiently diverse to cover African-Americans, Hispanics, and Native Americans, as well as people of European descent.

In summer 2002, by a close 10-7 vote, the President's Council on Bioethics voted in favor of a four-year moratorium on U.S. research cloning. "Moratorium" does not sound so bad. "Ban" is a synonym for moratorium. In fact, the Council proposed a temporary ban on a potentially promising line of research.

Several countries in the world have already adopted this fifth and most radical option, such as Belgium, with its new law. The British Parliament approved Option 5 in January 2001. California—and in January 2004, New Jersey—are the only states in the US that have enacted policies similar to the policy of the United Kingdom. Asia, China, India, and Singapore are adopting or have adopted this policy. Israel accepts Option 5, and Sweden is considering this option. With the exception of Arkansas and probably Virginia, all of the unshaded or lightly shaded states in Figure 6 either implicitly or explicitly permit the creation of embryos for research purposes through cloning. California and New Jersey are the two states that expressly permit this kind of research.

What is the Moral Status
of a Five-Day-Old Human Embryo?

Probably the most central and debated ethical question surrounding human embryonic stem cell research is this: What is the moral status of a five-day old blastocyst, or human embryo, either *in vitro* or in frozen storage? Aristotle thought there were several stages of ensoulment during human embryonic and fetal development. He saw no *human* ensoulment before forty days of age. In fact, I regret to say, Aristotle thought that male fetuses received their souls at forty days and female fetuses only at ninety days. Aristotle's views were mediated through the Jewish tradition and through a particular text in the Hebrew Bible—Exodus 21:22, a passage that talks about what the legal penalty should be if two men fight, accidentally strike a woman who is pregnant, and cause her to miscarry. The way that this text was translated into Greek fit well with Aristotle's view. It was thought that if the fetus was unformed (or unensouled), one merely paid a fine; if it was a formed or ensouled fetus, the person who accidentally struck the women was guilty of homicide.[8]

In the Jewish religious tradition, there is virtual unanimity that one has no strong moral obligations to early human embryos. In fact, during the first forty days, the human embryo is said to be "like water." In Islam, only a tiny radical minority disagrees with this view. The predominant position in Islam is that either until forty days, or even until four months, one has no strong obligations to human embryos.

The Catholic tradition has changed over time. Saint Augustine accepted Aristotle's view of developmental stages, as it was mediated through the Septuagint, the Greek translation of the Hebrew Bible. He wrote that early in pregnancy a fetus does not have any sentience (cannot feel pain, is not aware) and that one has no strong moral obligations to the fetus—or at least, that the unformed fetus is qualitatively different from the later, formed fetus, which has a human soul. Pope Pius IX changed this teaching in 1869. The new view since that time has been that one should protect human embryos from the time of fertilization forward.[9] That is the official teaching of the Catholic Church; there is, however, dissent on this point among some Catholic theologians. Eastern Orthodoxy accepts the view that one should protect the embryo from the time of fertilization forward. Within Protestantism, as on most issues, there is a spectrum of views about our obligations to early embryos.

What about Eastern religious thought? The best evidence on this topic has been provided by the Singapore Bioethics Advisory Committee, which carefully surveyed the various religious groups in that island state. The committee found that the spokespeople for Buddhism and Hinduism said, "If the research is to promote human health, we have no problem with research on early human embryos." The Sikh tradition and Taoism were opposed.

Insights from the Anabaptist Tradition

How can one relate this very modern topic to the Anabaptist vision? None of the Anabaptists, obviously, talked about basic biomedical research, so the best one can do is try to extrapolate from some of the themes or emphases in the Anabaptist and Quaker religious traditions and other left-wing Reformation groups to see whether they provide a direction on this topic. A first lesson I draw from the Anabaptist vision and the Anabaptist approach to a topic like human embryonic stem cell research is this: Seek to maintain a clear separation between religious bodies, especially churches, and the coercive power of the state.

I draw from this lesson the implication that one ought to avoid establishing by law the religious position of conservative Christian groups regarding the moral status of early human embryos, or the moral permissibility of research on early human embryos. Think about Judaism; think about Islam; think about Hinduism and Buddhism. They do not view this issue in the same way that conservative Christian groups do. To them a restrictive policy on human embryo research probably feels like the imposition of a conservative Christian view on people who do not share that religious perspective.

What is known about public opinion on this matter in the United States? I think it is fair to say that there is either a small majority or a small plurality who favor human embryonic stem cell research. A Gallup poll taken in May 2003 found that fifty-four percent of the people surveyed said that medical research using stem cells obtained from human embryos is morally acceptable. Thirty-eight percent said it was morally wrong.[10] In another poll published in 2003, the question was asked, Do you favor or oppose research that uses stem cells from human embryos? Seventeen percent said they "strongly favor." Thirty percent said they "somewhat favor," so forty-seven percent were in favor. Twenty-one percent said they "somewhat oppose." Twenty-three percent said they "strongly oppose," so a total of forty-four percent were opposed.[11] Forty-seven percent to forty-four percent is a rather even division of opinion. To impose a law that says this kind of research cannot be done on religious grounds seems to me to be breaching the separation of church and state.

There was an ironic situation situation at the United Nations in the early 2000s. The United States and the Vatican were trying to get the UN to adopt a draft convention banning both research cloning and reproductive cloning. The U.S. argued vigorously that these two topics should be linked. Many Europeans (for example, representatives of Belgium, Germany, and France) said, "Why not focus on reproductive cloning? We can all agree that there should be a convention outlawing reproductive cloning." The U.S. said, "No. We want to ban *both* research cloning and reproductive cloning." The Organization of the Islamic Conference came up with the compromise formula. Many members of the conference did not want to see this kind of research banned, so the conference proposed that the whole issue be put off for two years. That procedural motion, spearheaded by the Islamic states, prevailed by one vote in early November 2003.[12]

A second consideration one can draw from the Anabaptist vision is this: Give special consideration to those who are the weakest and most vulnerable. Who are the most vulnerable? Who are the weakest in this situation? One definitely should include those who are afflicted with serious diseases, like Parkinson's disease or juvenile-onset diabetes or spinal cord injuries. The treatments are not just around the corner, but one goal of the research is to help people who have these kinds of illnesses and injuries.

Should five-day old human embryos also be included among the weakest and most vulnerable? There are arguments about the very early undifferentiated state of the five-day old embryo that can be brought to bear against giving them this high status and this level of protection. At the very least, one has to compare the good that can be done for people with serious illnesses and injuries versus the harm that will be done to the embryos that are used in the research. I think here of the laudable work of an agency like Mennonite Disaster Service (MDS) and how it goes to the site of floods or hurricanes and helps people rebuild their lives. In my view, it is not unfair to view the work being done by John Gearhart and others in this field as a kind of forward-looking strategy that aims to treat major human diseases and disabilities, and if possible, even to prevent them.

A third and final guideline I draw from the Anabaptist tradition is that one should promote justice in the entire world and not just in advanced industrialized societies. Here I think of the worldwide relief efforts of the Mennonite Central Committee (MCC) and the American Friends Service Committee as models. Ann Graber Hershberger and I had the privilege of serving in a Mennonite Voluntary Service work camp in Greece during summer 1961, digging ditches to bring fresh spring water into a village that otherwise had contaminated drinking water. This type of constructive work on behalf of people in need is very consistent with—in fact, it is an imperative that can be said to grow out of—the Anabaptist religious tradition.

It is very early to know how things will go in the next ten, twenty, or thirty years of human embryonic stem cell research. It might appear as if it is only going to be a high-tech approach to medicine that is very expensive—one that will only be available in North America, Europe, and Japan, for example. However, consider the basic laboratory research that went into developing vaccines for smallpox and polio, or the discovery of penicillin, or the development of other antibiotics and antivirals. The research was performed at a certain point in history. One did not know at that time how useful the research would be, or for how many people. Nevertheless, in all of these cases the technology has spread around the world and has helped prevent disease or helped to cure serious disease—not that all infectious diseases are taken care of, by any means.

I want to acknowledge the concern that this might turn out to be something expensive and only useable in developed countries. However, we can respond to this concern by saying, "Let us be sure we have a sufficient diversity in the stem cell lines, so that all major populations in the world are, in principle, candidates for therapy, if the therapy, at some point, becomes a reality." Even better would be trying to engineer a universal donor cell that would be similar to type-O blood, so that one type of cell could be used by people in every part of the world and from every ethnic background.

The only report I have seen that really focuses on this justice question is one by an ethics advisory committee for the Geron Corporation. The report was done in 1999 and published in the Hastings Center Report.[13] Laurie Zoloth and Karen Lebacqz, two people trained in religious ethics, are members of that board; both of them repeatedly said, "Let us never lose sight of the justice question."

I propose two conclusions for consideration. First, any of the final three public policies I have considered—Options 3, 4, or 5—is compatible with the Anabaptist vision. My second and final conclusion is that people of faith, including those who share in the Anabaptist tradition, should be at the forefront in doing this research as scientists and in supporting this research as citizens. Perhaps a special emphasis Anabaptists can bring to the table is that the fruits of this research should not just be bottled up in wealthy countries but should be actively shared with those most in need in every part of the world.[14]

Notes

1. This graphic was prepared by Terese Winslow for a July 2001 report published by the National Institutes of Health and is reprinted with her permission. See National Institutes of Health, *Stem Cells: Scientific Progress and Future Research Directions* (Bethesda: NIH, June 2001), A-4.

2. This graphic was produced by Terese Winslow and Caitlin Duckwall for the aforementioned report and is reprinted with their permission. See p. C-2 of the NIH report.

3. This graphic was also produced by Terese Winslow for the same report and is reprinted with her permission. See the cover page of the NIH Report.

4. This photograph was taken by Joseph Conaghan at the University of California San Franciso and is reprinted with his permission. The photograph is also included in the NIH report at p. 13.

5. Committee on Science, Engineering, and Public Policy, National Academy of Sciences, National Academy of Engineering, and Institute of Medicine, adapted with permission from *Scientific and Medical Aspects of Human Reproductive Cloning* (copyright © 2002 by the National Academy of Sciences, courtesy of the National Academies Press, Washington, D.C.), 8.

6. David I. Hoffman et al., in association with the Society for Assisted Reproductive Technology and the RAND Corporation, "Cryopreserved Embryos in the United States and their Availability for Research," *Fertility and Sterility* 79, no. 5 (May 2003): 1063-9.

7. Ibid.

8. For this history, see John T. Noonan, Jr., "An Almost Absolute Value in History," in *The Morality of Abortion: Legal and Historical Perspectives,* ed. John T. Noonan Jr. (Cambridge: Harvard University Press, 1970), 6-18.

9. On this change in perspective, see Noonan, ibid., esp. 36-46.

10. Gallup Poll conducted May 5-7, 2003; results published May 14, 2003, by the Roper Center for Public Opinion Research.

11. Virginia Commonwealth University, Center for Public Policy, *Life Sciences Survey 2003* (Richmond: The Center, 2003), 8-9.

12. On this topic, see LeRoy Walters, "The United Nations and Cloning: A Debate on Hold," *Hastings Center Report* 34, no. 1 (Jan-Feb 2004): 5-6.

13. Karen Lebacqz et al., (the Geron Ethics Advisory Board), "Research with Human Embryonic Stem Cells: Ethical Considerations," *Hastings Center Report* 29, no. 2 (March-April 1999): 31-6.

14. For an updated and expanded version of this presentation, see LeRoy Walters, "Human Embryonic Stem Cell Research: An Intercultural Perspective," *Kennedy Institute of Ethics Journal* 14, no 1 (March 2004): 3-38.

CHAPTER TEN

An Ethic of Caring

Beryl H. Brubaker

*Dr. Beryl H. Brubaker is provost at Eastern
Mennonite University. She received her doctor of science in nursing from the University
of Alabama at Birmingham. She has served
in many roles at Eastern Mennonite
University since 1970, including professor of
nursing, chair of the nursing department,
grant writer, vice-president for enrollment,
and academic provost before being named
provost in July 2004. She co-edited*
Bioethics and the Beginning of Life *with
Roman Miller in 1990 to publish presentations of a 1987 forum at Eastern Mennonite.*

A couple conceives to produce an embryo to provide stem cells for
transplantation into a sick child. Officials in a country in Africa consider whether to import genetically modified corn seed. Food companies try altering genes to increase the vitamins in lettuce. Scientists
determine that tobacco can be used to make vaccines against disease.
These radical changes are taking place all around us. The ability to
reengineer the genetic makeup of plants and animals creates enormous possibilities with potentially profound consequences for
human beings and the world we live in. Grappling with the ethical
implications of technological innovations must be seen as urgent
work in the twenty-first century. Shall we do what is possible to do?
What ought we to do, given the opportunities biotechnological research has made possible?

Any of us comes to such a discerning task with eyes seeing
through a particular worldview that comes out of our experience.

My background in nursing has helped shape my particular perspective and worldview. Sometimes this perspective feels very much in tandem with an Anabaptist framework.

Ethicists propose a variety of approaches to making decisions about what one ought to do or ought not to do. For instance, ethical theorists ask what principles can be applied to any situation or they focus on the consequences of various actions. In this chapter, however, I explore the concept of caring as a framework for ethical decision making, specifically decisions about biotechnology issues. Persons using a caring framework have frequently been critical of traditional frameworks, as will be seen in this review.

Nursing and Care

A number of scholars have theorized that caring is the essence of nursing. Before considering caring as an ethical framework, I will look at how nurses have viewed caring within the practice of nursing.

Several theorists have been particularly prominent in viewing caring as central to nursing practice. One of the earliest was Madeleine Leininger who defined care as "those assistive, supportive, or facilitative acts toward or for another individual or group with evident or anticipated needs to ameliorate or improve a human condition or lifeway."[1] Similarly, she described caring as the "direct (or indirect) nurturant and skillful activities, processes, and decisions related to assisting people in such a manner that reflects behavioral attributes which are empathetic, supportive, compassionate, protective, succorant, educational and otherwise dependent upon the needs, problems, values, and goals of the individual or group being assisted." Much of Leininger's work has related to the development of knowledge about caring practices in different cultural settings and providing culturally congruent care.[2]

Jean Watson also developed a theory of human care for nurses in practice. She views caring in terms of a moral ideal "directed toward the preservation of personhood and humanity of both nurse and patient."[3]

Patricia Benner has written extensively on aspects of care and caring. According to Benner and Wrubel caring "means that persons, events, projects, and things matter to people."[4] Inherent in this thinking is the understanding that not all things matter equally; some are deemed more important than others. Caring by the client, then, determines what is stressful and what strategies help the client to cope. In turn, caring is requisite to expert nursing (or other) practice because it allows the practitioner to notice symptoms and responses to intervention (because they matter), as well as enabling the client to accept help (because someone cares). Further, what is perceived as caring by clients depends on the context because different situations call for different interventions. Benner and Wrubel noted that the word caring fuses thought, feeling, and action.

Sr. M. Simone Roach proposed that caring manifests itself in five C's: compassion, competence, confidence, conscience, and commitment."[5] In other words, caring is expressed "in compassionate and competent acts; in relationships qualified by confidence; through informed, sensitive conscience; and through commitment and fidelity. . . . "

Janice Morse et al. conducted an extensive review of nursing literature to see how nurses were defining caring. They found that caring is conceptualized in five ways in nursing: 1) an innate human trait, 2) a fundamental value or moral ideal (i.e., to preserve the dignity of the patient), 3) an affect or feeling, 4) the feelings and behaviors that occur within the nurse-patient relationship, and 5) discrete nursing interventions.[6]

Other nurses have considered caring in terms of an ethical framework. Sara Fry, in a book of published papers presented at the annual conference of the International Association for Human Caring, summarizes various ethical models of caring, which she identifies as cultural, feminist, humanistic, obligation, and covenant.[7] A cultural model of caring relates caring actions to cultural norms. The feminist model looks at the place of caring within the female perspective in moral development. The humanistic model requires caring because of the dignity of human life. Fry described the obligation model as emphasizing compassion, doing good and providing benefit. Finally, the covenant model of caring "emphasizes the presence of fidelity in relationships. Fidelity between persons stems from the covenant made between persons when they stand in particular relationships to one another: mother and child, teacher and student, nurse and patient." Fidelity implies fulfilling one's duties to the person to whom one owes loyalty because of the relationship.

Jean Watson, in addition to defining nursing in terms of caring, embraces an ethic of caring for making moral decisions.[8] She, like many other nurses, is critical of traditional ethical frameworks used in the medical world. She observes that

the ideals of human caring that are rooted in receptivity, inter-
subjective relatedness, and human responsiveness help to coun-
teract the medical ethic of rational principle, fairness, and equity
that objectifies, detaches, and distances the professional from
the subjective world of the human experience. In other words, in
nursing and caring we are not concerned primarily with justification through ethical principles and laws in *general*.

She goes on to say that there needs to be space for feeling and
people need to be

protected from being reduced to the moral status of objects. . . .
[N]ursing ethics should be distinguished by its philosophy and
moral ideals that affirm the personal unique contextual experiences associated with human caring, inherent in nursing *qua*
nursing.

Practicing nurses resonate with Watson's views. Parker, after offering a particularly poignant story about a dying patient, pleads for
recognition of nurses' stories and emotional experiences. He tells of
an attempt to apply the usual biomedical ethical principles he saw as
calling for an objective, rational assessment speaking to rights, duties
and obligations. But then he tells of his conclusion that these are hollow and meaningless in a situation of intense suffering with little
hope for recovery. Therefore, he calls for moral reasoning that includes both the cognitive and affective domains to enhance the ability
to make decisions in situations that often do not allow for moral certainty. By admitting a role for both cognitive and affective aspects of
humanness, each aspect can correct and enhance the other.[9] This view
acknowledges limits to the applicability of moral principles in difficult situations. Further, while proponents of moral reasoning frequently assume an impartial stance on the part of the moral agent,
Parker insists that a deeply felt relationship is required to understand
individual needs and values and make good decisions in difficult situations.

Benner, Tanner, and Chesla also advocate for the development of
ethical knowledge through hearing the stories of expert practition-
ers.[10] "The practices and stories told within a community provide the
necessary background understanding for everyday ethical comportment and for formal ethical judgments." Further, "an ethic of care
must be learned experientially because it is dependent on recognition of salient ethical comportment in specific situations located in
specific communities, practices, and habits." These authors assert

that "in nursing, the dominant ethic found in stories of everyday practice is one of care, responsiveness to the other, and responsibility." Development of ethical understanding requires "emotional attunement" and relating in forms such as seeing, hearing, and responding.[11]

Ethics of Care and Compassion

These sentiments are not unique to nursing. Ethicist David C. Thomasma supports the idea that compassion is an important ingredient for making ethical decisions in illness situations.[12] He defines compassion as "the capacity to feel, and suffer with, the sick person—to experience something of the predicament of illness, its fears, anxieties, temptations, its assault on the whole person, the loss of freedom and dignity, the utter vulnerability, and the alienation every illness produces or portends" (131). Thomasma goes on to say that to experience compassion is to want to help, even to be willing to sacrifice for the victimized one.

These ideas are consistent with those of Davies, who goes even farther in defining compassion as a radical resistance to the type of dehumanization seen in Auschwitz.[13] Reminiscent of Benner and Wrubel (cited earlier in defining caring) and building on ideas similar to Thomasma, Davies insists that compassion combines cognition, affect and volition so the person sees another person's distress, is moved by it and acts on behalf of the person. It is marked by "a self-dispossessive attitude of mind which makes the particular virtues possible."[14] Compassion involves risk taking and selflessness in the face of extreme suffering of another person or group.

What compassion brings to the ethical situation, according to Thomasma, is concern for a particular individual's values and situation. Thus compassion changes the application of the major principles used by ethicists—beneficence, justice, and autonomy. To practice beneficence, the practitioner must go beyond avoiding harm to promoting the client's desires. Justice is not simply doing what is obligatory but what is merciful for this person. Autonomy is only achieved if the client is allowed to be a full participant in the healing process. In these ways Thomasma advocates an ethical approach that goes beyond rationalistic decision making to one that values a relationship and a person.[15]

Consideration of an ethic of caring leads us to Carol Gilligan's pioneering empirical work published in her 1982 book, *In a Different*

Voice.[16] Until her work, the ruling paradigm on moral development was Kohlberg's theory. What Gilligan discovered was that many females' approach to moral problems did not mirror those of the males interviewed in earlier studies by male theorists and upon whose responses moral theory had been built. She rejected the thesis that females are deficient in their sense of justice as some had concluded. Her studies suggested a new conception of morality where "the moral problem arises from conflicting responsibilities rather than from competing rights and requires for its resolution a mode of thinking that is contextual and narrative rather than formal and abstract."

Gilligan went on to say, "This conception of morality as concerned with the activity of care centers moral development around the understanding of responsibility and relationships, just as the conception of morality as fairness ties moral development to the understanding of rights and rules." The latter approach is concerned with principles of justice and calls for "the logic of equality and reciprocity," whereas the former approach "defines the moral problem as one of obligation to exercise care and avoid hurt."[17] Gilligan suggested that in the process of development persons move beyond the desire not to hurt others toward efforts to sustain relationships.[18] From her studies, then, Gilligan discovered the existence of an ethic of care where persons feel responsible in moral situations to discern what will make the world a better place, rather than how to protect peoples' "rights to life and self-fulfillment."[19]

For some time I have been uncomfortable with the language of rights. Jesus did not talk about people's rights. I am reminded of Jesus' story of paying the same wage to those who began work at the end of the day as those who started with the sunrise. Apparently, Jesus saw this situation not in terms of justice as fairness but in terms of justice as caring for people's needs. I recall Bible scholar Nancy Heisey at Eastern Mennonite University suggesting in an unpublished paper that Micah 6:8—"What does the Lord require of you, but to do justice, and to love kindness, and to walk humbly with your God?"[20]—can be viewed as a credible summary of the message of the entire Scripture. She then went on to define justice as right living in relation to our neighbors.[21] This portrays an understanding of justice as focusing not on rights, but on relationships.

Nel Noddings has applied the ethic of care to the educational environment.[22] Like Thomasma, she compares this ethic with the more traditional ethical approaches. In addition to focusing on relation-

The centrality of relationships lies in the responsibilities we carry toward the other. To make good moral decisions we must consider the nature of our responsibilities toward others affected by our decisions. Inherent in this discernment is an understanding of others' needs and values, that is, the particularity of the individuals in the situation. What matters to the individuals and groups involved? We cannot assume needs but must allow individuals to participate in defining their needs.

Further, an ethic of care will focus on sustaining relationships and communicating compassion. Both intellect and feelings are essential in the making and carrying out of moral decisions. Achieving the wanted outcomes may be difficult because of conflicting responsibilities, but there are ways to work at this even when it seems that some relationships must suffer. When this is true, expressions of compassion and attempts to be reconciling become especially important.

Often, as implied above, there are conflicts between one's responsibilities to various persons, so that one faces ethical dilemmas. For instance, responsibilities toward God may conflict with responsibilities as a citizen of one's country—as when Anabaptists who espouse a nonviolent approach to all of life are asked to pay taxes that support war. In some situations it may be difficult to prioritize one's multiple responsibilities.

An ethic of care will try to understand the web of relationships within their multiple contexts. This can be an arduous task because contexts are complex and the difficulties increase when multiple relationships are involved, as they usually are. I suggested earlier that dialogue is important for applying an ethic of care because it provides opportunity to more adequately explore the complexities of relationships. For Anabaptists, dialogue takes place within a group of discerning Christians who take biblical teachings seriously and listen to the voice of the Holy Spirit.

Application of Care Ethics to Cloning

How might an ethic of care as described here apply to the major issues of biotechnology? I will share some observations from an edited work on human cloning,[26] perhaps one of the most shocking applications of biotechnology, to illustrate the application of a caring perspective that considers responsibilities within relationships. The various authors in this book take different positions, some suggesting that human cloning would be acceptable and others categorically rejecting this technology. I make no claims for a comprehensive application of an ethic of care here but simply offer a few thoughts about relationships to enhance understanding of this framework.

Why might one try to clone a child? Let's suppose a couple has a child who needs a bone marrow transplant and no suitable match has been found. So the parents decide to produce a child with identical genes to be able to later transplant bone marrow from the newly conceived child into the child who is ill. Is this a good thing to do? What are the relationships that need to be considered here? Certainly a few pertinent relationships would be the parents' relationship to the children, the parents' relationship to God, the family's relationship to their church family, and the family's relationship to the society in which they live.

Author Brent Waters in the book on cloning referred to above expresses serious reservations regarding such an action because of our moral responsibility as parents to love each child unconditionally as a gift from God.[27] (Note that Waters does not categorically reject cloning, however.) This raises the question of whether a child should ever be conceived for instrumental purposes. How does this affect the child's sense of self-worth? Do our responsibilities to love our children allow us to produce a child who knows she was created to enable a sibling to live? Might this child always feel that she takes second place to a sibling and perhaps wonder if she is really loved? This could vary depending on the particular child, but we have no way of knowing ahead of time how the cloned child will respond.

There are wider relationships—with peers, with publics. Children created through human cloning in this generation will become objects of media attention. Peers may ridicule such a child as abnormal. Certainly, the community of faith will enter the dialogue and have a stake in the decision.

How would this action to produce a child affect one's relationship with the Creator God? Would the action of "designing" one's own child change the way we view children? Recall Waters' reference to children as a gift from God. But let's be honest and ask this: Do most modern parents indeed view their "naturally" conceived children as a gift from God or rather as a product of their own sexual activities? Are there lines we should choose not to cross, towers of Babel that will be too detrimental to God-human relationships? Or is human inventiveness unlimited in the search for cures for the world's ills? Does it depend on the particular illnesses? That is, are some illnesses so destructive and the means of cure so limited that human intervention is justified?

We also could pose a situation where cloning is used to reproduce a genius or a successful athlete, rather than to help an ill child. Again, we could project a variety of relationships and responsibilities but certainly a primary one would be with the cloned child. Editor Cole-Turner suggests that cloning to produce a set of wanted characteristics would likely create burdens no child should need to bear.[28] This is particularly true because we know that cloning an organism does not result in identical organisms, even though the genes are identical, because environmental influences interact with genes to create unique individuals. So what would it mean to become a disappointment because as a cloned person you did not measure up to expectations? Would a caring framework disallow such a cloning?

These brief illustrations signify the tremendously difficult and complex issues we face with the biotechnological possibilities in today's world. Granted some issues are less daunting than human cloning. However, many have potentially significant consequences that may not be predictable. It is essential that we seriously consider the issues arising from biotechnology, rather than allowing changes to occur without careful reflection and deliberation in the community of faith.

Like most theories or frameworks, an ethic of care has been criticized. Is it really an ethical theory, and how does it stand up to alternative, traditional approaches? I will not attempt a critique here but will refer the reader to a 1998 issue of the *Journal of Medicine and Philosophy*, where several authors have considered its status as a theory.[29]

I believe an ethic of care is a valid perspective for viewing the challenging moral issues that face us in a world revolutionized by technology. This way of thinking is in many ways consistent with an Anabaptist Christian worldview where people and relationships matter. A caring framework can at least stand alongside more traditional ethical frameworks. At most it may suggest a more helpful lens for viewing difficult moral issues.

Notes

1. Madeleine M. Leininger, ed., *Care: The Essence of Nursing and Health* (Thorofare: Slack Incorporated, 1984), 4.

2. Madeleine Leininger and Marilyn R. McFarland, *Transcultural Nursing: Concepts, Theories, Research and Practice,* 3rd ed. (New York: McGraw-Hill, 2002).

3. Jean Watson, *Nursing: Human Science and Human Care: A Theory of Nursing* (Norwalk: Appleton-Century-Crofts, 1985), 75.

4. Patricia Benner and Judith Wrubel, *The Primacy of Caring: Stress and Coping in Health and Illness* (Menlo Park: Addison-Wesley Publishing Company, 1989), 1.

5. Sister M. Simone Roach, *The Human Act of Caring: A Blueprint for the Health Professions* (Ottawa: Canadian Hospital Association Press, 1992), 57.

6. Janice M. Morse et al., "Concepts of Caring and Caring as a Concept." *Advances in Nursing Science* 13, no.1 (1990): 1-14.

7. Sara T. Fry, "The Ethic of Care: Nursing's Excellence for a Troubled World," in *A Global Agenda for Caring*, ed. Delores A. Gaut (New York: National League for Nursing Press, 1993), 175-9.

8. Jean Watson, "Introduction: An Ethic of Caring/Curing/Nursing *qua* Nursing," in *The Ethics of Care and the Ethics of Cure: Synthesis in Chronicity*, ed. Jean Watson and Marilyn A. Ray (New York: National League for Nursing, 1988), 1-3.

9. Randy Spreen Parker, "Nurses' Stories: The Search for a Relational Ethic of Care," *Advances in Nursing Science* 13, no. 1 (1990): 31-40.

10. Patricia Benner, Christine A. Tanner, and Catherine A. Chesla, *Expertise in Nursing Practice: Caring, Clinical Judgment, and Ethics* (New York: Springer Publishing Company, 1996), 233.

11. Ibid. 161.

12. David C. Thomasma, "Beyond the Ethics of Rightness: The Role of Compassion in Moral Responsibility," in *The Crisis of Care: Affirming and Restoring Caring Practices in the Helping Professions*, ed. Susan S. Phillips and Patricia Benner (Washington, D.C.: Georgetown University Press, 1994), 123-43.

13. Oliver Davies, *A Theology of Compassion: Metaphysics of Difference and the Renewal of Tradition* (Grand Rapids: William B. Eerdmans Publishing Company, 2001), 10-5.

14. Ibid., 18.

15. David C. Thomasma, "Beyond the Ethics of Rightness: The Role of Compassion in Moral Responsibility," in *The Crisis of Care: Affirming and Restoring Caring Practices in the Helping Professions*, ed. Susan S. Phillips and Patricia Benner (Washington, D.C.: Georgetown University Press, 1994), 133.

16. Carol Gilligan, *In a Different Voice: Psychological Theory and Women's Development* (Cambridge: Harvard University Press, 1982), 19.

17. Ibid., 73.

18. Ibid., 149.

19. Ibid., 100.

20. Micah 6: 8

21. Nancy R Heisey, "The Case for Micah 6:8: Another Look at the Theme Verse of the Global Village Curriculum," unpublished paper, Eastern Mennonite University, Harrisonburg, Virginia, July 2002.

22. Nel Noddings, *The Challenge to Care in Schools: An Alternative Approach to Education*, Advances in Contemporary Educational Thought Series, ed. Jonas E. Soltis (New York: Teacher's College Press, 1992), 21.

23. Martha A. Carpenter, "Tutor or Tyrant?" in *Current Issues in Nursing,* 4th ed., ed Joanne Comi McCloskey and Helen Kennedy (St. Louis: Mosby, 1994), 758-62.

24. Dennis P. Hollinger, *Choosing the Good: Christian Ethics in a Complex World* (Grand Rapids: Baker Academic, 2002).

25. Joel James Shuman, *The Body of Compassion: Ethics, Medicine, and the Church* (Boulder: Westview Press, 1999), 77.

26. Ronald Cole-Turner, ed., *Human Cloning: Religious Responses* (Louisville: Westminster John Knox Press, 1997).

27. Brent Waters, "One Flesh? Cloning, Procreation, and the Family," in *Human Cloning: Religious Responses*, ed. Ronald Cole-Turner (Louisville: Westminster John Knox Press, 1997), 78-90.

28. Ronald Cole-Turner, ed., "At the Beginning," in *Human Cloning: Religious Responses,* ed. Ronald Cole-Turner (Louisville: Westminster John Knox Press, 1997), 119-30.

29. *Journal of Medicine and Philosophy* 23, no. 2 (1998).

CHAPTER ELEVEN

Eugenics, Genetic Screening, and the Slippery Slope

Ruth Schwartz Cowan

Dr. Ruth Schwartz Cowan is an historian of science, technology and medicine. She is Janice and Julian Bers Professor of the History and Sociology of Science at the University of Pennsylvania and professor of history emerita at the State University of New York at Stony Brook. Professor Cowan spent spring 1999 as senior Fulbright scholar on the island of Cyprus where she studied the mandated genetic screening programs there. Dr. Cowan received her Ph.D. from The Johns Hopkins University.

Since the 1970s, when genetic testing and genetic screening began, many people have worried that these procedures represent the beginning of a slippery slope, a slope that leads down to a very particular kind of pit, a pit to which the word "eugenics" is often attached. My goal is to assess whether that is a reasonable or unreasonable fear—and how far along the slope we have actually slipped, if we have slipped at all.

If the top of the slope is a world in which no one ever attempts to influence the genetic character of the next generation, we have certainly begun a descent, but from what? There is plenty of evidence that at least from the beginning of recorded history some people have been unwilling to leave the character of their offspring entirely to "fate" or "the luck of the draw" or "God's will." Are there more such people today? Or is our ability to influence the biological character of future generations simply more efficacious? If we don't know where the top of the slope is, how can we measure the distance we have fallen? We've had more than enough time (about forty years) to assess our situation on the slope, but we don't seem to have reached a consensus. What is it, precisely, that makes some people of good will and good sense able to happily contemplate a future with more and better genetic testing—while others tremble in dismay? What does it mean to have finally reached the bottom?

Eugenics

The people who couple post-1945 genetic testing with pre-1945 eugenics are sure they know the answer to that last question: The bottom is what American and German and Scandinavian governments did on the urging of powerful eugenicists. We were there once before, these folks say, and we are on our way back there again. I am not sure they are right; in fact, after studying the history of eugenics and this history of genetic screening, I am pretty sure that they are wrong. Historians do ethics this way: by comparing, contrasting, and analyzing how people have behaved in the past, we feel that we can draw what might be called pragmatic ethical lessons for the present and the future.

The eugenics movement began in the latter part of the nineteenth century in England. The founder of the movement, Sir Francis Galton, was Charles Darwin's first cousin.[1] Very soon after reading his cousin's book, Galton began a study on a not exactly surprising topic: the inheritance of intelligence. His enterprise was statistical; using biographical dictionaries he calculated the frequency with which eminent people were related to each other and then compared this with the frequency of the relationships in the general population. Galton's method was fraught with problems, but his conclusions were firm and unequivocal: talent and character must be hereditary.[2]

Following the publication of this initial research, Galton launched (at his own expense) a fairly extensive set of studies; he collected data on the inheritance of many human characteristics, among them height, mathematical ability, and religiosity. His method remained statistical, or, to use his own term, *anthropometric*; he measured and counted and compared the data from one generation with the data from another. His conclusions were always hereditary; no matter what he studied he found that the influence of heredity was always more important than the influence of environment. Finally, in 1883, he published a book reporting on his researches: *Inquiries into Human Faculty.*

In this book Galton used the word *eugenics* for the first time; he made it up by combining the Greek roots *eu*, meaning beautiful, and *gene*, meaning birth or inheritance. He hoped eugenics would be "the science of improving human stock by giving the more suitable races or strains of blood a better chance of prevailing speedily over the less suitable."[3] In Galton's formulation eugenics was—as it continued to be long after his death—both a scientific research enterprise and a political program. The science of eugenics would learn more about human traits and about how they are passed from one generation to another. The politics of eugenics would apply this knowledge in such a way that those who possessed the best traits would be able to outbreed everyone else. Darwin's theory of evolution by natural selection was built into Galton's eugenics; if people with good traits managed to outbreed people with bad traits, then the whole human stock would evolve in a positive direction, just as those animals and plants with the best adaptations go on to form new, improved, species.

The English, who gave birth to the idea of eugenics, pursued it as a scientific program, not a political one. The politics of eugenics were put into action, particularly in the United States, Germany, and Scandinavia, in the first half of the twentieth century.[4] There were two parts to the eugenic political program. The first part, which was called positive eugenics, involved encouraging the better people to breed more. Positive eugenics, insofar as it was enacted—which wasn't very far—is not what is being referred to when, today, people worry about the slippery eugenical slope; few people want to repeal the income tax deductions (in the U.S., for example) for children and other dependents. Few object to family allowances and subsidized day care (in Scandinavia, for example)—all of which were originally advocated as eugenic initiatives.

The second part—negative eugenics, preventing the breeding of the "unfit"—is another story altogether. In the United States, a very large number of states had instituted mandated sterilization laws in the early twentieth century. These laws permitted (and in some instances required) physicians and bureaucrats who managed homes for the feeble-minded, and medical and administrative personnel in prisons, to recommend to state courts that a person be sterilized. Between 60,000 to150,000 Americans were sterilized under these eugenic laws. [5]

Eugenics was also taken up by legislatures in Scandinavia. In several countries the sterilization of mentally deficient individuals was authorized. In all, eugenic abortion became legal. Decision-making authority over abortion was vested in a panel of physicians. If the panel concluded the pregnant woman had a family history of a genetic disease or that there was a great likelihood that the fetus would become a disabled, deformed, or a seriously ill infant, then an abortion could be approved. [6]

Germany took eugenic legislation to the bottom of the slope.[7] In Germany, after the advent of National Socialism, eugenic courts were established. Ministers, teachers, and physicians were required, on penalty of a fine and/or incarceration, to report to the court families or individuals in which alcoholism, epilepsy, feeble-mindedness, or homosexuality was evident. The court could then remand those individuals for sterilization. In addition, a court could remand individuals to sex-segregated institutions, so those individuals could be prevented from breeding.

Genetic Screening

Since the 1970s, three types of genetic testing and screening programs have developed, not just in the affluent countries of the world, but also in some nations that are struggling to emerge from poverty. One type is population screening of newborns: a drop of blood is taken from the heel of newborn babies and subsequently tested biochemically for the presence of a genetic disorder. In the United States, mandated genetic screening for phenylketonuria (PKU) began in the 1960s; today all states mandate testing for five or six other disorders and some states test for as many as twenty-two.[8] Newborn screening is also mandated in many European countries and is available for babies born in hospitals in some parts of the developing world. The majority of these tests are diagnostic; they are done to alert parents and physicians to a disease state that can be meliorated therapeutically. Some tests, however, are for diseases which can be neither cured nor meliorated; they are done to alert parents to their status as carriers of the disease gene.

A second type of screening involves testing children, adolescents, and adults. Often this is carrier screening, done to determine whether the individual is a carrier of a particular single gene recessive disease (such as sickle cell anemia, Tay-Sachs disease, or cystic fibrosis). Heterozygotes are more or less asymptomatic; carrier screening is done not to improve their health but to allow them to make informed reproductive decisions. Screening of children, adolescents, and adults also can be done for dominant conditions that do not appear until middle age (such as Huntington's disease) and for some multifactorial conditions (such as the forms of breast cancer that are now called BRAC 1 and BRAC 2).

To be screened in this fashion is, in a medical sense, easy and no more painful, nor time consuming, than having some blood drawn. In psychological and social senses, however, this screening can be extremely problematic because it makes people anxious (they fear their identities are "tainted") and sometimes leads to various forms of discrimination (in employment, in some cases; for insurance coverage in others; in marriage prospects for yet others.) Nonetheless, whatever the consequences, today most people who decide to be tested and most people who make that decision for their children, do so voluntarily.[9]

Finally, there is screening of the fetus: prenatal diagnosis. Prenatal diagnosis has become a standard aspect of prenatal care in the developed world since the middle of the 1970s. Many, many Americans under the age of twenty-five have been screened as fetuses. Most were screened for Down's syndrome or spina bifida—but many were also screened for particular diseases for which one or both of their parents were known to be carriers, like Tay-Sachs disease or sickle cell anemia.

There are four different types of prenatal screening: amniocentesis (in which fluid, containing floating cells, is removed from the amniotic sac), maternal blood screening (in which tests are done for circulating biochemicals and also, recently, for fetal cells), ultrasound examination (which allows certain anatomic deformities of the fetus to be seen), and chorionic villus sampling (which biopsies one of the fetal membranes). Prenatal diagnosis can test for chromosomal abnormalities (such as the trisomy which causes the dominant form of Down's syndrome) or for the various changes in DNA which lead to disease or disability; it can also be used to test for certain chemicals that indicate disease states in the fetus. Prenatal diagnosis can also be used to determine the sex of a fetus.

Sometimes prenatal diagnosis is done so that necessary therapies can begin promptly, but in the vast majority of cases, no therapy is possible, and positive prenatal diagnoses lead to decisions to abort. One of the most controversial aspects of prenatal diagnosis—even among people who are not opposed to abortion per se—is prenatal diagnosis and abortion for gender. Initially, the test for gender was used to identify males who were at risk for one of the sex-linked disorders (like hemophilia) but shortly it started to be used just to test for gender, particularly in those parts of the world (India and China, for example) and among those ethnic groups in which there is a marked preference for male, or at least first-born male, children. There are some locales in which prenatal diagnosis is thought to be responsible for a profound and growing imbalance in the sex ratio at birth.[10]

Before proceeding to describe one particular genetic screening program at length, I'd like to take this brief survey of modern genetic screening one step farther, to identify the various social actors—the various types of people—who have been responsible for advocating, establishing, and sustaining these kinds of programs.[11] First, there are legislators. All newborn screening programs in the United States and Western Europe have been established and funded by legislatures. Every form of genetic screening is mediated by health care professionals, so wherever and whenever medical care is publicly funded, legislators have both authorization and monetary control over genetic screening. Much of the research which preceded these screening programs was paid for by public funds, authorized by legislatures. Thus legislators have been crucial social actors in the creation and the maintenance of these programs; in virtually all the countries in which legislatures have played a role in genetic screening, the legislatures themselves are democratically elected—which means that legislators have been, insofar as they ever do, expressing the public will in their support of genetic screening.

Physicians have also been active in creating genetic screening programs, particularly those physicians who care for persons and families afflicted with genetic disease. In their efforts to prevent these diseases—where genetic screening is done for informed reproductive decision making, it is a form of preventive medicine—these physicians have been allied with the parents of afflicted children, parents who have frequently joined together in disease advocacy groups: The Cooleys' Anemia Association, the Association to Help Retarded Citizens, the Association for Research on Sickle Cell Disease, the Tay Sachs and Allied Disorders Association (to name just a few such groups) have all been active in advocating genetic testing and in helping to pay for the research that was needed to get it started. In addition to clinicians and parents, physician researchers have also played crucial roles in genetic screening, in part because they have done targeted research intended to develop genetic tests and confirm their reliability as predictors.

Some decision makers were unquestionably guided by profit motives. Business executives have made decisions to manufacture and market testing instruments, ranging from massive ultrasound machines to tiny fiberoptic biopsy probes. Medical geneticists and specialists in what has come to be called maternal-fetal medicine enhance their professions, as well as themselves, by advocating for genetic screening. Hospital administrators have made decisions to purchase these instruments and to set up clinical practices and services to use them—undoubtedly calculating the financial advantages of these outpatient services. In the United States, insurance executives have made decisions to cover the costs of the tests—undoubtedly after calculating the balance between the cost of the test and the cost of the illness "prevented."

Finally, ordinary people have voted with their feet to sustain genetic testing. Millions of women have requested amniocentesis when pregnant, even when their insurance companies would not pay for it. Millions of adults have volunteered to have their blood drawn so that their carrier status could be tested. Millions of parents have agreed (where their agreement is sought) to have their newborn babies tested. Millions of women have decided to terminate the pregnancies—oftentimes very much wanted pregnancies—on the basis of genetic diagnostic results, even some women who were, until the time they had to make the decision, very much opposed to abortion.[12]

Some scholars have argued that women who make this abortion decision are compelled to do so by economic and social factors over which they have no control. This may be true, but what is also true is that there is only one jurisdiction (China) in which the compulsion to terminate the pregnancy of an afflicted fetus comes from a governmental mandate. Thus, most of the decisions that people have made to participate in genetic screening have been voluntary. People may not have been fully informed about the consequences of their decisions, but they were not compelled by a government, employer, or an insurance company to make them. Such requirements for testing have been outlawed in just about every jurisdiction in which they were once enforced.

Thus, the decisions to create, sustain, and participate in modern genetic testing programs are what we might call *diffused* decisions.

Decision-makers came from many different sectors of society. Decisions have been made by very different social actors, participating in many different kinds of social institutions, operating in many different social environments: legislators in Springfield and Washington, Oslo and Jerusalem, Bangkok and Madrid; affluent parents in London and poor parents also in London; American insurance company executives and Chinese physician researchers; clinicians who are government employees and physicians who are self-employed; public health administrators in places that are affluent as well as places that are not; prospective parents in Nicosia, Paris, Hamburg, and Los Angeles; business managers in many companies, large and small, local and global; and, finally, individuals at risk for many different kinds of diseases. All have played a role.

In short, many different people have agreed—in many different ways—to the creation and maintenance of genetic screening. Before assessing whether these programs are good or bad or somewhere in between, it behooves us to understand *why* so many people have behaved in this fashion, what their reasons were, and what their ethical justifications were. How did it come to pass that eugenic activities have continued, for so many years, even after the horrors once visited upon people in the name of eugenics have been publicly revealed?

Genetic Screening in Cyprus

Cyprus is an island in the eastern Mediterranean, just north of Egypt and south of Turkey. It is the second largest island in the Mediterranean (about the same size as Long Island) but because of its location—between the Middle East and Europe—it has been historically significant for several millennia. Today, Cyprus is governed by two independent national governments at odds with each other. The southern two-thirds of the island is the Republic of Cyprus; it is almost universally recognized as the official government of the island and is represented in the United Nations. The Republic of Cyprus was created in 1960, when Britain gave up control of the island and helped establish a federal, democratic republic. All the current citizens of the Republic are of Greek ancestry. They speak Greek and virtually all adhere to the Cypriot Orthodox Church, the established church of Cyprus. The Orthodox churches are autochthonous; although they share theological and liturgical traditions, they are separate entities with separate governing bodies.

The northern third of Cyprus is called the Turkish Republic of North Cyprus. North Cyprus was established after a decade of civil war and UN monitoring (1964-1974), the invasion of Turkish troops (summer 1974), and the forced resettlement of Cypriots (1975-1976). During the resettlement period, all the Greek-speaking citizens moved to the south and all the Turkish speaking citizens moved to the north, no matter where they owned property or businesses. All the current citizens of North Cyprus speak Turkish and are of Turkish ancestry, descendents of the Ottoman bureaucrats who ruled the island for centuries before it was ceded to Britain in the 1880s. North Cyprus does not have an established religion; most inhabitants are secularized Muslims. North Cyprus has its own president and legislature, all democratically elected, but it is financially and militarily dependent on Turkey, which is the only country in the world that recognizes it diplomatically.

The size of these two feuding populations is a matter of considerable dispute, but rough approximations suggest that there are probably three times as many Greek Cypriots as Turkish. Greek Cyprus has emerged from poverty in the half century since Britain left. Turkish Cyprus is much further behind, its economy crippled by the lack of trading partners, emigration, and the instability of the Turkish economy on which it is dependent.

These two countries, the Republic of Cyprus and the Turkish Republic of North Cyprus, have the only two mandated adult genetic screening programs in the world. In spring 1999, I went to Cyprus, under the aegis of the Fulbright Commission, to interview the people—on both sides of the Green Line—who had set up these programs and who were enmeshed in them. Before I left for Cyprus, I imagined that my project would help me to understand what it was like to live at the bottom of the slippery eugenic slope and I did not expect to like what I saw. By the time I left, I had changed my mind.

The mandated genetic screening programs on the island of Cyprus address a disease called ß-thalassemia. Thalassemia exists everywhere in the world where malaria once existed; today there is a considerable amount of ß-thalassemia in the United States, especially in the families of recent immigrants from Southeast Asia. The disorder is one of the hemoglobinopathies, a blood disease. It is a single-gene recessive; the mutated gene that causes the disease prevents production of the chain in adult hemoglobin.

Afflicted babies are homozygotes; they have two copies of the mutated genes. This means that each of their parents is a carrier, a heterozygote. Each time two carriers conceive, there is a 25 percent chance that the resulting embryo will be a homozygote. The population of Cyprus has one of the highest carrier rates for -thalassemia in the world; 1 in 7 Cypriots is a carrier—which means that 1 in 49 marriages on the island is between two carriers.

A baby born with ß-thalassemia has a life span of about five years; death is both agonizing and slow. By about six months, parents recognize something is wrong with their baby; the child is listless and pale, very sleepy, and slow to grow. By the age of two or three the child's abdomen is protruding and the facial bones have developed in an odd way, making the child's face unusually broad and the eyes unusually protruding. The child is very small and its skin has a gray pallor. No matter how well fed, the child continues to waste away slowly; the child becomes bed-ridden and then dies, almost always before reaching its sixth birthday.

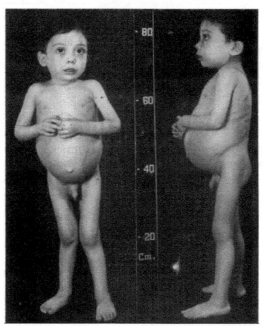

Fig. 1. Young thalassemic male with characteristically protruding abdomen[13]

Thomas Cooley, the Detroit pediatrician who first described this peculiar, fatal form of anemia in the 1920s, discovered that the children he was treating had very abnormal red blood cells. What he was unable to figure out—indeed no one could have figured out until the chemical structure of the various hemoglobins had been elucidated in the 1950s—was that these children's bodies could not make adult hemoglobin; they lived out their short lives on fetal hemoglobin, which cannot carry enough oxygen to support the metabolism of a growing child.

Even before physicians understood the underlying cause of the disease, they began to attempt a therapeutic regimen of regular transfusions to provide the child with red blood cells that could sustain some approximation of normal metabolism. By 1960, pediatricians who cared for thalassemic children in the United States and Britain (where there were well-organized blood banks) knew that with regular, monthly transfusions of concentrated red-blood cells beginning at about six months, a child's life could be extended into adolescence. The child would still be small and pale, but the hypertrophied spleen and the distorted facial bones (both the result of the blood-making tissues in the body working overtime) would not develop. Unfortunately, these teenagers struggled against iron overload in their tissues, the result of so many transfusions of concentrated red blood cells. But the struggle was rarely successful for long. Where transfusion therapy was regularly available, thalassemic children were now dying in their teens. In places like Cyprus, where there was no blood bank, most thalassemic children still died before reaching their sixth birthday.

In 1960 an iron chelating drug, deferoxamine mesylate, or Desferal, came on the market. This drug combines with elemental iron in the body to create a water soluble compound which can be excreted. By 1970, doctors in Britain had come to the conclusion that if Desferal therapy was administered several times a week, transfusion dependent thalassemics might be able to live into their twenties—and maybe even beyond. Adult hemoglobin would come in through transfusion and excess iron would be removed by chelation.

There were then, and still are, two very significant problems with transfusion/chelation therapy. Chelation is generally done three times a week. A hypodermic needle containing the drug is inserted under the skin, then the drug is slowly infused, over ten-twelve hours, using a portable battery-powered pump. The best therapeutic approach is to start administering Desferal when the child is six months old and to continue it, three times a week, for the remainder of the person's life. In childhood the parents must do the injecting; sometime in early adolescence, children generally take over the painful chore themselves.

Either way, compliance is extremely difficult, painful, and emotionally fraught. Imagine what it means to develop parent-child trust when, from six months on, the parent is sticking a needle into the child and causing pain. Imagine what it means to be an active teenager, having to accept responsibility for such an arduous therapeutic regimen, constantly being reminded by over-solicitous parents. The therapy for ß-thalassemia is almost, but not quite, as bad as the disease.

A second problem with Desferal therapy is that it is now and was then enormously expensive, much more than any average family can afford. In the early 1970s the cost of sustaining a child on Desferal amounted to one half the average income of a Cypriot family. In Britain the cost of treatment was covered by the National Health Service, but in Cyprus, when the treatment first came into use, only the wealthiest families could afford to purchase the drug.

In those years, eighty to eighty-five babies with thalassemia were being born on the island every year. Since the civil war had been raging since the mid-1960s, the economy of the Republic was in shambles. Greek Cypriot babies were being cared for in the central hospital in the capital, Nicosia; Turkish Cypriot babies, if they were cared for at all, received transfusions at one of the British naval bases close by a Turkish settlement. In 1971, after being lobbied by an association of parents and physicians, the Public Health Department of the Republic had agreed to cover the costs of Desferal therapy, although, since by then the Turkish community had seceded from the Republic, only thalassemics of Greek descent would actually benefit.

In 1972, a World Health Organization (WHO) consultant, one of the pediatricians who had helped develop Desferal therapy, was invited to the island. Her report made an argument that was already patently clear to the pediatricians on the island: if babies with thalassemia continued to be born and people with thalassemia were now able to receive therapy that would sustain their lives into middle-age, then the island would reach a critical impasse in a decade or two, even if the civil war was resolved. Sometime before the turn of the millennium, the cost of caring for the thalassemics—with both transfusion and Desferal therapy—would take up the entire health department budget, leaving no funds to care for any one else. Worst still, sometime before that, at the then-current rate of overall population growth, every Cypriot citizen over the age of eighteen would have to give blood every six weeks to satisfy the needs of the thalassemia patients.[14]

Something had to be done. To make two rather long stories short, to reduce the number of babies born with thalassemia, both the Turkish Cypriots (who by then had their own government and their own national health service) and the Greek Cypriots had developed, within a decade, independent, mandated genetic screening programs for the disease. Today if a couple wants to marry, on either side of the Green Line each person must be screened and counseled at a thalassemia clinic. Both national clinics are located in Nicosia, the capital of both governments. Nicosia is the last divided city in the world. The clinics are completely independent of one another and they cannot even communicate with each other by telephone.

In Turkish Cyprus the legislature mandated screening in 1979. A marriage license will not be issued unless both parties have been screened and counseled. Marriages between two carriers are permitted. Every pregnancy resulting from such a marriage can be monitored by prenatal diagnosis at government expense. In 1979, this was being done by sending pregnant carriers to London where a sample of the fetus's blood was drawn out of the umbilical vein. Today it is done on the island by DNA analysis on chorionic tissue biopsied before the end of the first trimester. Every pregnancy found to be afflicted can be terminated, if the couple so wishes, also at government expense. Abortion is not required; the government commits to caring for thalassemics born after the screening program began in the same way that it cares for thalassemics born before 1979. On the other hand, almost all pregnancies with an afflicted fetus are terminated.

All these aspects of mandated screening are similar in the (Greek) Republic of Cyprus, with one exception: the mandating authority is the Cypriot Orthodox Church, not the government. In the early 1970s, with the support of what was then called the Pan-Cypriot Anti-Anemia Foundation (now the Thalassemia International Foundation), the pediatricians in charge of the Thalassemia Clinic in Nicosia began a campaign for voluntary screening. Over the course of the next several years, they were able to reduce the birth incidence of thalassemia significantly, but not completely. The effort involved was also enormous and detracted, they felt, from their clinical responsibilities.

Since virtually all marriages in Cyprus are performed by priests of the Orthodox Church, they knew that only a program approved by the church would be effective. Consequently, parents and physicians met with church officials, and in 1984 the church instructed its priests not to perform marriages unless both parties had been screened and counseled. The Cypriot Orthodox Church, like all the other Orthodox churches, is adamantly opposed to abortion. The church mandate is for screening and counseling before marriage. The abortions performed consequent to a positive prenatal diagnosis are paid for by the National Health Service and performed in a publicly funded hospital. As in North Cyprus, carrier couples may marry. They are not required to abort afflicted pregnancies and thalassemic babies born after the screening mandate receive the same care, at public expense, as those born before.

| Year | Thalassaemia major | | | Percentage fall | |
	Total births	Expected	Actual	Due to fetal diagnosis	Due to avoidance of pregnancy
1974	8594	54	51	0	5.5
1975	8039	51	48	0	6
1976	9259	59	37	0	37
1977	9188	58	37	5	31
1978	9644	61	27	10	46
1979	10372	66	25	33	29
1980	11087	70	19	39	34
1981	10780	68	10	66	19
1982	11578	73	8	55	34
1983	10900	69	7	65	25
1984	11200	71	2	73	24

Table 1. Numbers of babies born with thalassemia major in Cyprus, 1974-1984[15]

As shown in table 1, both mandated programs have been successful from the point of view of the people who designed, organized, and advocated for them. Since 1985, only a small handful of Cypriot babies have been born with thalassemia; one was the result of a false negative diagnosis, two were children of parents who refused prenatal diagnosis, and one was the child of two thalassemia patients who decided to marry. No one on the island, on either side of the Green Line, has formally objected to either of the programs, with the exception of a few Greek Cypriot obstetricians who will not perform the abortions.

As with all other genetic screening programs, the decisions to create, administer, and support these two mandated premarital programs were socially diffused. Many people, playing many different social roles, participated: legislators, physicians, public health officials, parents of afflicted children, and priests. In spring 1999, I made an effort to interview a sample of these individuals, both Turkish and Greek, to ascertain the reasons for their support. I found that each group of people expressed a different sort of ethic but their ethics all converged on the same pragmatic conclusion: in our particular situation, mandated genetic screening—eugenics—is unquestionably the right thing to do.

The physicians treating the children with thalassemia were the professionals who pushed hardest for the screening programs. I interviewed many physicians in both parts of Cyprus in 1999, including all the pediatricians who had been or still were in charge of the thalassemia clinics. Each of these physicians had cared for thalassemic babies before Desferal therapy was possible; since they administered transfusion services, they knew the children, the parents, and the siblings of these babies very well. "You cannot imagine the suffering," they told me. Whether Turkish or Greek, whether in their eighties or in their fifties, these physicians basically gave me the same rationale for their support of screening: "To end suffering for the family. I'm a physician; it's my job to reduce suffering for people. I couldn't reduce the suffering of those dead babies. I can't reduce the suffering of my current patients, but I can prevent further suffering, and screening is the way to do it."[16]

One physician, who is devoted to the ideals of socialized medicine, went further. "Everybody who talks about socialized medicine," he remarked, "says that one of its main virtues is that it can focus on preventive medicine; we can do things through public health that just can't be done in fee-for-service medicine. For thalassemia, the screening program is the only way we can achieve prevention."[17]

Cypriot legislators and public health administrators also made decisions concerning the thalassemia screening programs. When I asked legislators or public health administrators why they authorized these screening programs or payment for the prenatal diagnosis and abortion, they replied in terms of utilitarian ethics: "Because we cannot afford to care adequately for an increasing population of these people and because the risks of preventing the birth of a thalassemic child were minimal compared to the risks of continuing therapy at the increasing level that we anticipate. The greatest good for the greatest number."[18]

The parents of Greek thalassemic children began banding together in an association in the early 1970s; Turkish parents followed suit later in the decade. Their initial goals were to lobby the government to cover the costs of Desferal therapy and to create a blood bank; they were also active in the campaigns to encourage blood donation and to inform the public about the genetic nature of thalassemia. The parents subsequently became strong supporters of voluntary, then mandatory, screening. Several Greek parents were part of the delegation that visited the Archbishop's Council to plead for mandatory screening. Several Turkish parents organized the lobbying campaign that led to mandatory screening in the North.

When I asked them why they had supported screening, which their own children might regard—as some American opponents of prenatal diagnosis have argued—as a discriminatory practice, I found their response surprising: "I'm a parent; my responsibility is to care for my child. My child requires a lot of expensive care, all the time. If we didn't stop the birth of more babies with this disease, then, sooner or later, my child's care was going to be rationed, or I was going to have to pay for it myself—and I can't afford to do that. Screening protects my child's health."[19]

I did not ask the patients I interviewed for their reactions to the screening programs. In North Cyprus the children who started Desferal therapy in the 1970s are now adults, and they have gained control of the association their parents started, In the Republic of Cyprus, the patients now have their own, active, subcommittee. Both associations remain strong supporters of screening. Every year the Thalassaemia International Federation (headquartered in Cyprus) sponsors workshops to teach physicians and technicians from countries with high prevalence how to organize their own screening programs. In Cyprus most thalassemia patients express their feelings about screening by voting with their feet. Now adults themselves, many have married. Virtually all have been very careful to pick noncarriers as their partners; all the children of such a marriage will be carriers but none—because the disease is caused by a recessive gene—will be afflicted.

I did not have the opportunity to interview the archbishop or any of the priests of the Cypriot Orthodox Church who participated in the Church's decision to mandate screening. I did however, get two accounts, from a physician and a parent who participated, of the arguments that were made at the crucial meeting in spring 1984.[20] They recall three. First, that the Archbishop, as shepherd to the flock of believers, should do what he can to reduce the level of suffering in the population. Second—and crucially—that a mandated screening program, coupled with prenatal diagnosis, would reduce the number of abortions being performed on the island; carrier couples who discovered their status when they had their first child with thalassemia were terminating all subsequent pregnancies, but couples who had been screened and who had fetal testing available were only terminating twenty-five percent of such pregnancies. Third, that carrier couples who were now resolutely childless would feel free to have children—and thus increase the flock—if they knew they could have children without thalassemia. To put the last two arguments in more ethically relevant language, a mandated screening program for thalassemia would be, in the Cypriot context and in pragmatic terms, both pro-life and pro-natalist.

In short, the mandated genetic screening programs on the island of Cyprus seem, *to the Cypriots*, to be both politically correct and morally right. The programs were developed in a democratic political context; decision making was decentralized and diffused. Many parties with vested interests—physicians, parents, patients, public health officials, even members of the church hierarchy—advocated for the programs and continue to support them. Because each population (Turkish and Greek) is relatively small and because carrier rates are relatively high, almost everyone knows someone with thalassemia and something of the suffering that the disease brings in its wake. In addition, special efforts were made to provide population education through school curricula, lectures and brochures, newspaper articles, and television shows so that Cypriots would know how screening programs can reduce that suffering.

Unlike the eugenic programs of the past, what is mandated in these Cypriot programs is only the *test* for carrier status; both carriers and patients are left free to make their own reproductive decisions after being tested. Crucially, economic support is provided both for those who decide that test results will alter their reproductive decisions *and* for those who do not. No one is required to undertake prenatal diagnosis or to terminate a pregnancy; all patients receive care at public expense, no matter how they came to be born with the disease.

Also unlike the eugenic programs of the past, these mandated genetic screening programs were not undertaken "for the good of the race" so much as for the good of the families that carry the gene. The programs were not imposed upon these families. To the contrary,

166 ❖ *Viewing New Creations with Anabaptist Eyes*

members of affected families helped create the programs and continue to sustain them politically and financially.

Utilitarian ethics—the greatest good for the greatest number—was only one of several ethical arguments that motivated the organizers and advocates of mandated screening. Some people acted out of a desire to reduce suffering, others out of a desire to protect their children, others to reduce abortion rates. Yet others saw mandated genetic screening as a form of positive eugenics, encouraging carrier families to have more and healthier children. Under earlier eugenic programs, people who carried deleterious genes or traits were treated as enemies of good health. Under these Cypriot programs, people who carry deleterious genes or who suffer from genetic disease, are welcomed and encouraged to be fully functioning, fully contributing members of their communities.

The Cypriots are fully aware of what was done, early in the twentieth century, in the name of eugenics. They are also fully cognizant of the nature of genetic disease and the suffering it can bring. As a result, they have carefully crafted a genetic program meant to give eugenics a good name, a program which uses genetic means to achieve a genetic end but which avoids the moral mistakes made by earlier eugenicists. In the process they have taught us all that the bottom of that slippery slope can be a place to welcome, a place we need not fear.

Notes

1. There is a vast literature on Galton and on the eugenics movement. A good place to start is, Daniel J. Kevles, *In the Name of Eugenics* (New York: Knopf, 1985).

2. Francis Galton, "Hereditary Talent and Character," *Macmillan's Magazine*, 12 (June, 1865) 157-66; (August, 1865) 318-27.

3. Francis Galton, *Inquiries into Human Faculty* (London: Macmillan, 1883) 24-5.

4. On the eugenics movements in different countries see Diane B. Paul, *Controlling Human Heredity, 1856 to the Present* (Atlantic Highlands: Humanities Press, 1995) and Mark B. Adams, *The Wellborn Science: Eugenics in Germany, France, Brazil and Russia* (New York: Oxford University Press, 1990).

5. Phillip Reilly, *The Surgical Solution: A History of Involuntary Sterilization in the United States* (Baltimore: The Johns Hopkins University Press, 1991).

6. Gunnar Broberg and Nils Roll-Hansen, *Eugenics and the Welfare State: Sterilization Policy in Denmark, Sweden, Norway, and Finland* (East Lansing: Michigan State University Press, 1996).

7. The literature on German eugenics is also vast. One good place to start is Robert N. Proctor, *Racial Hygiene: Medicine Under the Nazis* (Cambridge: Har-

vard University Press, 1988).

8. For information about newborn screening, go to the American Academy of Pediatrics, Newborn Screening Fact Sheets, at http://www.aap.org/policy/01565.html.

9. A good review of these screening programs can be found in Lori B. Andrews, *Future Perfect: Confronting Decisions about Genetics* (New York: Columbia University Press, 2001).

10. Andrews, *Future Perfect,* also discusses prenatal diagnosis.

11. This analysis is based on my own research, soon to be published (by Harvard University Press) under the title, *Bad Genes, Good People: The History and Politics of Genetic Screening.*

12. Rayna Rapp, *Testing Women: Testing the Foetus* (New York: Routledge, 2001) discusses attitudes toward abortions consequent on prenatal diagnosis.

13. From T. Cooley, P. Lee and E. R. Witwer, "Anemia in children with splenomegaly and peculiar changes in bones; report of cases," *Am J Dis Child* 34 (1927): 347-63.

14. B. Modell, "Report on Thalassaemia in Cyprus," (copy of a typescript, dated 1972, given to the author by Michael Angastiniotis in 1999). See also WHO Working Group, "Community control of hereditary anaemias: Memorandum from a WHO meeting," *Bulletin of the World Health Organization* 6, no. 1 (1983): 63-80.

15. From, M. A. Angastiniotis, S. Kyriakidou, and M. Hadjiminas, "How thalasseaemia was controlled in Cyprus," *World Health Forum* 7 (1986) 291-7.

16. This quote is a paraphrase from several interviews.

17. Author's interview with Michael A. Angastiniotis, Director, Thalassemia Centre, Archbishop Makarios Hospital for Children, Nicosia Cyprus, April 18, 1999.

18. This quote is also a paraphrase from several interviews.

19. This quote is also a paraphrase from several interviews.

20. Author's interviews with Minas Hadjiminas, MD, retired Director of the Thalassemia Center, Archbishop Makarios Hospital for Children, Nicosia Cyprus and Panos Englezos, President of the Thalassemia Internation Foundation, March and May, 1999.

CHAPTER TWELVE

Crosscultural Approach to Biotechnology

Kabiru Kinyanjui

Dr. Kabiru Kinyanjui is the Senior Program Specialist for International Development Research Center in Kenya. Previously he was a Senior Research Fellow and Director of the Institute for Development Studies for the University of Nairobi.

*A*lthough biotechnology provides rays of hope, there are also many questions to raise, particularly in the African context. One cannot fail to be impressed by the complexity and sophistication of research on biotechnology in the United States and Canada. However, we need to recognize that sophistication and advancement create a major gap between countries of the northern and southern hemispheres.

I discern a major gap between African society and the system of knowledge seen in biotechnology. There is a major cultural distance between the system that produces the biotechnological knowledge and the people who may use it, particularly when this knowledge is transferred to a continent like Africa. That cultural distance becomes much more clearly defined when these technologies are tried in our context without raising very fundamental questions about the appropriateness of biotechnology. Biotechnology is driven in the United States by the profit motive, which in my African context distorts our ability to feed ourselves and to deal with hunger on the continent.

Biotechnology operates in the context of power. Presently, this power is concentrated in the northern hemisphere within transnational corporations. Developing countries, such as those in Africa, find themselves on the receiving end of that particular power. It is important to recognize that power needs not only to be in the hands of the professionals but also needs to be questioned by communities, by civil society, and by governments in the South.

Who made the decision on a particular biotechnological intervention? Do we see a whole range of people making decisions on how this intervention is going to be carried out so that it has a positive impact on society? When researchers, politicians, professionals, physicians, parents, and children work together making those kinds of decisions, it is a very positive thing. In the African context, the ability of the politician, the professional, and the community to act together to make those kinds of decisions is essential. However, the tendency of those who propagate the ideas of biotechnology is to work with professionals and ignore communities. They ignore what communities have learned over the ages, whether it is provisions of the seeds or the indigenous knowledge of agricultural methods that they have acquired.

The second crosscultural element in biotechnology is seen in the thalassemia case study in Cyprus, where a partnership was established between communities, government, professionals, and the international health organization. There was common understanding of the need for and value of intervention in the occurrence of thalassemia. This particular success occurred because the partnership transcended the cultural and religious sensitivities. This success indicates the necessity of a partnership that transcends culture and differing values so that people can make difficult decisions that benefit the whole society.

We need to recognize that the social injustices and inequalities in societies will not go away with the introduction of biotechnology. The United States has enormous power to introduce biotechnology and carry out research. However, when the technology comes to us, the inequalities which exist between the north and south will not go away. The technology will not rid us of hunger and poverty. We must recognize that technology by itself cannot deal with the issues of inequality, which need to be incorporated into the decision-making processes.

As evidenced by the thalassemia case, it is necessary to create an informed society, which is part of dealing with issues of biotechnology. It is also important to build the necessary capacity for biosafety, which will bring the kind of partnership that is required. Let us build a partnership for the responsible and creative utilization of biotechnology that benefits a majority of people in a continent like Africa—a partnership which involves the private sector, communities, government, and civil society so that they can see the commonalities and understand how this will serve the majority of the people.

CHAPTER THIRTEEN

Emerging Biotechnologies: A Historical Perspective

Carl D. Bowman

Dr. Carl D. Bowman is professor of sociology at Bridgewater College and director of survey research at the University of Virginia's Pew Center on Religion and Democracy. He has authored books and articles on Brethren history, including Brethren Society: The Cultural Transformation of a Peculiar People. *He obtained his Ph.D. in sociology from the University of Virginia.*

Compared to other scholarly and professional lenses, the lens of the historian is neither practical nor pragmatic. History can be exacting to the point of pedantry or sweeping to the point of sloppiness. It does not predict the future, though it may slow the repetition of past mistakes. It is not linear, though we often think of it in linear terms. History accumulates, taking us on a journey in which our pathways crumble behind us. Existentially, history is the wellspring of memory. Culturally, it is the repository of heritage. As an arena of scholarly inquiry, history usually examines past realities from the vantage point of an ever-shifting present. Yet in the context of this presentation, I must comment upon the present from the vantage point of a shifting past.

What can taking the long view—historical farsightedness— teach us? First, that defining our concepts broadly (biotechnology, for example) highlights the continuity between past and present events, shrinking the uniqueness of the moment, and tempering our natural tendency toward chronocentrism: my generation, our mission, our discoveries.

A historical rendering of the term *biotechnology* does not begin with "cloning" or "genetic engineering." Historians might even cite the automobile, which is a legs-supplement, or the slingshot, an arm extender, as examples of biotechnology. The car, after all, stands alongside in vitro fertilization in our ongoing project of overcoming basic human limitations. If biotechnology were defined as "anything that alters or extends an individual's biological capacities," the list would be lengthy indeed. Yet even if we narrow our scope to technologies that manipulate living things themselves, the historical list includes using yeast for bread, circumcision, inoculating children by infecting them with mild strains of disease, tanning beds, hair dyes, the cup of coffee I carry to class, and cloning cats. Thus seen, recent biological discoveries and their technological derivatives accomplish the same thing their precursors have done for ages. They attempt to overcome human limitations in an effort to satisfy our deepest hopes and longings.

All of this leads to a second point, which is little more than a logical extension of the first: Much of what now seems new is not as new as it seems. New technologies have always satisfied human longings, solved problems, and extended capacities. As such, they have empowered people, extending their frontiers of thought and action, thus giving rise to new longings. None of this is particularly novel. New technologies often inspire prophecies about the future, some of which are fulfilled and some of which fade from memory. They spark fears. Some are well-founded, some are ungrounded, and many dissipate with time.

Consider the car. One hundred years ago some of our Anabaptist ancestors fretted about where the car might take them, others realized it would only go where you told it to, and still others worried about how it might affect communities and change the pace of life. Some concerns were warranted; some now seem foolish. One thing is certain: Those who first tinkered with horseless carriages could scarcely have imagined how their tinkerings, multiplied en masse, would alter the social geography of cities, affect the quality of the earth's atmosphere, or generate a demand for oil that profoundly impacts world politics. It began with a human longing to travel greater distances cheaply and to save time in the going. Who could have imagined the consequences? Who among us would give up our car?

Time and again, history reveals that the satisfaction of old aspirations spawns new ones, technological solutions to old problems generate new problems, technology sometimes offers solutions to problems that have barely flickered into our consciousness, and technologies often blur or transcend things that were once accepted as given. They thus alter our understandings of human nature itself. None of this is new.

A third lesson from history concerns the fact that while certain moral truths have endured longer than others, ethical wisdom and integrity have been shaped as much by history as they have shaped its course. I am not dressed plain; my grandfather once was. I will have a glass of wine with dinner; my father will not. Our Anabaptist ancestors rejected lightning rods because lightning rods seemed to wrest nature from God's grasp. My grandparents believed hardship could build character. My daughter echoed this sentiment when she made a poster for our fridge proclaiming, "If you want to keep your children's feet on the ground, put responsibility on their shoulders." Charity toward the destitute and downtrodden has a long history in the Anabaptist heritage. Honesty has a noble history as an ideal but a more tawdry history in practice. Even as we struggle to delimit what is ethical with respect to emerging biotechnologies, biotechnologies themselves will influence future understandings of what is ethical.

Recent biological discoveries and biotechnological innovations reflect our enduring hopes that the blind will see, the deaf will hear, the hungry will eat, the sick will be healed, the sad will be comforted, children will be disciplined and focused, loved ones will live long and productive lives, and we will be fruitful and multiply. They also reflect hopes that tummies will be tighter, memory will be sharper, muscles will be larger, the short will be made tall, the nervous and obsessive will relax, the old will become young, our daughters will be blond, and our destinies will be subject to our control. Some go so far as to take the biblical injunction to "be ye therefore perfect" where no one might have imagined it would go.

There is much here to consider and much that is disquieting. However, thinking historically, our disquiet should probably focus as much upon the expansion of human aspirations as it does upon our biotechnological attempts to satisfy them. Even so, the technologies themselves multiply and modify our aspirations, taking hope to unforeseen, imaginary places.

The fact that all of our dilemmas are old (in a sense) makes them no less compelling. Each generation must fight its own battles. Each generation in its own time charts the course of history. As they do, the paths they construct crumble behind them. Because they cannot turn back, they have laid the foundation for everything that will follow. Sometimes we build better than we know, and sometimes we build worse. In every case, our hopes and fears about the future contain wisdom and foolishness, prophecy and fantasy. This is a human limitation that not even biotechnology can alter: The future always differs from the sum of our imaginings.

CHAPTER FOURTEEN

Biotechnology Through the Discipline Lens of the Poet's Pen

Barbra R. Graber

Barbra R. Graber is professor of theater and chair of the theater department at Eastern Mennonite University. She received her MFA from the University of Southern California and was narrator for the award-winning ABC television special, "Journey to Forgiveness," that aired in 2002.

"This we know: the earth does not belong to man; man belongs to the earth. All things are connected like the blood that unites us all. We did not weave the web of life, we are merely a strand in it. Whatever we do to the web, we do to ourselves."[1] These words were penned in 1852 and credited to the legendary Native American Chief Seattle, but they express an ethical belief system about the nature of life for tribal peoples thousands of years before.

Long before the words *science, bioethics, biotechnology,* or *bio*-anything was in our vocabulary, our human ancestors contemplated life's questions about birth and death, creator and creation, sickness and health, freedom and dignity.[2] Their form of inquiry was not the world of academic conferences but the language of art, poetry, drama, story, dance, and music. Through these art forms they inquired into and pondered the great mysteries.

We are richer having added science to the well from which we ponder these things, but we do well to remember and seek out the

175

wisdom of the poets and artists who have contributed to this discussion from the beginning of time. They offer us a legacy of wisdom and a complimentary way of knowing. Thus, for our enjoyment and inspiration, and as a way of looking at biotechnology through the discipline lenses of literature, I offer the work of five poets: Delmore Schwartz, Walt Whitman, Denise Levertov, Wendell Berry, and Gerard Manley Hopkins.

Each poet explores some aspect of the questions surrounding our theme. Schwarz and Whitman express very different attitudes toward living in a body. Schwartz likens it to living with a "heavy bear," while Whitman praises the beauty of this earthly frame inhabited by spirit and soul. Levertov expresses the inevitable and universal bioethical conundrum of death and talks to grief as though it were a homeless dog. Berry warns against elevating human and scientific "genius" and calls us back to "an old love, an old intelligence of the heart..." (line 94). [3] Finally, Hopkins reminds us that in our search for perfection, there is beauty in the irregular and that the Source of this strange beauty is worthy of our praise. Herewith, an unexamined contribution to the worthy discussion at hand, from the pen of poets:

The Heavy Bear Who Goes With Me

The heavy bear who goes with me,
A manifold honey to smear his face,
Clumsy and lumbering here and there,
The central ton of every place,
The hungry beating brutish one
In love with candy, anger, and sleep,
Crazy factotum, disheveling all,
Climbs the building, kicks the football,
Boxes his brother in the hate-ridden city.

Breathing at my side, that heavy animal,
That heavy bear who sleeps with me,
Howls in his sleep for a world of sugar,
A sweetness intimate as the water's clasp,
Howls in his sleep because the tight-rope
Trembles and shows the darkness beneath.
— The strutting show-off is terrified,
Dressed in his dress-suit, bulging his pants,
Trembles to think that his quivering meat
Must finally wince to nothing at all.

That inescapable animal who walks with me,
Has followed me since the black womb held,
Moves where I move, distorting my gesture,
A caricature, a swollen shadow,
A stupid clown of the spirit's motive,
Perplexes and affronts with his own darkness,
The secret life of belly and bone,
Opaque, too near, my private, yet unknown,
Stretches to embrace the very dear
With whom I would walk without him near,
Touches her grossly, although a word
Would bare my heart and make me clear,
Stumbles, flounders, and strives to be fed
Dragging me with him in his mouthing care,
Amid the hundred million of his kind,
The scrimmage of appetite everywhere.[4]
—*Delmore Schwartz*

I Sing the Body Electric

The man's body is sacred and the woman's body is sacred. . .
Head, neck, hair, ears, drop and tympan of the ears,
Eyes, eye-fringes, iris of the eye, eyebrows, and the waking
    or sleeping of the lids,
Mouth, tongue, lips, teeth, roof of the mouth, jaws,
    and the jaw-hinges,
Nose, nostrils of the nose, and the partition,
Cheeks, temples, forehead, chin, throat, back of the neck,
    neck-slue,
Strong shoulders, manly beard, scapula, hind-shoulders,
    and the ample side-round of the chest,
Upper-arm, armpit, elbow-socket, lower-arm, arm-sinews,
    armbones,
Wrist and wrist-joints, hand, palm, knuckles, thumb,
    forefinger, finger-joints, finger-nails,
Broad breast-front, curling hair of the breast, breast-bone,
    breast-side,
Ribs, belly, backbone, joints of the backbone,
Hips, hip-sockets, hip-strength, inward and outward round,
    man-balls, man-root,
Strong set of thighs, well carrying the trunk above,
Leg-fibres, knee, knee-pan, upper-leg, under-leg,

Ankles, instep, foot-ball, toes, toe-joints, the heel;
All attitudes, all the shapeliness, all the belongings of my or
    your body or of any one's body, male or female,
The lung-sponges, the stomach-sac, the bowels sweet
    and clean,
The brain in its folds inside the skull-frame,
Sympathies, heart-valves, palate-valves, sexuality,
    maternity,
Womanhood, and all that is a woman, and the man that
    comes from woman,
The womb, the tears, nipples, breast-milk, tears, laughter,
    weeping, love-looks, love-perturbations and risings,
The voice, articulation, language, whispering, shouting
    aloud,
Food, drink, pulse, digestion, sweat, sleep, walking,
    swimming,
Poise on the hips, leaping, reclining, embracing, arm-curving
    and tightening,
The continual changes of the flex of the mouth, and around
    the eyes,
The skin, the sunburnt shade, freckles, hair,
The curious sympathy one feels when feeling with the hand
    the naked meat of the body,
The circling rivers the breath, the breathing it in and out,
The beauty of the waist, and thence of the hips, and thence
    downward toward the knees,
The thin red jellies within you or within me, the bones and
    the marrow in the bones,
The exquisite realization of health;

O I say these are not the parts and poems of the body only,
    but of the soul,
O I say now these are the soul![5]
—*Walt Whitman*

Talking to Grief

Ah, grief, I should not treat you
like a homeless dog
who comes to the back door
for a crust, for a meatless bone.
I should trust you.
I should coax you
into the house and give you
your own corner,
a worn mat to lie on,
your own water dish.
You think I don't know you've been living
under my porch.
You long for your real place to be readied
before winter comes. You need
your name,
your collar and tag. You need
the right to warn off intruders,
to consider
my house your own
and me your person
and yourself
my own dog.[6]
—Denise Levertov

Some Further Words

Let me be plain with you, dear reader.
I am an old-fashioned man. I like the
world of nature despite its mortal
dangers. I like the domestic world
of humans, so long as it pays its debts
to the natural world, and keeps its bounds,
I like the praise of Heaven. My purpose
is a language that can repay just thanks
and honor for those gifts, a tongue
set free from fashionable lies.

Neither this world nor any of its places
is an "environment." And a house
for sale is not a "home." Economics
is not "science," nor "information" knowledge.

A knave with a degree is a knave. A fool
in a public office is not a "leader."
A rich thief is a thief. And the ghost
of Arthur Moore, who taught me Chaucer,
Returns in the night to say again:
"Let me tell you something, boy.
An intellectual whore is a whore."

The world is babbled to pieces after
the divorce of things from their names.
Ceaseless preparation for war
is not peace. Health is not procured
by sale of medication, or purity
by the addition of poison. Science
at the bidding of corporations
is knowledge reduced to merchandise;
it is a whoredom of the mind,
and so is the art that calls this "progress."
So is the cowardice that calls it "inevitable."

I think the issues of "identity" mostly
are poppycock. We are what we have done,
which includes our promises, includes
our hopes, but promises first. I know
a "fetus" is a human child.
I loved my children from the time
they were conceived, having loved
their mother, who loved them
from the time they were conceived,
and before. Who are we to say
the world did not begin in love?

I would like to die in love as I was born,
and as myself, of life impoverished, go
into the love all flesh begins
and ends in. I don't like machines,
which are neither mortal nor immortal
though I am constrained to use them.
(Thus the age perfects its clench.)
Some day they will be gone, and that will be a glad and a holy
    day.
I mean the dire machines that run

by burning the world's body and its breath. When I see an air-
     plane
fuming through the once-pure sky
or a vehicle of the outer space
with its little inner space
imitating a start at night, I say,
"Get out of there!" as I would speak
to a fox or a thief in the henhouse.
When I hear the stock market has fallen,
I say, "Long live gravity! Long live
stupidity, error, and greed in the palaces of
fantasy capitalism." I think
an economy should be based on thrift,
on taking care of things, not on theft,
usury, seduction, waste, and ruin.

My purpose is a language that can make us whole,
though mortal, ignorant, and small.
The world is whole beyond human knowing.
The body's life is its own, untouched
by the little clockwork of explanation.
I approve of death, when it comes in time
to the old. I don't want to live on mortal terms forever, or sur-
     vive
an hour as a cooling stew of pieces
of other people. I don't believe that life
or knowledge can be given by machines.
The machine economy as set afire
the household of the human soul,
And all the creatures are burning within it.

"Intellectual property" names
the deed by which the mind is bought
and sold, the world enslaved. We
who do not own ourselves, being free,
own by theft what belongs to God,
to the living world, and equally
to us all. Or how can we own a part
of what we only can possess
entirely? Life is a gift we have
only by giving it back again.
Let us agree: "the laborer is worthy

of his hire," but he cannot own what he knows,
which must be freely told, or labor
dies with the laborer. The farmer
is worthy of the harvest made
in time, but he must leave the light
by which he planted, grew, and reaped,
the seed immortal in mortality,
freely to the time to come. The land
too he keeps by giving it up,
As the thinker receives and gives a thought,
As the singer sings in the common air.

I don't believe that "scientific genius"
in its naive assertions of power
is equal either to nature or to human culture. Its thoughtless
    invasions
of the nuclei of atoms and cells
and this world's every habitation
have not brought us to the light
but sent us wandering farther through
the dark. Nor do I believe
"artistic genius" is the possession
of any artist. No one has made
the art by which one makes the works
of art. Each one who speaks speaks
as a convocation. We live as councils
of ghosts. It is not "human genius"
that makes us human, but an old love,
an old intelligence of the heart
we gather to us from the world,
from the creatures, from the angels
of inspiration, from the dead—
an intelligence merely nonexistent
to those who do not have it, but
to those who have it more dear than life.

And just as tenderly to be known
are the affections that make a woman and a man
their household and their homeland one.
These too, though known, cannot be told
to those who do not know them, and fewer of us learn them,

year by year.
These affections are leaving the world like the colors of extinct
    birds,
like the songs of a dead language.

Think of the genius of the animals,
every one truly what it is:
gnats, fox, minnow, swallow, each made
of light and luminous within itself.
They know (better than we do) how
to live in the places where they live.
And so I would like to be a true
human being, dear reader—a choice
not altogether possible now.
But this is what I'm for, the side
I'm on. And this is what you should
expect of me, as I expect it of myself, though for realization we
may wait a thousand or a million years.[7]
—*Wendell Berry*

Pied Beauty

Glory be to God for dappled things –
For skies of couple-colour as a brinded cow;
For rose-moles all in stipple upon trout that swim;
Fresh-firecoal chestnut-falls; finches wings;
Landscape plotted and pieced – fold, fallow, and plough;
And all trades, their gear and tackle and trim.
All things counter, original, spare, strange;
Whatever is fickle, freckled (who knows how?)
With swift, slow; sweet, sour; adazzle, dim;
He fathers-forth whose beauty is past change:
Praise him.[8]
—*Gerard Manley Hopkins*

As we continue explorations and contemplations on bioethics,
may we be inspired to take our own journey into this brave new
world of biotechnology through the minds and hearts of artists and
poets.They have left a legacy of wisdom, a profound way of knowing, and an ancient and reliable approach to the pursuit of ethical
truth.

Notes

1. Chief Seattle. 1852

2. Leon Kass, ed, *Being Human: Readings from The President's Council on Bioethics* (Washington D.C.) 17 Jan. 2002, (accessed October 13, 2003) http://www.bioethics.gov/bookshelf.

3. Wendell Berry, "Some Further Words." *American Poetry Review* 31, no. 3 (May/June 2002): 29-30, line 94. Used by permission of Wendell Berry, all rights reserved.

4. Delmore Schwartz, "The Heavy Bear Who Goes with Me," in *Summer Knowledge: New and Selected Poems 1938-1958* (Garden City: Doubleday, 1959), 74-5.

5. Walt Whitman "I Sing the Body Electric" in *Leaves of Grass* (New York: The Modern Library, 1921), 85, 87-8.

6. Denise Levertov, "Talking to Grief," in *Poems 1972-1982*, Copyright © 1978 by Denise Levertov, reprinted by permission of New Directions Publishing Corporation.

7. Wendell Berry, "Some Further Words." *American Poetry Review* 31, no. 3 (May/June 2002): 29-30.

8. Gerard Manley Hopkins, "Pied Beauty" in *The Poems of Gerard Manley Hopkins*, 4th. ed., ed. W. H. Gardner and N. H. Mackenzie (London: Oxford UP, 1967), 69-70.

CHAPTER FIFTEEN

Biotechnology Through the Lens of Public Policy

Laura E. Powers

Dr. Laura E. Powers works for the Office of U.S. Foreign Disaster Assistance at the U.S. Agency for International Development in Washington, D.C. She serves as the agriculture and livestock technical advisor for the office and spends about half of her time traveling internationally, primarily in the Horn of Africa. She received her Ph.D. from University of Florida, Gainesville, and did postdoctoral work at Colorado State University.

Advances in biotechnology are creating new challenges to policymakers, including issues of regulation, oversight, and the role of government in science. These issues are leading many citizens to ask questions about whose business it is to safeguard what is at stake and who policy-makers listen to when they make decisions.

The basic premise of policymaking is that decisions should be neutral, not based on the ethics of one particular group alone. To achieve this neutrality within the policy arena, bioethical controversies often avoid areas of morality and ethics and are reframed in terms of maximizing human good and minimizing harms. Safety and benefits play more important roles than ethical or moral beliefs in making policy decisions.

It is these ethical and moral questions, however, that are driving the increasing policy concerns about biotechnology. The challenge lies in how to insert theological and philosophical views into policy

186 ❖ *Viewing New Creations with Anabaptist Eyes*

discussions while still ensuring that the resulting policies are neutral. However, even language itself is not morally neutral (e.g. how we define genetic information is defined by values), and even values within one defined worldview may sometimes compete. Therefore, it is not enough to simply acknowledge the existence of many different worldviews and to then try to find ethical overlap within various moral and religious traditions.

In addition, the role of economics in policy decisions should not be underestimated. Individuals or companies with vested interests in the success of biotechnology often attempt to push their agendas forward, claiming that consumer ignorance or emotional reaction is all that stands in the way of their support for biotechnology. These same individuals seek to educate consumers by talking about safety issues alone. However, education about the safety of biotechnology does not address the ethical issues involved, and informed citizens may still have ethical concerns they wish to express to decision makers.

When trying to influence U.S. policymaking, citizens with ethical concerns must still translate those concerns into the terms lawmakers use. Generally, concerns about human life are not yet integral to policy justification, but there is some indication that this is changing. Many ethics advisory boards are now inviting theologians and philosophers to testify as they wrestle with biotechnological issues and are incorporating these perspectives in their reports. However, most policy recommendations still are based solely on issues of human good and safety. Until other moral and ethical viewpoints become integrated into the decision-making process surrounding technology, the policies that result from these discussions will never truly represent the will of the people that will be affected by the technology.

CHAPTER SIXTEEN

Biotechnology Through a Nursing Ethics Lens

Arlene G. Wiens

Dr. Arlene G. Wiens is professor of nursing at Eastern Mennonite University and is chair of the nursing department. She received her Ph.D. from the University of Virginia. Her nursing experience began as a nurses' aide in long-term care. Other experiences have been in critical care units, a step-down unit, a psychiatric setting, a rehabilitation hospital, community clinics, and nursing education settings. She remains active in nursing at the state and local level.

*N*ursing is a human science that focuses on maintaining wellness and the diagnosis and treatment of the human response to disease, across the life span. Nursing can best be theorized and exemplified as the art of other-oriented caring through states of both wellness and illness.[1] Nurses walk with their clients from conception to death, through health, illness, times of great joy and profound losses and pain. Nurses guide patients through the wellness/illness continuum. Because nurses deal with human responses to illness, ethical behavior is a complex, multifaceted phenomenon.

I frame my discussion of the nursing discipline ethics lens by using the American Nurses Association (ANA) Code of Ethics[2] and the International Council of Nurses (ICN) Ethical Concepts Applied to Nursing.[3] Both codes emphasize respecting human dignity (customs, values, beliefs, self-determination, and so forth). According to J. R. Ellis and C. L. Hartley, the ICN code includes a specific statement about technology: "The nurse, in providing care, ensures that use of technology and scientific advances are compatible with the safety, dignity and rights of the people" (358). The board of the International Society of Nurses in Genetics (ISONG) based its position statements on these codes.

Protection of client confidentiality, informed consent, managed care, and allocation of resources were the major ethical issues reported by genetic and oncology (cancer) nurses in a survey conducted by J. N. Cassells and others.[4] These nurses expressed concern about a lack of prepared providers to counsel patients and the possibility that patients are receiving insufficient information to understand the impact genetic testing may have on their lives. ISONG emphasizes additional concerns, including privacy of genetic information, ensuring the protection of vulnerable populations, respecting an individual's and/or family's right to choose, and the elimination of discriminatory insurance practices.[5]

Autonomy, or self-determination, is a challenge in all healthcare settings. It is often labeled noncompliance by caregivers who disagree with a client's decisions. Nursing places a strong emphasis on mutual planning and goal-setting with the client. Nursing ethics includes the responsibility of the nurse to be present with the client in such a way that the client can be helped to make the choice that truly reflects his or her own desires.

Autonomy becomes increasingly complex in relation to genetics technology, where there are competing rights. Several of these rights are addressed in questions on the U.S. government web site concerning the Human Genome Project (HGP). [6] Who has a right to participate in decisions—the entire family or the individual? Should parents make decisions for children who are minors in relation to anticipated adult diseases? ISONG expresses great concern about the role of insurance companies. Will insurers ultimately decide for persons who cannot afford testing or subsequent therapies? ISONG supports a person's right to accept or reject genetic testing.[7]

Informed consent is foundational to self-determination. As knowledge increases and becomes more complex, the power differential between the provider and the patient expands. ISONG believes that for an informed decision to occur, discussion of the benefits and risks, including the potential psychological and societal injury by stigmatization, discrimination, and emotional stress, in addition to emotional or physical harm, must be addressed.[8]

ISONG (2002) identifies vulnerable populations because of the complexity of the science of genetics. They include "children, individuals with hearing and language deficits or conditions limiting communication (for example, language differences and concerns with reliable translation), cognitive impairment, psychiatric disturbances, persons from minority populations, clients undergoing stress due to a family situation, those without financial resources; clients with acute or chronic illness and in end-of-life, and those in whom medication may impair reasoning."[9] Nurses are in a unique position to serve as genetic counselors in their role as guides through the wellness/illness continuum. Nurses are educated to be especially aware of the needs of vulnerable populations.

Nursing codes also emphasize that the nurse must maintain competence. This is consistent with the concept of fidelity in which nurses promise to provide competent care in whatever setting they practice. The profession has few graduate programs in genetics. Because nurses are the last line of defense for patients in a healthcare system that does great good as well as great harm, it is crucial that nurses become more knowledgeable in genetics.

If nurses look at healthcare history to predict the future in relation to autonomy, informed consent, and fidelity, the outlook is less than positive. As noted earlier, genetics and oncology nurses identified managed care as a major ethical dilemma. In many managed care settings, where nurses are repeatedly offered fewer resources than are needed to provide quality nursing care, the nurse is valued for completion of tasks, not for being one who informs or guides the patient. In addition, too often there is a pervasive attitude in the healthcare system that all the technology available should be used. This often conflicts with a patient's right to choose. It also can result in conflicts among providers, or between providers and the family or patient.

In my experience, nurses are less focused on saving a life at all costs and are more focused on what the machines or treatments *do to* the patient, rather than what they *do for* the patient. Nurses believe in comfort care as a form of healing. Luthringer noted that the "closer you are to the bedside, the less defensible a win-lose scenario."[10] Nurses are the closest people to the bedside of a patient and are acutely aware that, as Luthringer said, "self-righteously waging a war on behalf of patients is self-defeating. The patient will be the first casualty." Experienced nurses are often skeptical of technological optimism. We have seen too many broken promises and too much damage done.

Distributive justice is a principle about which nursing has great concern in relation to genetics. According to Muin Khoury "nine of the top ten leading causes of death, most notably chronic diseases, such as cancer and heart disease, have genetic components resulting from the interaction of genetic variation with modifiable risk factors."[11] This offers great opportunities for nurses in public health to combine testing with education. Again, if the past is any indicator, our nation chooses not to spend its money on public health. Rather, end-of-life care given during the last six months of life takes up major portions of the healthcare budget. On the opposite end are the technologies that have made it possible to save very small babies, many of whom will cost their families and the nation phenomenal amounts during the child's life span. At the same time, public health departments are short of funds to carry out programs that benefit a greater number of people for much less money.

Furthermore, ethical dilemmas will ensue as genetic therapy is used in diseases that also require modifying lifestyle behaviors. North Americans have not been very accepting of modifying lifestyle behaviors. Will gene therapy be refused if behavior is not modified? ISONG is concerned that insurance companies may potentially refuse policies and therapies to persons with certain genetic conditions.[12] In addition, other forms of discrimination are possible, especially if certain genetic illnesses are prominent in already marginalized populations. Employers may require genetic testing and not hire, or may eliminate employees with high-risk problems. Nurses are ethically responsible for speaking to policy makers so laws are passed that will protect the public, protect privacy, and provide access to the new genetic therapies.

The ANA's Code of Ethics states that "the nurse's primary commitment is to the patient, whether an individual, family group, or community."[13] Luthringer asserts that the ideal is that patient wellbeing is the sole concern of treatment personnel. While patients are the primary concern of any responsible caregiver, they cannot be the full concern.[14]

Nurses function in complex organizations and in multiple roles. They practice as part of a team, whether they are working in a high-tech environment such as a neonatal intensive care unit or a lower-tech public health environment. Luthringer argues that because the moral context of patient care is one of competing legitimate concerns, "conflicting obligations come with the territory" (12). Obligations to the team, nursing profession, employers, insurers, families and the patient are very real for nurses. Therefore, according to Luthinger "loyalty cannot be singular when reality is plural" (15).

Competent treatment depends on functional relationships. Research has shown that morbidity and mortality decrease in intensive care units when nurses and physicians engage in effective communication, a mark of functional relationships.[15] This research supports what many nurses already know; functional relationships are essential to protect patients from harm in healthcare settings.

As biotechnology advances, nurses will continue to collaborate with the healthcare team. However, the profession is always cognizant of the value that what the patient truly desires should be honored. When that person is unusually vulnerable, nurses will speak loudly on his or her behalf at all levels of the healthcare system from research to policy to practice.

Notes

1. M. Histand, "Philosophy of Nursing." Unpublished Paper September 2003. (3 pages).

2. American Nurses Association, "Code of Ethics for Nurses with Interpretive Statements" (Washington D.C.: American Nurses Publishing, 2001).

3. Janice Rider Ellis and Celia Love Hartley, *Nursing in Today's World*, 8th. ed. (New York: Lippincott, 2004), 358.

4. J. N. Cassells et al., "An Ethical Assessment Framework for Addressing Global Genetic Issues in Clinical Practice," *Oncology Nursing Forum* 30, no. 3 (May/June 2003): 383-90.

5. International Society of Nurses in Genetics, Inc., "Access to Genomic Healthcare: The Role of the Nurses." September 9, 2003, http://www.global-referrals.com/about/position_statements/genetics_healthcare.html, 1-3, (accessed Oct. 10, 2003).

6. "Human Genome Project Information: Ethical. Legal and Social Issues." http://www.ornl.gov/sci/techresources/Human_Genome/elsi/elsi.shtml, (accessed Oct. 30, 2003).

7. International Society of Nurses in Genetics, Inc., "Privacy and Confidentiality of Genetic Information: The Role of the Nurse." October 9, 2001, http://www.globalreferrals.com/about/position_statements/
privacy.html, 1-3, (accessed October 30, 2003).

8. International Society of Nurses in Genetics, Inc., "Informed Decision Making and Consent: The Role of Nursing." September 30, 2000, http:www.globalreferrals.com/about/position_statements/consent.html, 1, (accessed October 30, 2003).

9. International Society of Nurses in Genetics, Inc., "Genetic Counseling for Vulnerable Populations: The Role of Nursing," Oct. 10, 2002, http:www.globalreferrals.com/about/position_statements/vul_pop.html, 1-4, (accessed Oct. 30, 2003).

192 ❖ *Viewing New Creations with Anabaptist Eyes*

10. George F. Luthringer, "The Ethics of Ordinary Time" in *The Ethics of the Ordinary in Health Care*, ed. J.A. Wortley (Chicago: Health Administration Press, 1997), 19.

11. Muin Khoury, "Genomics and Disease Prevention," http://www.cdc.gov/genomics/about/welcome.hm, 1 (accessed Oct. 30, 2003).

12. International Society of Nurses in Genetics, Inc., "Access to Genomic Healthcare: The Role of the Nurses," Sept. 9, 2003, http://www.globalreferrals.com/about/position_statements/genetics_healthcare.html, 1-3, (accessed October 10, 2003).

13. J.R. Ellis and Celia Love Hartley, *Nursing in Today's World*, 8th. ed. (New York: Lippincott, 2004), 9.

14. George F. Luthringer, "The Ethics of Ordinary Time" in *The Ethics of the Ordinary in Health Care*, ed. J. A. Wortley (Chicago: Health Administration Press, 1997), 19.

15. S. Gordon, *Life Support: Three Nurses on the Front Lines* (New York: Little, Brown and Company, 1997), 283.

CHAPTER SEVENTEEN

Natural Selection or Genetic Modification? Biotechnology and Business

Mike E. Baker

Mike E. Baker is Senior Vice President, Pennington Seed, Inc. Oregon Division. He served as president of the Oregon Seed Trade Association and the Oregon Seed Council and chair of the Oregon Seed Council's Seed Production Research Committee from 1989-1995. He is currently working on a degree in international business at Linfield College.

*T*he assumption is often made that nature employs an evolutionary system, wherein beneficial mutations and genetic alteration of organisms result in actual genetic changes that survive and are passed on in a population, allowing the organism to thrive. This chapter describes the case of toxic alkaloids in naturally grown grasses and how nature's method of biotechnology was a healthy and economically beneficial.

Following the Dust Bowl years of the 1930s and 1940s, there was a drive to increase livestock production in areas with thin, rocky soils in the Midwest, mid-Atlantic, and Piedmont areas of the United States. The challenge was to find a pasture system suited to the climate and soils that would require few crop inputs. Farmers wanted to find a grass that would survive and grow nearly all year long.

The solution was found on a Kentucky farm that was growing

tall fescue. Tall fescue is a grass that produces edible forage despite repeated winter ice and snow storms, extreme wet and dry conditions, humidity, and nasty bugs. To survive, tall fescue requires a symbiotic endophyte fungus that lives within the plant.

However, the tall fescue solution came with a serious side effect—endophyte toxicity. Caused by alkaloids in the plant, this condition causes vaso-constriction of the circulatory system in the extremities of susceptible animals, leading to elevated body temperatures in summer, reduced body temperatures in winter, stillbirths, thickened and/or retained placentas, and in extreme cases, frozen flesh. Endophyte toxicity also causes a condition known as fescue foot, which is the loss of hooves, tails, and ears due to inadequate blood flow.

Tall fescue with endophyte is the least costly, most resilient forage grass in the United States. It is the most productive pasture grass on over 35 million acres of thin and rocky soils from eastern Kansas/Oklahoma/east central Texas to the Atlantic Ocean. Fescue toxicity is estimated to cost livestock producers millions of dollars in losses each year. The alternatives, however, require more energy inputs and resources for stand replacement, cut-and-carry forage production on arable land, and continuous movement of livestock to minimize grazing damage.

Much research was conducted in the late 1980s and early 1990s to study endophyte fungi and the range of alkaloids produced by these endophytes. Among the alkaloids produced in our fescue research were two of particular importance: peramine and ergovalene. While ergovalene was the most detrimental to domestic livestock, peramine was detrimental to insects that ate the plant and spread disease. Once we understood the problem—the presence of ergovalene alkaloids at above 250 parts per billion in the diet—we just needed to find a way to prevent the right endophyte from producing ergovalene without harming the fungus. The wanted andophyte needed to keep producing the beneficial alkaloids and providing the other services it does for its grass host.

E- (endophyte-free) seeds are produced easily by storing seed at ambient temperature and moderately high humidity for for over eighteen months, which causes the endophyte to die. Plants grown from E-seeds host no living fungi and produce no toxic alkaloids. However, plants without an endophyte fungus partner live only one to two years in the transition zone unless managed very carefully (i.e. animals cannot graze on it much from May through October). This grazing restriction is not a favored option for most livestock producers. The endophyte gives the plant benefits that allow it to thrive in extremes of weather and abuse by grazing livestock and insects. Without endophyte, there are serious stand losses. The challenge was to find or create an endophyte fungus that will produce all the alkaloids that give benefits to the plant but do not produce any of the alkaloids detrimental to livestock.

Studying the natural relationship between organisms brings up an ethical question: Is waiting on the evolutionary system that nature employs a better ethic than understanding the genetic and physiological controls of how the alkaloids are produced and manipulating those parts of the genetic code to accomplish some good? If the genetic code of the right endophyte fungus could be tweaked just right, we could have a near-perfect solution. If we can afford it, why not do it? If it pays dividends and is good for the environment, the animals, and the producers, we simply need to determine the cost of learning the code and making the modifications. Using biotechnology, we can transform the organism, while allowing a cost-benefit equation to guide us. However, MaxQ endophyte was developed by nature as a genetically modified fungus that symbiotically produces non-toxic alkaloids, thereby increasing pasture productivity. while we could have done this in the lab, nature did it for us in the field.[1]

I put into poetic form some reflections on the path researchers took to bring MaxQ to market—

> Two roads diverged in a grassy field
> And I . . . more ethical than most,
> I looked to nature as my aid
> To find a plant, the perfect host,
> To nurture one to live therein
> Who'd bring no harm to common beast.
> I went to deserts far away
> Where life was struggle, strain, and luck,
> To find a place where drought and pest and heat bore down . . .
> But beast lived not.
> For there would be the perfect place,
> For God to do a perfect work.
> A fescue there would need the aid
> Of endophyte to beat the odds . . .
> To beat the pests, the heat, the drought,
> But had no need to beat the beast.

And sure enough, God's work was done.
For MaxQ waited patiently to serve mankind
So naturally that horses, cattle, sheep, and goats
Could live both full and healthy life
Without the harm to inner parts.
So now I ask you—weigh the thought . . .
If God had not and we knew how
Should we have helped or done without?
God help us know . . . God help us now.

Note

1. See http://www.fescue.com/info/maxQ.html.

CHAPTER EIGHTEEN

The Farmer's Future: Biotechnology from an Agricultural Perspective

Carole L. Cramer

Dr. Carole L. Cramer was professor of plant pathology and physiology at Virginia Tech and co-founder of CropTech Corporation and Biodefense Technologies, Inc. She is currently the director of the Biosciences Institute at Arkansas State University.

*U*nlike many people represented in this book, I have not thought much about the broader implications of biotechnology. Since I have mainly focused on what I am doing in the research laboratory, these presentations have been an excellent education in thinking about the bigger picture of biotechnology. I recognize that for many of us, stem cell research and genetic disease is easy to put aside if it is not in our family. However, our food supply is fundamental.

Agriculture spans all the way from subsistence farming to complex agri-business. Agriculture involves many persons, including farmers, food producers, and marketers. Agriculture is an extremely complex global enterprise with issues of international trade and different cultures.

I will look at how biotechnology impacts the farmer. Take, for example, the commodity farmers growing corn in Iowa or soybeans in Illinois. They have bought into biotechnology, because it brings them significant benefit. However, their world is now being turned on end because of acceptance or non-acceptance of their products on the global market. Issues of labeling, traceability, and full segregation have significant impacts. Every spring, farmers must decide whether they are going to plant genetically modified (GM) seeds or not, and consequently wonder if they will be able to sell their products. These issues are significant for them as they try to build their farming enterprise. The small farmer in rural America is at risk. Some farmers are needing to sell their farms and find other work to make a living.

Farmers are exploring the concept of specialty uses. In Arkansas I was surprised to find that the rice farmers are now changing the way they handle rice. They used to burn the stubble down to make plowing easier the next year. Now, many of these farmers are leaving the stubble in the fall and renting their land to duck hunters. By leaving the rice stubble, farmers make more money in the duck hunting industry than they do in farming. Farmers view new crops, high value pharmaceuticals, and specialty crops as ways to have enough participation and value to keep their farms going.

Looking at the subsistence farmer in Kenya, for example, another set of issues surrounds the need for biotechnology. The technology must be provided to them in a context consistent with their culture and ability to use their agricultural traditions.

Farmers see the numerous potential impacts of new technologies, however, and it is unclear what the result of some of these impacts will be. In this situation, a whole lot of tails are wagging the dog. Producers themselves have issues. Will consumers trust the food supply? Trade issues continually emerge. Within the next couple of years, for the first time in history, the United States may be a larger food importer than exporter. As our relationship with our food supply changes, new issues suddenly arise.

I sit on a panel in the Biotechnology Industry Organization (BIO) that is looking at the controversies of plant-made pharmaceuticals. We had many discussions with the grain and corn producers saying they are extremely uneasy about human genes going into our crops. There would be huge commercial consequences if these were to cross into the food supply. Stringently controlling how we contain our crops, BIO member companies agreed not do field trials in major production areas that are growing the crop being used for the trials. For example, the people growing corn with these genes will notdo it in major corn-growing regions.

We agreed on this standard and put it out publicly. We were immediately attacked by Iowa legislators, who said this policy robs the farmers in Iowa of the ability to participate in this potential high-value use. We were trying to do the best we could to insure good stewardship, but we immediately got trounced because we were not taking account of the economic implications.

Education is critical when dealing with these issues. We need to understand not only the science of what is going on, but also the implications. Discussions like this bioethics conference are important. Education and realistic discussions of the issues and concerns are critical. We are all still looking at the consequences of Monsanto's arrogant approach to biotechnology, as detailed in Daniel Charles' book, *Lords of the Harvest*.[1]

We also must look at historical advances such as the invention of the automobile and recognize that new technology is not intrinsically less safe than old technology. We simply do not have the experience to know what long-term issues biotechnology in agriculture poses. Caution and wisdom are good, but looking at a technology's ability to do benefit is also important.

My favorite example of how to think of the risks and benefits compares new techniques with existing technologies. The alternative to genetic engineering for some of these agricultural features is classical breeding. Hypothetically, I have a tomato species suffering from a fungal disease. Normally, I go to Peru for germ plasm, because that is where there is much more wild diversity and where the tomatoes were originally bred. I know that in Peru there is a wild tomato species resistant to the fungus. Think of the wild tomato as the wolf and the cultivated tomato as the French poodle. I cross these two because I need the disease resistance from the "wolf." The offspring are "wolfish poodles," so I continue to cross back to the poodle, trying to get rid of as much of the wolf as I can. Literally, I have just brought 30,000 genes in from the tomato and selected for the one that is resistant to the fungus. I do not know what those other 29,999 genes are, so I am taking a risk in traditional breeding.

There are many examples of classical breeding selecting for the perfect vegetable or fruit but carrying something toxic back in the process. We do not want to throw the baby out with the bath water, but we do want to insure the safety of our food supply and use this technology as wisely as possible.

Note

1. Daniel Charles, *Lords of the Harvest: Biotech, Big Money, and the Future of Food* (New York: Perseus, 2002).

CHAPTER NINETEEN

Menno Simons, Anabaptism, and the Promises of Biotechnology

Lawrence E. Ressler

Dr. Lawrence E. Ressler is Vice-President of Academics and Student Development at Tabor College in Hillsboro, Kansas. He has had nineteen years of experience as mediator, family counselor, social worker, and social work professor. He served as a past president of the North American Association of Christians in Social Work. He received his M.S.W. from Temple University and a Ph.D. from Case Western Reserve University.

*P*ersonal experiences color one's understanding of events, and that is certainly the case for my reflections. I am an Anabaptist Mennonite. That is, I trace my faith heritage to the Dutchman Menno Simons. Menno Simons was a priest who renounced Catholicism in 1535 and joined the young and outlawed Anabaptist movement. As a result, he lived the last twenty-five years of his life as a fugitive, eventually dying in the small city of Wustenfeld in northwest Germany, which was not his home.

What seems to be less well known is that the final impetus for Menno Simons' departure from the Catholic Church was a personal family tragedy. Menno's brother, who had joined a zealous group of Anabaptists called the Munsterites, was one of three hundred people killed in the government squelching of an insurrection. With his brother's death, Menno could no longer stay quiet about the erroneous thinking that surrounded him.

A century and a half after Menno died in 1561, my grandfather seven generations removed was sentenced to prison for his faith in France. He escaped while being taken to prison and eventually made his way to Pennsylvania in 1715. The family's faith heritage remained strong for another two centuries into the twentieth century when my grandfather suffered permanent injury at the hands of United States military personnel during World War I for refusing to wear a uniform. This history has had an important impact on how I see the promises and perils of biotechnology.

Intimately linked to my Mennonite tradition is the profession I have been involved in for the past twenty-five years—social work. I went into social work because I wanted to help people in need. I thought I was smart; I could get paid to do what Jesus called all Christians to do—feed the hungry, and clothe the naked, among other things. I could have eternal security and money, too. (I am not sure about the eternal security at this point, but I have discovered social work is not where one makes money.)

From my experience as a social worker, I draw from the stories of hundreds of individuals and families I have worked with and whose lives were in turmoil. Usually, as their stories unfolded, I found a tangled web of biological, psychological, sociological, and spiritual issues. I could see how biological forces twisted people's hands, confused what they wanted to say, hindered their ability to understand, distorted their emotions, undermined their will to live, and overwhelmed the family bonds of love. The best I could do with respect to biology up to this point was to encourage them to find ways to compensate, suggest they find meaning in their situation as best they could, and tell them to take Prozac.

Now I learn that biotechnology might be able to help. How can I say no? Why would I say no? With many stories of families with which I have worked ringing in my ears, the helping impulse in me wants biotechnology to be an answer. Yet there is something deep within me, whispering of trouble, that tells me to be disturbed about biotechnology and the industry that drives it.

My first concern stems from the history of persecution in my faith tradition and my family. For all of biotechnology's potential, I am reminded of that quip by British historian Lord Acton that "power corrupts, and absolute power corrupts absolutely." As scientists unravel the powers of creation never known before and as they get to the very essence of life, despite all the good that could come from biotechnology, there is no reason to believe that biotechnology will be used only for good. History and Scripture suggest otherwise. In a new and frightening way, the power associated with biotechnology will be concentrated in the hands of a few with special knowledge and skills. Minority thinkers, odd-looking people, and those who disagree should be prepared for oppression that is as powerful and unimaginable as the very good that can be found in technology.

My second concern has to do with two little letters—™—we frequently see in products that emerge from the biotechnology industry. Jesus talked a lot about money, and he reminds us about the significant choice we must make between serving God and serving money.[1]

In 1989, when the Berlin Wall was dismantled and the Soviet empire collapsed, one of the authors of *Habits of the Heart*[2] made this insightful statement in a public lecture I attended, "The fall of communism does not vindicate capitalism. Capitalism has its own seeds of destruction." The business practices of Microsoft, the rampant greed of Enron executives, and pollution at Love Canal are not aberrations in history. They are reminders of a seamy side of human nature that has existed in the past and is at work in the boardrooms and intentions of some who promote biotechnology even now. The profit potential that exists in the biotechnology industry will produce yet another choice between God and money.

History suggests that more than a few will choose money, and many will suffer as a result. Amid all its affluence, it is shameful that the United States is not able, even now, to provide for the hungry and sick. Without a doubt, the concentrated power inherent in biotechnology will exacerbate the problems of globalization and may even dwarf them as it introduces what I will call "creationalization."

What do I suggest? I believe the drive to understand is part of what it means to be created in God's image. Like clockwork, as children, we begin to ask "Why?" because we are wired to want to understand.

The Scriptures also remind us that human beings are predisposed to turn from God and lean to their own understanding.[3] The result is trouble. It is here that Mennonites have made a historic contribution and have something to offer even today, which I will emphasize in my final comments.

For some reason I was not introduced to the writings of Menno Simons at any point in my education at a Mennonite high school, a Mennonite college, or in my many years attending a Mennonite church. It was not until my mid-thirties that I actually read Menno Simons directly. I was surprised by what I read.

I discovered that Menno Simons was not principally a pacifist. He was not a strong proponent of simple living, and his primary interest was not social justice. History has highlighted these elements, all of which are true; however, Menno Simons actually said relatively little about these things in his writings.

What did he write about? Read any of the writings of Menno Simons and one is immediately impressed with the passion Menno had for the Bible and the impact it had on his life. He was radical all right, radically committed to the Scriptures. Menno Simons's favorite verse, found at the beginning of all of his writings, was 1 Corinthians 3:11: "For no one can lay any foundation other than the one that has been laid; that foundation is Jesus Christ." He was a fugitive because he was determined to follow Christ as he understood Christ's teachings in Scripture. He would not be denied. He was also evangelical. Menno took every opportunity in his writings to call all people, but especially those in power, to repent and follow Christ.

How do I suggest we respond to the biotechnology issues that confront us? First, the community of faith needs to have the same passion for Scripture that Menno Simons and my ancestors had. We must study Scripture diligently and look at the issue of biotechnology through that lens, as well as through other lenses. Doing so will not provide us with simple solutions, but it will keep us on track. Like Anabaptist Mennonites in the past, we must have a commitment to live a life that honors God and that does not conform to this world, but is transformed by the renewing of our minds,[4] no matter what the cost. If we adhere to this commitment, we must refuse some aspects of biotechnology, even if they are possible. The Amish have it right in this regard. A radical commitment to Scripture will bring us to social justice, to simple living, and to a peace position, and it will sustain us through troubled times and confusing issues.

Second, we must do what Menno Simons and Mennonites have done historically; that is, we must call for others to pick up their crosses and follow Christ.[5] This call includes both those who are developing new technology, as well as those in power who develop the policies related to its distribution and consumption. Not only should we call for a personal commitment to Christ, we should also encourage those in the biotechnology industry to be involved in a community of faith in which they can discover what God calls them to do. Doing so will not necessarily make things easier, but it will provide the leaven and the salt needed as the technology develops and as decisions are made. It will allow for the spirit of God to guide them.

We may not be clear about what we should do in many of these complicated issues at this point, and we may not agree. Nevertheless, we must pay attention, study the issues, and pray for God's wisdom. When the issues are clear, I trust we will be willing to speak to the truth regardless of the world's reaction. Even more importantly, we must boldly call for all to follow Christ and allow this commitment to transform their work for the glory of God and the good of others. Although inviting others to trust in Christ will not solve all of life's problems, such a call will move things in the right direction.

Notes

1. Matt. 6:24.
2. Robert Bellah et al, *Habits of the Heart: Individualism and Commitment in American Life* (Berkeley: University of California Press, 1996).
3. Prov. 3:5.
4. Rom. 12:2.
5. Matt. 16:24.

CHAPTER TWENTY

The Face of Overpowering Knowledge

Randall L. Longenecker

Dr. Randall L. Longenecker is a clinical associate professor of family medicine and the associate rural program director at The Ohio State University College of Medicine and Public Health. In 1998, Dr. Longenecker established a rural residency program in family medicine. He now teaches a series of bioethics courses for the Ohio State University family practice residency programs and is vice-chair of the bioethics committee. He received his M.D. from the University of Pennsylvania.

As a self-taught, bedside bioethicist living in the swamp of clinical practice, the "Ethics and Biotechnology" conference reaffirmed for me the importance of being a part of both a community of knowledge and a community of wisdom, rather than attempting to possess this awesome knowledge for myself alone.[1] In the face of overpowering knowledge—an avalanche of new information every year, every day—my patients and I can easily find ourselves frozen into inaction.

The mass of data is so overwhelming I must become the material interface for my patients, bringing my own values and filters to the data and into the clinical encounter. From an ethical point of view and in real-world application, biotechnology is quite complicated!

In our society, knowledge is often equated with power. Therefore, giving knowledge is considered empowering. For example, knowledge of my cholesterol level before I have a heart attack can potentially galvanize me into effective action. The knowledge gained from genetic screening, however, is a different matter. It is less clearly useful knowledge. In addition to the task of making the complex simple, translating this knowledge into practice places some very difficult ethical obligations upon the physician, especially the duty to cause no harm.[2]

As a family physician who still delivers babies, I am aware of the ethical dilemmas that face women and their families when, through advances in biotechnology, they are offered genetic screening early in pregnancy. In 1997, for example, a National Institutes of Health Consensus Development Group of experts recommended that all couples who are pregnant or even considering pregnancy be offered carrier screening for cystic fibrosis.

The test available to us in our office screens for thirty-four of the more than 900 known mutations of the seventh chromosome, mutations which can result in varying severities of the clinical condition we call cystic fibrosis (CF). CF is a condition that even with optimal treatment carries a life expectancy of thirty to forty years. Currently there is no definitive cure, although biotechnology holds forth the promise of gene therapy in the not too distant future.

As a prenatal screen, the test is usually offered to the mother in early pregnancy, often at the same time as alpha-fetoprotein (AFP) screening and genetic amniocentesis—tests that, incidentally, carry their own ethical imperatives for informed consent. A positive CF test identifies the mother as a carrier. Then, if the baby's father is also tested and identified as a carrier, the couple has a roughly one-in-four chance of having an affected infant. The infant can then be tested prenatally and aborted if the couple so desires. Alternatively, the newborn can be tested immediately following birth for the purpose of early diagnosis and aggressive treatment of associated conditions.

Because the screen does not test for every mutation, however, a negative test does not remove the possibility that this couple could have an affected child. In fact, a negative test can have widely varying interpretations depending on the couple's ethnicity. Among those of Caucasian or Northern European descent where the test identifies ninety percent of the mutations, a negative test reduces a carrier risk before testing of one-in-25 to a carrier risk of 1-in-241. Among Asian populations, in which the test only identifies thirty percent of the mutations and in which CF is uncommon, a negative test only changes the carrier risk from one-in-90 to a posttest risk of 1-in-128.[3]

In clinical practice, how do I explain all of this to an expectant couple and get their informed consent—in two minutes or less and amid a prenatal visit crowded with other important tasks? What do I include in my discussion of benefits and harms? The cost of the test? Whether their insurance is one that covers it? Do I go on to explain the intervention cascade that this simple blood test can set in motion? What about distributive justice—that getting this expensive test "simply for the purpose of knowing" could in a systemic way deprive someone else of needed medical care for the purpose of surviving?

As an individual of Anabaptist heritage and faith, I have grown up and live with an uncommon perspective on the nature and limits of knowledge and power in medicine.

First, more knowledge and more power are not necessarily better. In an upside-down kingdom, less is sometimes more. Some knowledge can certainly be empowering, but too much knowledge is not. One patient described to me an overwhelming session with a genetic counselor following a positive AFP screen as "the worst day of my life!"

Second, knowledge without action, like faith without works, is lifeless. To simply know the future (as in genetic testing for Huntingdon's Chorea) without the ability to do something about it is not necessarily life giving, and is potentially breath-taking. It is not enough "to know"—one must "know how." Biotechnology in clinical medicine, except in a few instances, has not reached the point of "knowing how" in a substantive way.

Finally, "knowing how" is a communal endeavor, worked out in interaction with others—ear toward heaven and toward each other and hand to the plough until we "get it right."

The challenge for today's clinician is to take the massive amounts of data to which we have access and somehow distill that information into a form or package that is useful to patients. I want my patients to have enough information to make good, informed decisions, but not so much information that they are overwhelmed, distracted, and paralyzed into inaction.

Simple rules or heuristics that I find useful in practice, though they may not be easy, include—

- begin and end with a question—inquire about the patient's values and understanding, avoiding a long discourse on genetic testing if the woman does not want to know;
- employ metaphor—compare the test or the risk to something else already known, placing the information in personal context;
- explicitly acknowledge the uncertainty—"We're a little better than predicting the weather, but not much";
- Explain the intervention cascade—i.e. there may be more tests, each with costs and risks of their own;
- always be thoughtful, yet action-oriented—"What will you do, and what do you want me to do with the information we get? With whom will you share it?"

My ethical challenge as a physician is to proffer empowering but not overpowering knowledge in small, manageable, and relevant doses at the appropriate moment and in the appropriate way. From the specialists, researchers, and other experts among us, I ask for useful knowledge, and from my community and my God I ask for the wisdom to employ it well.

Notes

1. E. Schall, "Learning to Love the Swamp: Reshaping Education for Public Service," *Journal of Policy Analysis and Management* 14, no. 2 (Spring 1995): 202-20.

2. R.M. Ewart. "Primum Non Nocere and the Quality of Evidence: Rethinking the Ethics of Screening," *Journal of the American Board of Family Practice* 13, no. 3 (May/June 2000): 188-96.

3. T Brown and E. Langfelder Schwind. "Update and Review: Cystic Fibrosis," *Journal of Genetic Counseling* 8, no. 3 (June 1999): 137-62.

CHAPTER TWENTY-ONE

Biotechnology and Agriculture: An Anabaptist Response

Emerson D. Nafziger

Dr. Emerson D. Nafziger is professor of crop production extension in the crop sciences department at the University of Illinois, where he conducts applied research and extension programs in field crop management. His recent international work has involved soybean management in South Asia. He received his Ph.D. in agronomy at the University of Illinois at Champaign-Urbana, studying herbicide effects on plants and plant cells in culture.

My ancestors left Switzerland in the 1830s, bought swampland in northwestern Ohio, cleared heavy forests, and drained swamps to farm. While they left various occupations in the Old World, some of them were accomplished farmers, even when forced to farm marginal land at higher elevations. Family legend has it that my father said he would never farm without horses. Less than a decade later, he farmed without horses. My grandfather had a generator for electricity before most others in the area. We used chemical fertilizers, herbicides, and hybrid corn seed within a few years of their availability. Mennonites were then (and most remain) innovative and technologically advanced in their farming methods.

While some in the community delayed using modern farming inputs and practices for their own reasons, there is little evidence that new farming methods were ever resisted officially by the Mennonite churches of the area. Buttons were forbidden during some periods of Amish Mennonite history, but tractors and cars were fine. Acceptance of useful new things was not restricted to farming. Many of us remember lining up for polio shots in the 1950s once this miracle vaccine was available. If some viewed such things as against the natural order, the benefits were so obvious and great that they showed little interest in protesting. We prayed, but also showed faith in new technology.

While I believe most Anabaptist farmers have a greater-than-average sense of the need to protect and nurture the soil and environment, most have felt free to consider the use of new technology and to use it if it seems to confer an advantage. Stories of farmers who became too big and lost their wealth as a result are still used as cautionary tales, but those who succeed in expanding the size of land holdings while using the latest in technology are not generally ostracized. As far as I can tell, there is no official church position on the accumulation of wealth by farmers or anyone else, though ostentatious displays are not always considered acceptable.

Against this cultural background and theological silence, what practical reasons could we name as a basis to resist the advantages offered by biotechnological crop developments? As a pragmatic person, I find few. Yes, we do have to trust that governmental regulations and testing requirements will keep us from disaster, environmental and otherwise. This has been true for decades, and standards have risen with time, spurred by tragic instances like thalidomide use, which prompted the formation of the Food and Drug Administration (FDA).

Farmers engaged in some appalling practices in the early days of farm chemical use, including the use of toxic and long-lasting chlorinated hydrocarbon insecticides on millions of acres where they were not needed. However, we have learned from past mistakes, and today's herbicides and insecticides are safer than those used forty years ago. Required testing before release of new pesticides (including those like Bt produced in plants) is extensive and stringent. Methods of integrated pest management have been introduced, and most of today's farmers are committed to minimizing soil loss and damage to the environment. Biotechnological innovations that reduce chemical use can help to fulfill this commitment.

There is little theoretical or demonstrated support for the argument that transfer of genes from another species to a crop species will result in cataclysmic ecological disasters. I leave it to others to comment on this from human and animal sides of the issue, but plants are rather tame and immobile parts of creation, not good candidates to take over the world or even a sizeable chunk of it. Most crops are, in fact, not well suited for survival on their own. Corn is one of the most human-influenced of all crops and cannot survive on its own. Soybean and wheat pollen moves little from plant to plant, and these crops have no relatives with which to cross in most places. Early biotechnological scares about "Frankenfoods" and walking tomato plants have not materialized, nor will they.

Another common concern has been that use of a transgene like that for Bt will cause widespread insect resistance, thus ruining the usefulness of the insecticide. After six years of use on millions of acres of corn, insect resistance to Bt has not yet been reported. This may be due in part to the requirement for non-Bt plantings near Bt corn, done to reduce the chances of resistance development. I fully expect such resistance will some day be found, requiring new management approaches, including new Bt strains in plants. Roundup® herbicide-resistant soybean enables the use of an effective and environmentally benign weed management system on some seventy percent of United States soybean acres, though its use does result in gradual selection of more tolerant weed biotypes. Practices to manage pest resistance have been required as part of the release of Bt crops in the United States.

Ironically, crop genotypes produced using such "natural" methods as chemical- or radiation-induced mutations have attracted almost no protests of the sort that have greeted biotechnological products. As a method, mutation breeding is rather crude and ineffective. Most mutations are lethal, few are useful, and almost none are for what we hope. Screening the world collections for useful traits is a tried-and-true method, but many useful traits simply do not exist in collections. While gene transfer is not as precise as it will become, it is a "directed" process and is much more likely to produce discrete, useful genetic changes than most alternatives. As long as we are careful to assure that transgenic crops do not carry harmful genes, we can view gene transfer as offering more potential than older genetic improvement techniques.

Millions of animals and humans have consumed biotechnological grain and products over the past five years, and there has been no known failure of the testing system to identify a real danger in such products to date. Even Starlink®, a transgenic corn type that appeared in foods despite not being approved for food use, was found in the end to have caused no health problem. This case resulted in payment of millions of dollars to farmers and led to the withdrawal of the gene from the marketplace, but it did not threaten the health of any consumer. None of this is surprising—our digestive systems effectively inactivate most of the genes and gene products (proteins) we consume.

I consider the impediments to use of demonstrably safe biotechnological innovations to be of greater ethical concern than exposure to possible dangers from using such developments. The development of the so-called "golden rice," with increased levels of iron and vitamin A, has not been vigorously pursued partly because of vocal opposition. The introduction of Bt in cotton, corn, and rice has been slow and uneven for the same reason. Given the evidence that such developments are no threat to the environment or to consumers, opposition to them seems to be paternalistic and unethical, unless one subscribes to lifeboat ethics. It is not a stretch to suggest that the same approach in medicine would have left a substantial portion of the world's population to die from smallpox, plague, malaria, and other natural diseases instead of using unnatural palliatives such as vaccines and antibiotics.

We must use biotechnology carefully, but given the promise that it holds to alleviate human suffering, failure to use it is the real ethical risk we must not take. Instead, we should be actively promoting the development and use of the best biotechnological products (current and future) if we are serious about helping the poor and powerless in the world.

CHAPTER TWENTY-TWO

Biotechnology and Public Policy: An Anabaptist Response

Timothy S. Jost

Timothy S. Jost, J.D., holds the Robert L. Willett Family Professorship of Law at the Washington and Lee University School of Law. He is co-author of a casebook, Health Law, *used widely throughout the United States in teaching health law and of a treatise and hornbook by the same name. He holds a J.D. with honors from the University of Chicago.*

For many of us who have identified ourselves as Anabaptists during the past half century, an important faith tenet has been belief that God has called us to pursue social justice. Both Jesus and the prophets emphasized this theme. Jesus began his public ministry by quoting from the prophet Isaiah: "The Spirit of the Lord is upon me, because he has anointed me to bring good news to the poor. He has sent me to proclaim release to the captives and recovery of sight to the blind, to let the oppressed go free, to proclaim the year of the Lord's favor."[1]

The early Anabaptists also underscored the importance of mutual aid and, indeed, were charged with being communists because of their concern for the poor among them. Menno Simons, for example, faulted Christians of his time for living ostentatiously when other members of the church were living in poverty, and he claimed as a distinctive characteristic of the Anabaptists their care for the poor.[2]

A real concern for us as Anabaptists must be, therefore, Who will have access to all of the wonders that biotechnology promises us? Will access be rationed strictly on the basis of wealth, or insurance coverage, which in our society is often a proxy for wealth, or will all have access to these possibilities? If we are all to have access, there will have to be provision for public funding to pay for care for some of us, and probably eventually for most of us. Currently over 45 million Americans lack health insurance, while 70 million have no insurance for drugs.[3] Those most at risk for being uninsured are the poor and racial minorities. All other developed countries provide public insurance to assure access to medical care, and virtually all cover prescription drugs. However, if public insurance programs are to be viable, there must be some controls over the cost of technology and probably over access to technology as well.

Our current problems with the cost of biotechnology and access to it are widely recognized and are visible in our experience with pharmaceuticals. Expenditures for retail prescription drugs increased at a rate of 16.4 percent in 2000, 15.7 percent in 2001, and are expected to increase at double-digit rates through the rest of this decade.[4] While drugs still represent a relatively small part of national health care expenditures (a bit over 10 percent), the burden of drug costs falls disproportionately on a small number of people with chronic diseases.[5]

Median per capita drug expenditures for the elderly in 1998 were about $895 per person, but for the most expensive one percent, they were about $6,597.[6] The high cost of drugs means a lack of access to needed medications for many people. A recent eight-state study of Medicare beneficiaries found that 25 percent of uninsured beneficiaries failed to fill at least one prescription during 2001 due to cost, 27 percent skipped doses to make their medications last longer, and 20 percent spent less on other basic needs to afford prescription drugs.[7]

If this is the case with existing pharmaceuticals, how much more likely is it to be true of the costly new products that we hope will be discovered and developed through biotechnology? A great hope of genetic research, for example, is that we can develop drugs to help small subpopulations for whom current drugs are not helpful or are even perhaps dangerous. Indeed, some of the most promising applications of stem cell research would only help individual patients. Given the high cost of developing such products, however, they are likely to be available only to a fraction of the nation's population, and virtually inaccessible to most of the world's people.

If access to technology is to improve, its cost must be brought down. However, it is well known that drug manufacturers, which increasingly dominate the biotechnology industry, have very high profit margins. During 2002, U.S. drug companies had the highest after-tax profits as a percent of revenue (17 percent) of any firms represented in the Fortune 500. Drug companies produced more than half of the total net profits of all Fortune 500 companies.[8] Even if one considers return on assets, which might be a more accurate representation of their true profits, drug manufacturers came in first among the Fortune 500 at 14.1 percent for 2002.[9] Because drug manufacturers are granted effective monopolies on new drugs both through patent protection and through statutory market exclusivity periods (which block Food and Drug Administration, FDA, marketing approval for some generic substitutes even after patents expire or for products or uses that are not patentable), they are able to charge prices far above competitive levels.

Manufacturers justify their high profits by arguing that such returns are necessary to finance research and development. There is some truth in this—drug research is expensive and risky, and the drug development process is protracted and often disappointing. Drug company research and development costs tend to track profits, and countries that have placed strict limits on drug prices have seen drug research lag.[10] Research with respect to genetically engineered products is likely to be even more costly.

However, this argument also has been oversold. Drug companies currently spend far less on research and development of new products than they do on administration and on advertising and marketing of their existing products—including expensive but dramatically successful direct-to-consumer advertising of prescription drugs.[11]

Moreover, a high percentage of medical and health research and development in the United States, over one third, is funded directly by the American taxpayer.[12] The National Institutes of Health (NIH) funded in part the development of 52 of the 77 cancer drugs approved by the FDA by 1996, while the NIH or FDA contributed to the development of 45 of the 50 top-selling drugs approved by the FDA between 1992 and 1997.[13] Pharmaceutical companies have also profited from generous tax benefits, which have heavily subsidized their research efforts.[14] It is only fair that the public realize some of the benefits of its investment, including members of the public who cannot otherwise afford access to drugs.

We need to find a strategy that balances innovation with access. First, the federal government should enforce federal rights already recognized in the Bayh-Dole Act to assure that products developed through federally funded research are made available to the public "on reasonable terms."[15] It is simply unjust to allow pharmaceutical companies to make huge profits based on public investments and to deny much of the public access to those products.

Second, we should take measures that redirect the energies of pharmaceutical companies toward research and away from wasteful expenditures. The United States is one of very countries that permits direct-to-consumer advertising, which costs billions of dollars every year. If more money is needed for research, this money is already available.

Third, we need to establish a national health insurance system that provides universal access to the benefits of biotechnology, while assuring those who create and produce it a fair, but not exorbitant, return on their investment. This, I submit, would be a proper public policy agenda for Anabaptists to advocate in the United States at the outset of the twenty-first century.

Notes

1. Luke 4:18-19.

2. *Menno Simons, "Reply to False Accusations (1552)" in The Complete Writings of Menno Simons*, ed. J. C. Wenger (Scottdale, Pa.: Herald Press, 1956), 558-9.

3. Center for Policy Alternatives, "Playing Fair: State Action to Lower Prescription Drug Prices." (Washington, D.C.: Center for Policy Alternatives, 2000), http://www.stateaction.org/cpa/publications/pub.cfm?ID=112 (accessed June 2003).

4. Katherine Levit et al., "Trends in U.S. Health Care Spending, 2001," *Health Affairs* 22, no. 1 (Jan/Feb 2003): 154, 156; and Stephen Heffler et al., "Health Spending Projections for 2001-2011: The Latest Outlook," *Health Affairs* 22, no. 2 (March/April 2002): 207, 209.

5. John A. Poisal and Lauren Murray, "Growing Differences Between Medicare Beneficiaries With and Without Drug Coverage," *Health Affairs* 20 no. 2 (March/April 2001): 74, 80.

6. Uwe Reinhardt, "Perspectives on the Pharmaceutical Industry," *Health Affairs* 20 no. 5 (Sep/Oct 2001): 136, 140.

7. Dana Gelb Safran et al., "Prescription Drugs and Seniors: How Well are the States Closing the Gap?" *Health Affairs Web Exclusive*, www.healthaffairs.org/WebExclusives/2105Safran.pdf (accessed May 2003).

8. Public Citizen Congress Watch, 2003, 2003 Drug Industry Profits (2003), 1.

9. Ibid.

10. See F.M. Scherer, "The Link Between Gross Profitability and Pharmaceutical R&D Spending," *Health Affairs* 21, no. 5 (Sept./Oct. 2001): 216; and see Patricia M. Danzon, "Making Sense of Drug Prices" *Regulation* 23, no. 1 (spring 2000): 56.

11. See Families USA, "Profiting from Pain: Where Prescription Drug Dollars Go." July 17, 2002, http://www.familiesusa.org/PPreport.pdf (accessed July 2003).

12. Michael E. Gluck, "Federal Policies Affecting the Cost and Availability of New Pharmaceuticals." Kaiser Family Foundation, 2002, http://www.kff.org/content/2002/3254/GluckFinalReportweb3254.pdf, p. 40. (accessed July 2003).

13. Ibid., 20.

14. Ibid., 23-5.

15. P. Arno and M. Davis, "Why Don't We Enforce Existing Drug Price Controls? The Unrecognized and Unenforced Reasonable Pricing Requirements Imposed on Patents Deriving in Whole or in Part From Federally Funded Research," *Tulane Law Review* 75, no. 3 (Feb. 2001): 631-93.

CHAPTER TWENTY-THREE

Bioethics: How Will Anabaptists Respond?

Graydon F. Snyder

Dr. Graydon F. Snyder now retired, lives in Hyde Park, Chicago. Educated at Manchester College, Bethany Theological Seminary and Princeton Theological Seminary, he was dean and professor of New Testament at both Bethany Theological Seminary and Chicago Theological Seminary. His interest in bioethics derives from working with Bethany Hospital in Chicago and with the Association of Brethren Caregivers. He has written several books on medical ethics, including Tough Choices, *and* Health and Medicine in the Anabaptist Tradition.

*L*ike most of my peers in this book, I would like to make some disclaimers. I am not a scientist, so I cannot verify any of my statements about biotechnology. I am not an economist, so I cannot fathom the intricacies of profit-making and corporate decision-making. I am a theologian—and my task here is to clarify the basis on which bioethical decisions would be made in the Anabaptist tradition.

First, where do we derive authority for decision-making? For Anabaptists comprising the left wing of the Reformation or the free church, ultimate authority does not come from the political world. Nor does authority lie with the magisteria, the designated, learned officials as they interpret the Christian tradition, the creeds, and Scripture. Authority comes from the faith community and is led by the Holy Spirit and study of the Scripture as it makes contextual decisions.

Belief in the authority and cohesiveness of the faith community results in quite distinctive ethical directions, which include nonviolence in relationships, preservation of human life, a call for reconciliation both in and out of the primary community, respect and concern for those who may be peripheral, and service for those who need help. For Anabaptists these directions point to the coming of the sovereignty of God. Anabaptists are much less concerned about a divine order in creation.

Fetal Tissue

When covenant community is central, persons are identified by the role they play rather than any inherent individual identity they bring to that community. The same is true of the family. Mothers, fathers, and children are functional parts of a family. Mothers and fathers are identified by having children, and children are identified by having parents. They have no family identity apart from that. Consequently, Anabaptists define the beginning of life when the fetus has the function of a child.[1] Since Anabaptists are not creation-oriented, life does not begin with conception, the joining of a sperm and an ovum to create an embryo. An embryo in a Petri dish, or a frozen embryo, is not a child. It only becomes a child in the womb of a mother. When the mother knows there is a fetus, experimental use of that fetus would destroy a member of the family—excluding, of course, accidental abortion. Ancient religious traditions have put that time of awareness at forty days.[2] However, as long as the embryo remains in the laboratory it is not a person. Allowing the embryo to develop into a fetus does not change that. Consequently, some Anabaptists do not object to the use of fetal tissue as it forms various body tissues.[3] Quite the contrary, because Anabaptists care for those with physical difficulties, disease, or aging problems, they welcome the use of stem cells and fetal tissue to improve well-being.[4]

Cloning may have some value in the reproduction of animals and in the creation of particular stem cells, but a human being is a unique person in the family structure. Reproduction of an identical person in the same family will stress its inherent identity rather than its function as child in relation to a family. For that reason many Anabaptists will not favor human cloning.

Plant Genetics

Environmentalism is yet another problem. Anabaptists are concerned about the function of the natural, not the preservation of the natural.[5] The development of hybrid grain began about 1920, and by 1940, most seed corn was hybrid. For many years, Anabaptist farmers have dealt with genetically altered crops, especially corn. It has not bothered them that the corn is not the same as that found in the Garden of Eden or even as what Great-Grandfather Burkholder planted in Pennsylvania. Anabaptists are primarily end-time oriented—rather than retrodirective, that is, driven to preserve or duplicate the past. Primary reasons for genetic alteration are to increase crop size by decreasing the chances of plant disease and to develop plants that produce more and better results. In any case, genetically altered plants result in more food for a world that is hungry. Theologically speaking, Anabaptists seek to help those in need.

The people of the world are starving as the population grows, arable land decreases, and fresh water continues to be scarce. Each year in the United States, over one million acres of arable land disappear into the urban sprawl. Of course, there is more than one solution to these problems, but certainly the genetic alteration of food plants must be one. For example, the use of trehalose with rice, the major grain supply for much of the world, can allow the plants to withstand extended drought.

We use and eat genetically altered foods everyday. To be sure, anything may be possible, though whether it is useful, necessary, or even detrimental is a serious issue. Seventy-five percent of soybeans and thirty-four percent of our United States corn is genetically altered.[6] However, around the world, many of these crops are rejected—nicknamed "Frankenfood" by some. Much of the rejection is political, though with some good reason there is also fear of genetic consequences. Nevertheless, the discovery of DNA and how to alter it has to be one of the most significant events of history.

The theological issues cannot be discounted. While Anabaptists side with environmentalists against abuse of the land and the air, they side more with those who would curtail starvation.[7] For some Anabaptists, personal sin has no meaning. Sin must be communal. To allow children to starve is a corporate sin. The rejection of genetically altered grain in starving Zambia appears contrary to the will of God. The rejection of genetically altered grains by Europe seems like the sin of political pride. By sin, I mean actions that may block the availability of necessary food for very hungry people in South Asia or sub-Sahara Africa. It may also block the development and sharing of plants that can withstand otherwise unfavorable circumstances.

Pharmaceutical Drugs

Related is the issue of creating pharmaceuticals by genetically altering plants, that is, inserting a medically useful gene into the DNA of an edible plant. It could be less expensive than animal-created pharmaceuticals and will make certain drugs more available. Already some research chemicals are being produced by bioengineered plants, so pharmaceuticals cannot be far behind. Pharmaceutical drugs may not be a faith issue for Anabaptist types. The use of bioengineered plants to feed and heal the world seems theologically appropriate. The real issue is whether regular food crops might become contaminated by those genetically altered plants.

Use of Persons and Animals for Research

Anabaptists are willing to sacrifice themselves for future human good. Most famous were the conscientious objectors in World War II who allowed themselves to be used as human guinea pigs. Giving of one's life or suffering for another has significant Christological meaning for Anabaptists. Jesus gave himself up on the cross as a martyr—as one who expected his death to result in an end time change in society. Offering up one's self is one thing, but using another person or an animal raises a different theological issue. Do we have the right to ask or force someone to be used for research purposes? Clearly not. Memories of such tyrannies as that of Hitler have made it absolutely necessary that invasion of another person's body be done only by consent.

Do we have the right to use animals? Most Anabaptists are not vegetarians but use animals for food. They will probably accept genetically altered animals much as they accept biotechnological plants. An example would be genetically altered salmon that will mature in half the time needed for natural salmon. However, using animals for deadly testing and experimentation seems less defensible. I assume Anabaptists would accept experimentation with animals but not encourage it.

A watershed case is that of Harvard's Oncomouse.[8] She has been genetically altered so that she is cancerous, hence the use of the prefix "onco." The mouse is used to test cures for cancer. Furthermore her offspring are born genetically altered. Harvard has patented Oncomouse, as well as her offspring, and sells them for research to other institutions.

This practice has not been universally accepted. The first major conflict came from the Canadian churches, spearheaded by our quasi-Anabaptist relatives, the Canadian Quakers. Given the protest, Canada refused to recognize the patent of Oncomouse. The Christian argument was that God gave us dominion over the land and the animals but not ownership.[9] Oncomouse suffers for us every day. She has been described by some as a female Christ figure continuously crucified for the salvation of humans.

Do the ends justify the means? Anabaptists say no. We might reject patented ownership and sale of an animal, and even the reproduction of genetically doomed animals, but we need to approve the use of animals for important health research. Anabaptists are probably waffling somewhat on the principle that the ends do not justify the means.

In summary, I expect Anabaptists approve the use of stem cells and fetal tissue unless the tissue comes from an implanted fetus. However, abortion to gain stem cells will be rejected. Likewise, Anabaptists will consider cloning a rejection of family identity. Because of the increasing hunger and starvation in the world, Anabaptists will grow and share genetically altered crops. Failure to share with those in need is a sin. Because it will increase the amount of pharmaceuticals available, Anabaptists will promote the development of pharmaceutical plants—plants that, when processed or even eaten, will prevent certain diseases. Finally, Anabaptists will reject use of a human body for research unless the person has consented. With some hesitation Anabaptists will allow biotechnological research on animals but will balk at the sale of animals genetically altered to carry a terminal disease.

Notes

1. Conrad Brunk, "In the Image of God," in *Medical Ethics, Human Choices: A Christian Perspective* (Scottdale, Pa.: Herald Press, 1988), 29-39.

2. See Augustine, *Questiones. Exodus* 9.80. Bonnie Bullough, "Abortion," in *Human Sexuality: An Encyclopedia,* ed. Vern L. and Bonnie Bullough (New York: Garland Press, 1994).

3. "1987 Annual Conference Statement on Genetic Engineering," in *Minutes of the Annual Conference, Church of the Brethren 1987* (Elgin, Ill.: The Annual

Conference Office, 1987).

4. Dale Oxender, "The Biotechnology Revolution," *Brethren Life and Thought* 31 (1986): 223-36 (see 235-6).

5. John Howard Yoder, *The Priestly Kingdom: Social Ethics as Gospel* (Notre Dame: Notre Dame University Press, 1984), 155. James Wm. McClendon, Jr., *Ethics: Systematic Theology* (Nashville: Abingdon Press, 1986) 74-75.

6. *Chicago Tribune*, Jan. 25, 2004, 7. Based on data from the website Pew Initiative on Food and Biotechnology

7. Harvey F. Good, "Life with Genetic Engineering," *Brethren Life and Thought* 31 (1986): 249-51.

8. Donna Jeanne Haraway, *Modest-Witness, Second-Milennium; Femaleman Meets Oncomouse: Feminism and Technoscience* (New York: Routledge, 1997).

9. Lev. 24-25.

CHAPTER TWENTY-FOUR

Pastoral Concerns: Parental Anxiety and Other Issues of Character

Joseph J. Kotva Jr.

Dr. Joseph J. Kotva Jr. is the executive director of the Anabaptist Center for Health-Care Ethics (ACHE). He was a pastor for ten years, has a Ph.D. in theology and ethics, and has published numerous articles related to clergy ethics and medical ethics. He also served for several years on the ethics committee of a large hospital in eastern Pennsylvania.

The Case

Lyle and Judy Smith are Mennonites by conviction. Neither grew up in an Anabaptist-related church setting, but both are drawn to Mennonite convictions about following Jesus, discipleship, community, and so on. Judy is a schoolteacher. Lyle is primary caregiver for their seven-year-old daughter, Tiffany.

The Smiths live in a small, two-bedroom home in a quiet suburban neighborhood. They have a large yard and a park nearby. Their neighborhood includes two other families from their church and several children that are Tiffany's age.

Lyle and Judy recently decided to buy a new, much larger home in an exclusive development in a neighboring suburb. They are moving to get Tiffany into a better school system. Their current school system scores slightly below average in state tests and has above average class size. Although Tiffany is doing well in school, Lyle and Judy believe she could be doing better.

This move will put them geographically farther from both Judy's job and their church. The new house is expensive; to swing the payments, Lyle is getting a halftime job and they are significantly reducing their charitable giving. The Smiths also feel a bit guilty that the new house does not fit their ideals of simple living, but they are anxious to get Tiffany the best education possible. Lyle and Judy did not deliberate about this move with their small group or pastor. Instead, they announced the move during the Sunday service sharing time. This announcement was greeted after the service with many congratulations and several offers to help with the move.

This brief description of Lyle and Judy's decision will strike many as an odd place to start discussing pastoral concerns about biotechnology. I begin here to move our attention to the larger contexts in which our appropriation of this technology will take place. One such context is the anxiety exhibited by many Christian parents to do everything possible for their children to get ahead. Such parents are driven by the commendable desire to do right, but this desire (fueled by assorted social pressures) too often leads parents to make decisions at odds with the rest of their Christian commitment. Thus, although minimally aware of it, Lyle and Judy's move requires that they modify, if not outright reject, many of the Anabaptist-Christian convictions that brought them to the Mennonite church—including stewardship, simple living, and communal discernment.

Of course, the Smiths are not alone in loosening other commitments to fulfill their desire to do everything for their children. Most pastors know families where each child is involved in multiple extracurricular activities. These good parents worry that their children will miss out. Although often unnoticed by these parents, such programming means their children have little time for unstructured, imaginative play, and the family has little money and less time for church and its ministries.

My recognition of such parental anxiety and its resulting life choices leaves me doubly troubled when I consider the new powers coming with biotechnology. As parents within Christian communities, do we exhibit the habits, skills, convictions, qualities of character, and choices that will allow us to judge these new powers rightly? Or is it more likely that these new powers will further fuel our parental anxiety so we will genetically screen, select, and enhance our children with little regard for the effects on our lives together as a Christian community?

Questions of Character

As a pastor, I frequently consider a series of interrelated questions to evaluate our moral lives together: (1) Who does Christ call us to be? What qualities of character, types of relationships, patterns of behavior, and choices are expected from faithful followers of Christ? (2) Based on our habits, choices, and actions, who are we now with respect to that calling? (3) Are our current practices, patterns of behavior, relationships, and choices likely moving us toward or away from Christ's calling? (4) If we are contemplating some particular course of action, pattern of behavior, or choice, will it likely move us toward or away from Christ's calling? (5) In our life together, both within and outside the worship service, what practices, activities, social settings, discussions, and relationships can the congregation promote to encourage our growth toward Christ's calling?[1]

Directing these questions to the issue at hand is instructive. I believe shorthand answers would be something like the following:

(1) As church community and Christian parents, we are called to welcome all children with unconditional love as gifts from God. Jesus blesses children[2] and elevates children as models to be emulated.[3] Our own raised status is that of children of God.[4] Parents are instructed to care for their children,[5] and raising children is listed first among the good deeds of widows.[6] Born in the image of God, all children, healthy or sick, deserve our care.[7]

Yet our care for our children is to be limited by our faithfulness to God. God tests Abraham's faithfulness by calling for the surrender of Isaac.[8] Jesus tells us fidelity to him will bring conflict into the family, including between parents and their children.[9] We are told that the reward in heaven will justify the possible need to leave our children for Christ's sake.[10] In a typical hyperbole, Jesus says discipleship may even require us to hate our children.[11] In short, we are to love and provide for our children, but not at the expense of faithfulness.

(2) We are loving, anxious parents who frequently (though unconsciously) qualify our fidelity to Christ in the name of our children's enrichment and well-being.

(3) Many of our current patterns of behavior, such as moving to better school districts and over scheduling our children, likely reinforce our parental anxieties and willingness to sacrifice faithfulness. Each time we make such choices, we reinforce in ourselves and model for others the notion that our children's advancement is a preeminent concern. These distortions are further encouraged in all of us when such choices are met with congratulations and offers of help.

(4) We must recognize that parents already anxious for their children to get ahead have a built-in predisposition to avail themselves of various biotechnologies when they become available. Parents who see their children's advancement as such a preeminent concern are ill prepared to judge the Christian fidelity of such developments as genetic screening, selection, and enhancement. Parents face enormous social pressure to ensure that their children get ahead. In this climate, instead of careful Christian discernment, it seems likely that parental anxiety "will be readily exploited when they hear what other parents, more committed to their children, are doing to improve their offspring's [genetic] inheritance."[12]Moreover, it seems likely that our use of such technologies will further reinforce our anxious pursuit of our children's advancement. Even if the technologies themselves are morally acceptable from some supposedly "neutral" or "objective" perspective, when chosen by parents anxious for their children to get ahead, that choice will reinforce the tendency to make future choices out of the same anxious posture. In short, I believe that in the current context the arrival of these technologies will likely further corrupt our understanding of parenting and its relationship to Christian fidelity.

(5) The many parents who are/were missionaries and relief workers constitute one resource that might help move us toward a more balanced, Christian practice of parenting. Missionaries and relief workers spend significant time outside the anxious, competitive climate of North America. In addition, many have engaged in specific practices and made specific choices that reflect the priority of Christian fidelity over offspring advancement. Encouraging these folks to tell their stories in our midst is one Christian way to challenge our parental anxiety.

While many other things should be said about moving us toward Christ's calling regarding Christian parenting, I here note only one: The new powers of biotechnology again confront us with the need for communal discernment. We should be talking together about these issues before we ever confront them as choices, and we should repeatedly encourage parents in advance to bring such decisions to a communal forum that includes brothers and sisters free of parental anxieties. After all, Christ promised to join such gathered discernment.[13]

Conclusion

I was asked to address "pastoral concerns" about biotechnology. One tack on such concerns is to attend to the larger contexts in which we will appropriate that technology, an approach illustrated by focusing on parental anxiety. If space allowed, I would raise similar concerns about another dimension of parenting: our culture's tendency to view children as our right and our possession (a tendency seen in both the frequency of abortion and in many forms of reproductive technology). I fear that in the current context, the emerging biotechnologies will feed our tendency to view children as possessions rather than gifts.

I would raise similar concerns about our capacity for suffering and for justice. That is, I would argue that the rhetoric and expectations surrounding the emerging technologies will likely further degrade our already diminished capacity to recognize struggle and suffering as an inevitable part of finitude and of fidelity to Christ.

I would similarly argue that our capacity for justice is at stake. The technologies are largely emerging in an individualistic, consumer-oriented, capitalistic system that accepts high rates of child poverty and infant mortality, let alone the 43 million Americans who lack health insurance. Despite the best intentions of scientists and researchers, there are good reasons to believe that the inevitable limited access to these technologies will further the gross disparities in our system and further diminish our capacity to struggle for justice. In short, I am less pastorally concerned about the technologies themselves than I am about the contexts in which they are emerging and their likely negative effects on our Christian capacities to parent, to suffer, and to strive for justice.

Still, I remain hopeful, not because I believe in the inevitable progress of science or in the fundamental goodwill of our culture, but because I believe in God and God's church. If we are willing, the church can be the context in which we learn the skills and virtues (such as humility, wisdom, patience, integrity, and courage) necessary to chart these waters well. We can learn something about parenting from missionary and relief workers, and the church is full of similar resources through which God may yet teach us how to faithfully engage these new technologies.

Notes

1. Cf. MacIntyre's account of the tripartite structure of an Aristotelian ethic: Alasdair MacIntyre, *After Virtue*, 2nd. ed. (Notre Dame: University of Notre Dame Press, 1984), p. 52–55.

2. Matt. 19:14.

3. Matt. 18:13.

4. Rom. 8:16; 1 John 3:1.

5. Col. 3:21; Eph. 6:4; cf. 2 Cor. 12:14.

6. 1 Tim. 5:10.

7. Darrel Amundsen reminds us that early Christian attitudes toward children and newborns were strikingly different

from much of Greco-Roman culture: Darrel W. Amundsen, "Medicine and the Birth of Defective Children: Approaches of the Ancient World," in *On Moral Medicine: Theological Perspectives in Medical Ethics*, ed. Stephen E. Lammers, Alan Verhey (Grand Rapids: William B. Eerdmans Publishing Company, 1998), 681–92.

8. Gen. 22.

9. Mark 13:12.

10. Matt. 19:29.

11. Luke 14:26.

12. Ronald Cole-Turner, "The Era of Biological Control," in *Beyond Cloning: Religion and the Remaking of Humanity*, ed. Ronald Cole-Turner (Harrisburg: Trinity Press International, 2001), 11.

13. Matt. 18:20.

CHAPTER TWENTY-FIVE

Audience Questions: Perspectives

Does the ontological status (intrinsic nature) of the embryo change during development? (e.g. between day five and day six, or between day thirteen and day fourteen?)

LeRoy Walters: Clearly, this question has been debated from at least the time of Aristotle forward, and through most of human history it has been debated in terms of the abortion question. We have a new situation—since 1978—which is that embryos can be formed in vitro. We have a million babies in the world with the aid of in vitro fertilization as a reproductive technology. Therefore, I think it is unprecedented to question how we ought to look at an embryo (blastocyst) that is five days old. I see no way to avoid making a judgment about this. The answer is not evident from the fact that it has a genome or has potential; it is not evident from whether it has sentience or its level of differentiation or organization. We each have to make a judgment about whether, at this early stage of life, we will respect the entity, and if so, what the respect means. I tried to argue that whatever respect does mean, it is not disrespectful in carefully designed research to destroy some early embryos.

Conrad Brunk: I agree that all of the science in the world is not going to settle the question of what the moral status of a human embryo is. We will learn more biology, but the moral significance will still be contestable. The question is: When do we treat an entity as a person within our moral community? That is a moral question; it cannot be decided by science or by a philosophical or ontological argument. It is a question about what constitutes the moral community and what maintains our respect for each other and the future generations in the moral community. The question about how we treat an early term fetus should be viewed as a question of what impacts it will have on our understanding of the dignity of human beings.

Europe and North America have very different views regarding GM foods and stem cell research. What accounts for this difference?

LeRoy Walters: I would not want to defend some irrational views that are espoused and expressed in Europe. However, I do think there are certain actions the United States and American companies could have taken in the 1990s that would have put us in a better situation today. I think Monsanto at a certain point took the attitude that Europe would have to accept our products or we would beat down the doors. Even now the U.S. State Department works on sort of a brute force principle that we can get a coalition of nations ganging up on the Europeans and force them to accept our products. That is not very tactful or diplomatic, and it is not likely to succeed. I think if we had done a bit more testing of foods for safety early on in the same way we test drugs and biologics, we might have reassured people in Europe.

Conrad Brunk: The Canadian Biotechnology Advisory Counsel is dealing with this issue and we are caught between the United States and Europe. In Europe there was a public debate—generated and carried on by the political leaders—about GM crops and foods. That public debate took place *before* the products were introduced into the market and before it was a *fait accompli*. In both the United States and Canada, there was not public debate. Most people did not even know there was GM food in the food system before it was accomplished, and suddenly people were saying, "Do you know that sixty percent of the soybeans you eat are genetically modified?" As a result, the Europeans developed the very strong view that the way to deal with this issue was with labeling. And other countries—Japan, New Zealand, many others—have said, "Look, let's deal with this and the risk issues involved by letting the marketplace decide, and the marketplace can decide only if the marketplace has information."

This debate produced the demand for labeling; now we are in a situation where the United States is charging the rest of the world with impeding progress on this issue through this labeling requirement. Africans are refusing GM foods that could solve their problems of food scarcity because they will lose their market in Europe. However, to the rest of the world, it looks as if everybody has been faced with an American *fait accompli* on this issue. We could have had a system early on that segregated GM foods from non-GM foods and would have made the labeling problem much easier.

This battle will be fought hard in the next few years. Although of course I may be wrong, my prediction is that the labeling forces will win and that the United States and Canada—if they want to keep their international markets—will have to label GM foods. They will need to put in place a segregation system to keep these products separate to maintain the international market.

Those with juvenile diabetes, Parkinson's, and spinal cord injuries are mentioned as some of the most vulnerable in society. How does this connect with the ten-ninety gap in health research? That is, the World Health Organization (WHO) sponsored group says that 90 percent of the research done in health benefits only 10 percent of the world's population.

LeRoy Walters: There is a serious problem of injustice in the way we allocate funds for research on disease prevention and treatment; I think the First World is negligent in its approach to Third World diseases. Think about infant diarrhea and what could be done with clean water and inexpensive medicine. My hope is that, by some circuitous route, in the long run stem cell research may have a pay-off for the Third World like small pox vaccine or polio vaccine has had.

How does the Cypriot situation translate to the United States?

Ruth Swartz Cowan: I went to Cyprus thinking a mandated genetic screening program must be an offense to liberal principles and civil society. I found I was wrong. That caused me to return to the United States with a different perspective on the critiques and the advocacy for the genetic screening programs we have here.

I will provide one example. There is only one mandated genetic screening program in the United States, in California. Maternal alpha-theta protein screening is required; every provider who provides prenatal care in California must offer it.

There is a lot of criticism of prenatal diagnosis and consequent abortions, because they are discriminatory against the people who carry the condition being tested. One of the things I learned in Cyprus is that the Cypriots with thalassemia do *not* see it that way. They say, "There is one thing that discriminates against me; I have thalassemia." Thalassemics did experience discrimination. They could not get jobs. They could not be enrolled in some institutions of higher education. The parent association, the government, and various physician associations fought the discrimination hard. The thalassemics say, "It's one thing to discriminate against me as a person. It's not the same thing as discriminating against a fetus." The distinction to them is clear.

If we can no longer afford to give vaccinations to everyone in poorer areas, why does the United States spend so much money on the military?

LeRoy Walters: The United States now spends more on military matters than all other countries of the world combined. It used to be more than the North Atlantic Treaty Organization (NATO), but now it is more than everybody else in the world put together, and I see that as the deformation of our national budget and priorities.

What would you have done had you been a Zambian official? (asked in response to Laura Powers' assertion that she was not speaking for US AID) What other alternatives to getting the GM (genetic modification) grain were there in Zambia?

Laura Powers: In response to the first question, I would have cracked the grain; I would have milled it, and I would have accepted it, because the need to feed the children and the elderly suffering from this drought would have been far more important to me than some of the longer-term health questions. Having witnessed children in therapeutic feeding centers who would not make it until the next day, it is very hard for me to take the Zambian government point of view and say, "We are concerned about the longer-term food-safety issues, so in the meantime we will allow the suffering of these people." Again, I am speaking from the point of view of an American disaster worker, not from the point of view of a country that has a lot of history with the United States that may or may not be positive.

In response to the second question, the alternative (which happened) is that we shunted the genetically modified organism (GM) grain that was bound for southern Africa over to Ethiopia, which was also experiencing a severe famine. In place of that, World Food Program sent grain that was not genetically modified (grown in Europe and in other areas of the world) to southern Africa. It was just a matter of doing a shift; the GM product went to Ethiopia where it is not a problem. Non-GM product went to southern Africa.

What are the implications of proprietorizing technological products? What are the implications for justice issues? Can you speak about the lure of intellectual property and patents for biotechnology and how this lure becomes a driving force for business interests in biotechnology?

Mike Baker: When Pennington Seed looked at biotechnology, and said, "Look, we think that this set of good out there exists; we just have to go find it," the issue of patentability also came up. Whether one patents a GMO (genetically modified organism), or one that naturally occurs, the United States has made it possible to patent just about anything. The head of the corporation said, "Well, we need to protect those rights." It was the AgriSearch organization from New Zealand in partnership with the University of Georgia and Pennington that decided to patent this. We patented the way we *discov-*

ered it and *refined* it as well as the way we determined it is *safe*. The patent is now being contested, and it is in the United States court system to see whether we *can* protect this right.

Here is a real justice issue, because if one cannot afford this, the price jumps from $1 per pound seed to $4 per pound seed with the technology. If it is not affordable, then I have to go to Mennonite Economic Development Associates (MEDA) and see if they can set up a micro-loan program so the people *can* afford it. These technologies are expensive and corporations involved expect to make a profit. As my CEO says, "If we're not around, we can't do any good." Institutions have the idea, unlike Mennonites theoretically, that our immortality is of utmost importance. That is what public companies think: "We have to stay around. We cannot sacrifice and die."

Concerning the importance of the discerning community in our Anabaptist faith, what suggestions do you have for congregations or local conferences to begin to learn about biotechnology and its choices?

Joseph Kotva Jr.: The fact that the question is raised is a place to start. There is no reason people cannot go back to their congregations and say, "I think this is an important issue. How do we begin to talk about it among ourselves?" Sunday school classes are a good place to address the issue. Small groups, if a church has them, are a good place as well. If the pastor is willing to put in the time, there is no reason the issue should not be considered in a worship service itself. My own agency, the Anabaptist Center for Healthcare Ethics (ACHE), will be developing some materials that should prove useful.

Graydon Snyder: One result of this conference for me is that I will probably go back and ask the Church of the Brethren if I can write a four-program study on bioethics for Sunday schools and adult groups to study. The most powerful system is to find people who stand in need of genetic help and have them bring the case before a church or study group to talk about it.

There were strikingly different interpretations given of what Anabaptist theology and traditions would tell us about what to do with new biotechnology. Is it a sin to prevent new biotechnology from being introduced into the Third World communities of suffering? Or is it a sin to do so when we already have resources to feed the world and cure illnesses but are spending them to support an overly affluent lifestyle?

Lawrence Ressler: I am always encouraged when I look at the New Testament book of Acts to be reminded that the confusion we experience is not new. It is not easy to be the kingdom of God, or to know what we are to do today concerning these issues. What is important is that we talk about these issues. These kinds of conferences are important. The issues are enormously complex.

I truly understood the complex issues surrounding poverty when I went to Africa. One realizes how complicated the system is, so that on the one hand, to try to solve the problem actually creates unintended results that one never imagined when one was trying to do another wonderful thing. I do not see simple answers. What the Anabaptists did is commit themselves to be in serious dialogue about these things as groups. Search Scriptures, pray, and continue doing so. Believe that in the end, God's will shall be evident.

Graydon Snyder: When I read the New Testament, I do not see much fear of new things. I am not sure if fear should be a motif for us today.

I was surprised the questioner did not ask another question, which is, "How about the 89 billion dollars Bush wants for Iraq? How many millions of people would that save in the areas we suggested?" We can talk about solutions to the problem other than biotechnology.

A major barrier to acceptance of new technologies is lack of public understanding. When pneumococcal conjugate vaccine was introduced, I was excited, since I had seen a baby die of pneumococcal meningitis. But some parents were reluctant to use another new vaccine. How can the public be systematically educated?

Randall Longenecker: Being an Anabaptist, I would say we educate people one at a time. Being a clinician, that is often the way we do things. Education is recognized as the major challenge in biotechnology. There is an area being called "genethics," and a major challenge in relation to it is to increase the level of genetic literacy of the population in general. A second challenge is to ensure access to these things. It is a very difficult thing to do.

LeRoy Walters, in his first guideline, suggested a clear separation be maintained between religious bodies and the coercion of the state. In a similar vein, how might a clearer separation between public funding and private property of genetic research be achieved? How can churches impact this in specific ways?

Timothy Jost: I do not see any way to separate public funding and private research. There are certain goals that we want to achieve in our society, and we spend a lot of public money, particularly on biomedical research. It is unfortunate that private parties realize all of the profits to be made from that research. We need to explore alternatives that would allow us as taxpayers to benefit some from the benefits of that research, in terms of the profits that are shared. At least, we need to license those products to private companies with the understanding that they will make them available at a reasonable cost, which is what Congress has said should happen.

As far as the religious dimensions, I am not a theologian. I have not gotten very far in understanding how we can combine our belief in the separation of church and state with the understanding that we are supposed to witness to the state regarding issues that we hold to be important—one of which is taking care of the needs of the poor.

Randall Longenecker: One thing that really surprised me when I first became involved with federal grants was how little accountability there is for federal money. If you are going to take funds from the public, then you have to be accountable to the public.

Comment on the current situation concerning the discovery of the Bt transgene in Mexican native maize and the possible threat that this poses to the genetic diversity of maize. How do you think the transgene construct got to Mexico? What will be the impact?

Emerson Nafziger: What I think about it is clear. Some of you probably saw a National Public Radio (NPR) program on the U.S. maize. One of the more tragic things is what the North American Free Trade Agreement (NAFTA) is going to do to the Mexican corn producer. That is, they are going to release cheap, subsidized U.S. corn into the country, much to the detriment of Mexicans. Part of the U.S. corn that went into Mexico was taken off of a truck, and people planted it. I only saw part of that special, and a Mexican woman said, "Well, we just wanted to see how it would grow." Their experiment introduced Bt pollen into their atmosphere, in which they were growing more of the locally selected materials. Now they probably have Bt, and it is probably going to continue to be there because of the way their system works.

Genetic diversity in corn is an interesting topic. Someone said dogs and corn are the two most genetically tractable organisms on the earth. It is probably true. Corn is a human-produced crop. Its wild relatives are not agronomic, and there is not much concern about those. Bt is a small gene for resistance to an insect that may or may not trouble Mexican corn. I am not a geneticist, but I do not see a threat to the ability of people to continue to grow their local cultivars. If it does attack or kill insects that trouble their corn, they are probably even going to be a little more successful at it.

How will the discussions at this conference affect the meaning you give to "recognizably human" in your work or our work?

Randall Longenecker: I do not think we are anywhere close to the perfect baby that has been discussed. I do not think we are anywhere close to being perfected as humans. I think we will continue to be human in our imperfection and limitations. As powerful as this new technology is, it still does not hold a candle to the power of God.

Lawrence Ressler: My mother died voluntarily. She could have used some technology to prolong her life. My father and my mother decided she was ready to die. I still ponder this. She was only in her seventies, but because of a lung disorder that had developed quite rapidly, the quality of her life would have deteriorated. She was ready to die.

Part of biotechnology has the potential to prolong life; I do not know what to do with this, since death is part of life. There is a spiritual dimension to the technology that we can easily forget. There is the meaning of life and the search for connection. There is the ability to suffer and find meaning in suffering. I do not know that I can ever justify suffering and the making of suffering as a way to ensure that people find meaning in life, but it is clear that there is a whole part of life in which we learn to discover God amid suffering.

There is a spiritual dimension that we need to continue to search for amid the technologically promoted part of life that still does not capture the complete essence of what life is about.

Graydon Snyder: I am not sure you should define human life and human existence as necessarily involving pain, but as I read the Bible and study early Christianity, it is assumed that the move from life to death will involve pain.

How does commodifying one's human body affect one's being human?

Timothy Jost: I think it is part of being human, or at least comes very naturally to humans, to try to increase our individual welfare. Part of that has to do with trying to increase our physical well-being to improve our health, and that is something that all of us are interested in doing. Part of it also has to do with increasing our wealth, and that is something that we see happening throughout the Bible. It was a very big concern of the prophets and Jesus. There is a natural human tendency to try to find ways to increase wealth. Certainly to increase wealth by increasing other people's health is a natural response to that.

We must ask the questions, "How does the church respond? How does our government respond? How do we as the church witness to our government concerning how to respond?" Again, I think the teachings of Jesus or the prophets is that we should not just simply accept the drive toward accumulating wealth as naturally human, but we should try to stand against it in some ways when it leads to radical disparity in wealth and health.

Joseph Kotva Jr.: These are questions of theological anthropology. One of the things that has been theologically interesting to me for awhile is that Mennonites, even when we practice systematic theology, very seldom start with theological anthropology. We might eventually get around to it, but it is not where we begin. There probably are some good theological reasons for that. I am deeply concerned about the likelihood that the way the advances of biotechnology play out in our culture will affect the way we conceptualize what it means to be human, including whether or not we accept suffering as an inevitable part of humanity.

It does not even matter whether the technology delivers on its promise. What matters is the public perception of what is being offered. The rhetoric around so much of the biotechnological advances is promising us so much less suffering that we can get technological holds on things for which I seriously doubt there are technological solutions.

I was listening to somebody who works with geriatric patients the other day. The person said that as soon as we find a way to alleviate one issue, or eliminate one disease, another one immediately moves into its place. I am quite concerned about the public perception. Theologically, there are some ways we ought to be going. As Anabaptists, anthropology should be done Christologically. That is, whenever we are going to talk about what it means to be human, we have to first start talking about Jesus.

I am also personally struck by the Eastern Orthodox notions that personhood itself is a progressive notion. That is, *real* personhood is something that happens in theosis, at that endstage where we have achieved the kind of divinity God grants us, and that every part along the way has value because it is in relationship to God on the way toward theosis.

I would like to know if any of our speakers believe that human life begins at conception. What is the status of the early human embryo?

Joseph Kotva Jr.: Several speakers have suggested that the Anabaptist view is *not* that conception is the beginning of humanity, but they have also suggested we should be talking about these things in community. I was an integral part of the resolution on abortion that passed in Atlanta, Georgia, at the Mennonite Church Unites States

Assembly. A lot of our brothers and sisters *do* believe full personhood begins at conception.

One reason I am attracted to an Orthodox understanding of personhood is that it allows us to understand the dignity and value of different aspects of development without having to try and equate these things. However, I wonder if the question asked is the right question. I wonder if the questions are not, "What kind of people do we need to be to welcome children into the world? What practices are compatible with that?"

Graydon Snyder: No. Human life does not begin at conception, and to believe that humanity begins as a scientific act is wrong. Humanity begins as a communal act and a relational act, and it is simply wrong to define it as a scientific act. Let me go a step further and reverse the question. I do not believe that conception creates a human. However, if in anticipating a child, you set aside a room, put in a crib, buy the stuff for it, then for some reason reject the assumption of a child, you aborted even before the conception.

Timothy Jost: I have avoided this question for years, and I will probably try to continue to avoid it. I did find it interesting that the view that is *very* widely held in the Mennonite church has not been clearly expressed at this conference. That is, the view that life begins fully at conception and that an embryo is a human being, under no circumstances to be experimented on, aborted, or damaged. We should treat an embryo as a newborn child. I certainly have students in my classes who firmly believe that. Many people in the Mennonite church firmly believe that. If we did firmly believe that human life begins at conception, that would rule out in vitro fertilization as well as any kind of stem cell research.

As a country, we are clearly divided on this. Polls in the United States show that a majority of Americans are pro-choice and affirm *Roe v. Wade*. A majority of Americans also think that abortion is too freely available in the United States. I do not think we as a nation have reached a resolution on this question.

Lawrence Ressler: I have also tended to dodge this issue, and I have been mostly concerned that this seems to be a symbolic crusade attached to lots of other things, so I am not sure if the question itself is a pure question or a trick question. What does bother me is that the people who most vigorously argue this are not the people that are most vigorously arguing for carrying of children, for the social consequences, for hunger, for deprivation, and for many needs that we have. I wonder where the folks who are arguing that life is precious are when it comes to the redistribution of wealth and caring for the poor who are born. What I do not see is a consistent drive that says that in every stage of life we ought to make sure that the quality of life is as important as is the preservation of life at that particular moment. That always haunts me. Somehow, people get distracted and lose interest once a precious little child is born.

Part Three

Critique and Synthesis

CHAPTER TWENTY-SIX

Anabaptist Eyes on Biotechnology

Stanley M. Hauerwas

Dr. Stanley M. Hauerwas is the Gilbert T. Rowe Professor of Theological Ethics at Duke Divinity School. His work cuts across disciplinary lines, as he is in conversation with systematic theology, philosophical theology and ethics, political theory as well as the philosophy of social science and medical ethics. His book, A Community of Character: Toward a Constructive Christian Ethic, *was named one of the hundred most important books on religion of the twentieth century. He received his Ph.D. from Yale University and his D.D. from the University of Edinburgh.*

I begin with a disclaimer: I'm not an Anabaptist, nor the son of an Anabaptist. However, I have discovered that Anabaptists use me to say what they would like to say but do not want to say, fearing they will appear too combative. My remarks are critical but I hope constructive. Basically I shall try to address what is represented in these pages by reframing the discussion.

In particular I want to try to convince that a mistake is being made when anyone says that I am laying out the problems presented by the new technology about which we must make some ethical decision. The mistake is the assumption that "facts" can be determined by a disinterested reason on the basis of which value judgments are made. The distinction between facts and values is a necessary ideology that sustains liberal social orders through the creation of "experts" to whom we are supposed to grant authority irrespective of any further moral implications.

Morality and Ethics

It indicated in an earlier presentation that all are entitled to their own opinions but not to their own facts. Such a view exemplifies how that fact/value ideology works to make us responsive and dutiful members of liberal social orders. Morally, everything is entailed in the description, and no fact comes without description. Alasdair MacIntyre says in *Whose Justice? Which Rationality?*: "But facts, like the telescope and wigs for gentlemen, were a seventeenth-century invention"[1] and if we have left wigs behind we also ought to give up "facts" and "values." How descriptions work within certain determinative communities makes all the difference for how you understand what is going on in terms of the communities that make the descriptions intelligible.

Conrad Brunk quite rightly says that, for example, utilitarian and deontological ethical theories are inadequate. They only reflect the moral incoherence of this thing we call our society. When I talk about the development of that pseudo-discipline called bioethics—one of the great scams of the modern university—I point out that physicians started having so-called ethical problems which they attributed to development of technology. Actually, the ethical problems were due to the uncertainty of practicing medicine in a morally incoherent society. So physicians looked around and they discovered people with Ph.D's in ethics and thought, "Ah ha! Experts." These ethicists distinguished metaethics from normative ethics, to discover whether "right" or "good" is the primary moral term and whether such terms have natural or unnatural products. They then taught students they could be a non-naturalist utilitarian and/or a naturalist deontologist, though it turns out it does not make much difference.

Ethics courses in most colleges and universities teach students that there are two primary forms of normative theory within modernity: *teleological,* which means utilitarianism, and *deontological,* which means right triumphs over good. Most students discover that they want to be utilitarians when it comes to sex but deontologists when it comes to violence, which indicates that they are leading morally incoherent lives.

Then they get down to cases. For example, spelunkers are in a cave and the water begins to rise. "Fatty" goes out first but gets stuck in the mouth of the cave. You're all going to drown except for "Fatty." You then discover a stick of dynamite and matches. Utilitarians say, "Blow that sucker out of there—the greatest good for the greatest number." Deontologists say, "No, we all must die, never do a wrong that a good may accrue."

That is the way we ethicists have rushed in to try to give people an idea that we know what we are doing when we learnedly discuss such cases. We have also learned many descriptive terms from the scientists to help them feel we are really listening to them. The difficulty is that ethics itself is a disputed area, so the attempt to create something called ethics in modernity is a realm that must be distinguished from aesthetics and so on.

Issues of Rhetoric

Aristotle thought one of the most decisive moral characteristics of humans was how they laughed and what they laughed at. He made no distinction between etiquette and ethics. That seems to me to be right. When ethics becomes the realm of the expert, the result is the attempt to try to salve the conscience of modern people that they are in the moral game, and that game is to be found in the decisions they make. But I suggest that morality is constituted much more determinatively by the language we use, and that it is particularly important who the "we" is.

I represent what I call the "Tonto principle" of Christian ethics. The Lone Ranger and Tonto found themselves surrounded by 20 thousand Sioux in the Dakotas. The Lone Ranger turned to Tonto and said, "This looks pretty tough, Tonto, what do you think we ought to do?" And he said, "What do you mean 'we,' white man?" Now part of the whole process of the rhetoric of this conference has been the creation of the notion of "we," and as a result you have been co-opted into the notions of modernity that want to convince you that you are a player and an actor within the processes.

Let me give just a couple of examples of the rhetoric some of the people have used to illustrate the separation of expertise and ethics. For example, I heard someone remark that he doesn't know of any religion that doesn't want to make life better for their kids. You think, *Oh, I don't want to be part of any religion that doesn't make life better for my kids,* but you just heard Joe Kotva say he does not want to make life better for his kids. He is a Mennonite; he would not even know how. I take it that Mennonites want to live in a way that makes the way their children should live be dangerous. After all, you are raising them not to use the American flag in any demonstrative way.

Take Leslie Biesecker's comment—and I thought his presentation was quite illuminating—that they do not do genetic testing for abortion on Amish because it is not acceptable to their culture. Think about that phrase "to their culture." What produced that description? Would Beisecker have said that if he was dealing with a community of people who raised children for food? Would that culture be okay? The very presumption "to their culture" presupposes a cosmopolitan attitude whose point of view is superior to all other cultures and therefore respects cultural difference. That is the kind of cosmopolitanism that creates the pseudo-problem of relativism.

So language and grammar are all-important for the kinds of issues before us. Therefore, let me begin by noting a problem with the title of the conference and now this book, *Viewing New Creations with Anabaptist Eyes*. The problem is that "creation" is in the plural. There is only one new creation, i.e., the church of Jesus Christ. New things may be developments or innovations, but they are definitely not creations. The very fact that you use the language of creation underwrites Promethean assumptions that we somehow need to figure out what to do as human beings, since God is clearly no longer in the picture.

The assumption is connected with the general question James Peterson tried to deal with, "Should we play God?" I regard that question and responses to it as dramatically uninteresting, because we obviously intervene in all kinds of ways. You must act in the world in which you find yourself, and "technology" is but a name for that.

The important question that requires very close philosophical reflection is this one: "Is there a qualitative difference between some technology and another?" It simply is beside the point to note Jesus was a carpenter and therefore favored technology. That is the same kind of reasoning that suggests because Jesus drove the money-changers from the temple, he must think war is at times necessary.

Or take the innocent sentence with which John Gearhart began his talk: "We must listen to society." Part of what he was doing was rhetorically making you part of something called "society" and hoping to gain your willingness to support the kind of experimentation he is doing. Now no one has any idea what that strange subject called society is. At one time, you Mennonites didn't know you were a society; you just knew you were Mennonites, which is a great thing. My take on that is that I certainly do not want to be a society. I'm a Texan, which is a reminder that the very fact that you let a generic term like "society" determine your primary identification is already a way to make one then step back and think, *Hmm, somebody else's culture.* The language that we must listen to society is a mystification that lulls us into believing that we know what we are talking about.

Contemporary Society

Conrad Brunk was the only person who mentioned the political character of our lives; that is, he said we are liberals. That is certainly correct. What it means for us to be liberals is that we do not believe anyone should tell us what to do because we assume autonomy is the first characteristic of an appropriate social order in which there are no agreements about the goods. The morally incoherent nature of such a society makes the practice of medicine very problematic. That is one of the great issues before us.

Modernity names a time in which social orders are created that want to produce people who believe they should have no story except the story they chose when they had no story. Modernity calls that freedom. If you don't believe that is your story, I can ask you, "Do you believe that you ought to hold yourself or someone else accountable for decisions they made when they did not know what they were doing?" The obvious answer is no. Since that is our story, it has correlated with the institutional form of "You should have no story except the story you chose when you had no story."

The problem with that commitment is this: it makes marriage unintelligible. How could you ever know what you were doing when you promised lifelong monogamous fidelity? That is why Christians require you to be married before the congregation, where they witness the promises you made when you did not know what you were doing and can hold you to them. And if you think that makes marriage unintelligible, try having children—you will never get the ones you want. Since it becomes arbitrary why you are having children at all, and because you do not trust the convictions that you chose, you think you must bring children into the world in a manner that they do not have to suffer for your convictions. Thus we have the assumption that we should bring children up to make up their own minds.

A great problem in such a liberal social order is this: How do you secure cooperation between people who share nothing in common other than they have no story except the story they chose when they had no story? The answer is very simple. People *do* share the common belief that death is a very bad thing, and they're willing to work together with one another to keep death at bay as long as possible.

When I speak to lay audiences—that is, people who are not associated with medicine, because that is the only laity left that is interesting—I ask them how they want to die. People today want to die quickly, painlessly, in their sleep, and without being a burden. People do not want to be a burden because they do not trust their children. They want to die painlessly, quickly, and in their sleep because they do not want to know they are dying. So they ask physicians to keep them alive to the point that they do not know they are dying. Then they blame physicians for keeping them alive to no point. This is a wonderful double-bind game we are very good at playing.

Interestingly, a common prayer among medieval people was, "Dear God, save us from a sudden death." They wanted to be saved from a sudden death because what they feared was not death but God, and they did not want to go to God's judgment without having been reconciled with their family, church, and God. Now we fear death rather than God, so we want to keep death at bay as long as possible.

Medicine and Moral Training

The fear of death is the reason why the best moral training occurs today in the sciences and in medicine. I often point out that a kid can come to divinity school—they're actually not kids any more, they are often people who have already failed in another line of work before they get there—and they say, "I'm just not into Christology this year. I'm really into relating. I'd like to take some more clinical pastoral education." And we say, "Right, wounded healers are the best."

But if people went to medical school when they were kids and said, "I'm just really not into anatomy this year. I'm really into relating. I would like to take some more psychiatry," the professors would respond by saying, "Who do you think you are, kid? We don't care about your interest—take anatomy or ship out." That is real moral training.

Now why is it that medical school is so much more serious today about shaping people's lives than divinity school? The answer is simple: No one believes inadequately trained clergymen may damage their salvation, since people think nothing is really at stake in their salvation, but people do believe an inadequately trained doctor can hurt them. That explains why most of our lives—despite what we say about God and God's importance in our lives—are lived atheistically. The desire for modern medicine to save us from dying is exactly the desire to live in a world without God. The research imperative is fueled by a people bent on trying to get out of life alive. This imperative is why many insist that therapeutic gene therapy is not eugenics. But it is eugenics.

I thought Arlene Wiens and Randall Longenecker gave the classic accounts of what medicine is about. It is about caring for a patient under limits of their life and our lives together in a way that does not tempt them to be more than they are. The first commitment of medicine is do no harm. The second one, as physicians are trained, is to care for this patient in a way that transcends all other considerations. You are to care for this patient's body; he may be a vile child molester, but if he has a bad gall bladder, you do something about it. Those are extraordinary moral commitments that are internal to medicine.

However, a problem in modern medicine is that it has the power, given the research imperative, to turn certain kinds of conditions into illnesses that will help solidify the researchers' and the doctors' power. I know, for example, many of you like myself were chilled by an advertisement not that long ago in which a man was walking along the beach looking out over the ocean. He turns to the camera and says, "I face the existential crisis of my life. I've looked into the blackness, and I realize that I must take control of my life if I'm to live well. Tomorrow I'm going to see my doctor about my baldness." When did baldness become a bad thing? And when does it become subject to medical intervention? Increasing pressure is being put on medicine and research to underwrite the presumption that aging is an illness. When you go in that direction, you are in deep trouble.

Medicine and Ethics

A second example involves the ethics of in vitro fertilization (IVF). Why is the inability to conceive a child a subject for medical intervention? What kinds of people use IVF when adoption is always a possibility? Why is it so important that people think their children must be biologically linked? I think the development of IVF is extremely morally problematic, not because it is antithetical to the principles of a liberal society but because there is no reason for Christians to engage in IVF. Christians, whether they have biological children or not, have parental responsibilities.

"Is the embryo a human being?" is another example of a question that can only mislead. I agree with the panelists who tried to resist that as a straightforward question. Christian hope makes possible having children. As Christians, therefore, we want always to be in relation with people with whom we have had conception occur so that the existence of the child will not be rendered problematic. We hope it is a child, and I think the material conditions for that hope are clearly there.

As shown in these examples, science is a moral endeavor. The training of a scientist to believe negative results are as good as positive results is an extraordinary training in humility. That concept is difficult to accept when one is trying to get NIH funding. But science is certainly moral training, and it is shaped by the habits and expectations of people.

I think, therefore, we have to ask why we have gene therapy. We have gene therapy because we have the capacity to have gene therapy. In the same way, I asked one of my just war friends why we are at war with Iraq (a so-called elective war). The answer is: "Because we can be at war with Iraq." How did you get that "can"? Is the military power and capacity of the United States the result of just war reflection and practice? No, it is the result of Cold War presuppositions, so now you have a military that can let you do what you please wherever you want to do it. To assume that you only start doing ethical reflection when the decision confronts you is always to underwrite and legitimate what has gone before.

Again, why did we want to produce something like gene therapy? The question is never whether the techniques are moral or immoral, but why did you want to do it? Why did we want to clone Dolly? Because we can clone Dolly. These kinds of capacities must be subject to purposes beyond curiosity.

Why do we view our bodies as organ systems? Because this legitimates the kind of medicine that we believe we want. So the very knowledge itself always involves power relations. Therefore, I think you should resist Leroy Walters' attempt to advocate a public policy position. Promoting a public policy position tempts Mennonites again to become Constantinians. The first question for Anabaptists is, "By advocating or accepting the presumption that public policy is a 'good thing,' do I in fact underwrite the power of the state?" Please note I am not suggesting Mennonites must make a strong distinction between church and state. With Barth and Yoder I believe "the state" is to be understood christologically, and therefore with Anabaptists I think we know what the state ought to be about better than the state knows itself. So it is quite right to say that Mennonites may well have something to say about this or that "public policy," but what they have to say may not fit within the current policy options assumed by society.

Societal Issues

Conrad Brunk is right when he says we do not know what justice means, because one cannot have an account of justice without an account of the goods. When goods become value preferences—as they have within liberal social orders—that makes the idea of justice unclear. I always say America is the only country that had the disadvantage of being founded on a philosophical mistake, namely the notion of inalienable rights. Therefore justice assumes that you are providing a distribution of inalienable rights. Such an account of justice avoids the issues of the goods that need to be named in order for justice to have some rationality.

I thought Laura Powers put the issues well in her accounts of public policy. She notes that public policy in America must avoid strong convictions because such convictions will be conflictual. The whole point is to avoid conflict. Therefore the resort is primarily to language of harm, as if there were general agreement on what might count for harm. In such a morally incoherent context, Christians can contribute to the so-called public policy discussions by exposing the limits of those alleged modes of making decisions to avoid moral conflicts. The whole point of modern politics is to avoid the substantive issues over which there is no deep agreement. That is why abortion is basically taken off the political agenda. "Pro-choice" and "pro-life" are such unhappy alternatives because they do not get at the issue of how you understand children. Christians should ask if we are prepared for gene therapy when the current practice of abortion is so determinative for so many lives.

I say the "Yuppies" are the great monks of modernity because people think Yuppies decide not to have children because they would prefer a better stereo system. I do not think that is it at all. I think Yuppies do not have children because they do not see why they should pass on the meaninglessness of their own lives to a future generation. That is a certain kind of moral gesture and therefore one of the crucial issues we are facing is why people have children at all in the kind of social order in which we live. Laura Powers also noted that economics is so important it trumps ethics. However, economics is ethics. So it is one ethic trumping another ethic in their applications. We should be asking this: In a society as fearful as ours is, should we be engaged in IVF?

I found Ruth Cowan's presentation raised one of the hardest challenges. She talked about the development of eugenic discussions in the nineteenth century and how all the progressives in the nineteenth century were eugenicists. For example, Walter Rauschenbusch, the great Protestant social gospeler praised for being concerned about social justice, had very negative views about Catholicism. He pointed out that the Catholic church took their best talent and turned them into celibates, which meant the best part of the human race was not carried over to the next generation. He said that the deleterious effects are revealed in contrast to the great things coming out of the Protestant manse in which the talented reproduce children now for future generations. Progressives in the past (and present) can become eugenicists in a manner that may be quite problematic.

I do think (and I hope what you will not hear what I'm saying as medical Ludditism) that genetic family histories can be a useful means of therapy. What it will mean, however, as in Cyprus, is that love is not a sufficient reason to get married. That is a good thing that will make you step back and rethink what marriage is about. I point out in my classes that Christians married one another for centuries without knowing each other until the day of the marriage, even when they knew they were going to have sex that night. It was all right for them to have sex because it was being done in public, and they could be held responsible for any outcomes.

The deep problem about modern romantic conceptions of love legitimating sex is the privatization of sex, making accountability difficult. One of the most important things Christians can do is reclaim marriage as the appropriate context for sexual expression. As some of my neo-conservative friends say, pacifism is just so unrealistic. So I say, "Have you thought recently about lifelong monogamous fidelity?" If you think pacifism is hard, try marriage.

Finally, back to creation. We are all creatures. The assumption that we have an environmental problem, as Wendell Berry has pointed out, is still an indication of the problem because we are assuming we are not a part of "the environment." It becomes crucial for us to acknowledge that this is not nature dumb and dull, this is *creation*, which means all things have been created to glorify God. We should approach each plant with a kind of reverence because it is making sacrifices so that we may live.

I am not opposed to experimentation on animals, but surely Christians must pray before we start deciding to make a mouse not be able to walk on its back legs. We must pray to God that the sacrifice of this animal—just as we pray before every meal in thanks to God for the sacrifice it entails—is going to be for the glorification of God's kingdom. If such prayers were done in the lab, we would be reminded that we need not do everything we have the potential to do. As people who have been given the gifts of God's creation—suffering being one of them—we must restrict what we do in the name of technological innovation.

Note

1. Alasdair MacIntyre, *Whose Justice? Which Rationality?* (Notre Dame: University of Notre Dame Press, 1988), 357.

CHAPTER TWENTY-SEVEN

Technology, Justice, and Questions

Joseph J. Kotva, Jr.

Dr. Joseph J. Kotva Jr. is the executive director of the Anabaptist Center for Health-Care Ethics (ACHE).

*I*n a 1974 booklet for the General Conference Mennonite Church, Dwayne Freisen discusses "genetic surgery," that is, manipulation of genes themselves. He then writes, "Perhaps at this point you are saying, 'This is all wild and farfetched. What possible relevance could this have for me?' Probably, the same reaction would have been made by people in the year 1900 if someone would have described the possibility of nuclear energy or air transportation. The point is, we must try to anticipate technology, so as to make use of its opportunities. If not, we shall become slaves to technology and subject ourselves to the living hell on Earth."[1] This was a Mennonite in 1974 saying this.

In the intervening thirty years, as far as I have been able to determine, not a single Mennonite conference has tried to discern how Anabaptists should describe themselves in relationship to technology. I was struck by the good will and noble aspirations of the different presenters at the conference on which this book is based. That is worth mentioning because it is so easy to vilify those with whom we disagree. In the Mennonite church,recent debates about abortion and homosexuality have moved quickly from rigorous conversation and debate about how we should describe things to vilification.

If we discuss these issues with the seriousness they deserve, we will have significant heated disagreements. I pray that we will not shy away from the disagreements; I pray that we will not have to ask Stanley Hauerwas to speak every time we have to say difficult things to each other that we do not want to say ourselves, because we fear conflict. I pray that we argue out of Christian charity, humility, and patience. I pray that we will argue in ways that assume the best of those with whom we argue and that we have something to learn as well as offer.

During the conference proceedings, it struck me that there is little radically new in biotechnology. Carl Bowman, among others, pointed this out; many of the moral questions we are dealing with regarding the power of biotechnology look oddly familiar. However, I would suggest that they take on an additional urgency.

Our understanding of children, parenting, and family have been called into question through everything from freely-available abortion to the advent of public education. Public education did much to change the notion of parenting. In vitro fertilization certainly did something to notions of parenting. There is new urgency when we are presented with the power to screen embryos for disease or choose our children's physical characteristics and enhance their abilities.

We have previously discussed this question, but it has been taken to new levels, which is true of questions regarding distributive justice. Christians ought to have a notion of justice, even if broader society does not. I served on a hospital ethics committee in Allentown, Pennsylvania, for five or six years. I am struck every day with the absolute tyranny of autonomy. In the hospital setting, autonomy trumps almost every other value nearly every day. As people who believe in the authority of community and Scripture, we qualify autonomy. In the name of autonomy, society may one day choose everything from children to IQs. The question of autonomy may not be new; however, the powers we are developing through biotechnology force us to confront those questions in a deepened way.

Finally, I urge us to remember a lesson many learned from John Howard Yoder: We must always question whether we are asking the right question. We must always question whether we are being presented with the right question and description. I was fairly confident Stanley Hauerwas would make us wonder if we are asking the right questions, if we are framing them the right way, and whether or not we are using language that is clearly Christian or if we have adopted somebody else's language. Asking the right questions is a skill that needs to be nurtured. Therefore when someone presents us with a dilemma or new technology, we need constantly discern if the question and description are ones we ought to own.

Note

1. Duane K. Friesen, *Moral Issues in the Control of Birth* (Newton, Kan.: Faith and Life Press, 1974), 22.

CHAPTER TWENTY-EIGHT

Biotechnology and the Future

Conrad G. Brunk

Dr. Conrad G. Brunk is professor of philosophy and director of the Center for Studies in Religion and Society at the University of Victoria in British Columbia, Canada.

A number of general impressions came to me during the conference on which this book is based. The first was that I have been largely outside the Anabaptist debate on issues of biotechnology. In my work in Canada, I have been involved at the level of public policy. I spent the last ten years of my life working with the larger Canadian and international community on these issues, so I have been at many conferences. However, the EMU bioethics conference provided my first opportunity to reflect on how my own immersion in the Mennonite community has influenced my thinking about the many ethical issues raised by biotechnology.

With that as a context, even though the EMU conference was framed in terms of how one should look at these issues with Anabaptist eyes, the spectrum of opinions expressed there were as wide as anywhere I have seen. It is clear that much discussion needs to continue in our own church community concerning issues of biotechnology. I think the Anabaptist churches are far from moving toward an agreement on what direction the Anabaptist heritage is leading the church with respect to biotechnology. There was as wide a variety of interpretations of what Anabaptists would say about this or that issue at the EMU conference as I have seen in the larger secular society, and that in itself is a matter for further discussion.

I have seen one clear exception to this generalization. In the larger community in which I work, individuals strongly and unabashedly argue for advancement of the technology on the basis primarily of economic and market issues, intellectual property questions, and innovation for innovation's sake. At this conference, that has not been as strongly argued. However, it has been replaced by two values that I think are the most attractive and also the most seductive values for Anabaptists. Two things that Anabaptists believe in very strongly and have a near consensus about are that (1) food is a good thing, and the more food, the better and (2) health is a good thing and its promotion is a particularly virtuous, and even saintly, thing to which Christians should devote themselves.

These are great strengths of the Anabaptist tradition; they have produced the institutions of which Mennonites are most proud, such as Mennonite Central Committee, Mennonite Mutual Aid, and Mennonite Medical Association. However, these values are seductive in the sense that the almost unconditional commitments to them can also be the ones that may blind Anabaptists to the limits needed to respect the way in which Anabaptists pursue honorable goods. It is fair to say that the Mennonite and Anabaptist tradition has also been very concerned about the limits one places in pursuit of goods, and their whole nonresistance philosophy is based on that idea.

Soon after World War II, a French philosopher named Maurice Merleau-Ponty wrote a book called *Humanism and Terror*. In that book he reflected upon his own previous commitment to Marxist Socialism, from the perspective of the development of Stalinism in Russia and recent events in Nazi Germany. He reflected that when people become committed to the implementation of a new human future in which they will achieve some great human good, they become capable of carrying out the worst horrors and become drawn into the commission of great evils. Merleau-Ponty confessed his resignation from the Socialist ideals he had held because of his fear that his particular humanitarian ideal would draw him into the spiral of evil.[1]

That is dramatic language for this context, but because we as Anabaptists are so unconditionally committed to the production of food and to the alleviation of disease and starvation as quintessential Christian virtues, they may be the issues where we are most morally vulnerable; they may prevent us from seeing where we should be placing the limits on what we do in implementing the technological means to these ends.

There has been a great deal of talk here about the moral status of the human embryo. It is quite clear that Mennonites share the concern of many in the larger Christian community on that issue. The question of an embryo's moral status is a weighty one. However, there is a danger here as well. There is a tendency, especially in the United States, to put the whole moral weight of medical biotechnology on that issue. By doing that, attention is detracted from a whole set of other important issues one should be concerned about regarding biotechnology. I see that happening at the public policy level in the United States.

For example, LeRoy Walters discussed what happened at the United Nations when the United States effectively blocked an initiative to prohibit human reproductive cloning at the international level. There is a wide consensus currently in most of the world that such cloning should be prohibited. The United States did so by attaching the question of research with embryos to the issue, knowing that there was not a consensus on that question. Therefore, by tying the two issues together, they knew the original proposal would fail to win consensus; thus no restrictions would be placed on this technology.

The irony is that the United States government knows that by blocking any kind of legislation at the United Nations regarding biotechnology, many states are left in a situation where this research can go ahead without any restrictions. While the United States appears to be making a strong statement about standing firm on the question of an embryo's status (thus appearing firm on questions important to the religious right), the political effect leaves the United States research community in the least-regulated position relative to other countries with respect to both embryonic research and reproductive cloning. The Mennonite community ought to be concerned about this. It is an example of how putting the weight of the issue on an embryo's status can deflect attention from other serious concerns about biotechnology.

Regarding agricultural biotechnology, there have been many references in this conference to the fact that the Europeans are preventing a solution to the limited food supply problem (particularly in Africa) because of the position they have taken on genetically modified foods. There have also been comments that this is merely a reflection of European trade protectionism and is an immoral assault on the developing world. In the Anabaptist community, there can be more serious critical reflection on the tendency to blame problems on foreigners and blame another's actions on immoral motivations, while claiming that one's own actions are aimed at the human good. It is particularly interesting, because the United States has been among the most strongly trade-protected countries in the free-trade regime, as recognized by the World Trade Organization (WTO) ruling on trade tariffs in November 2003, which the American government will probably ignore. There is trade protectionism in both Europe and the United Sates.

There is an important ethical debate concerning biotechnology and how biotechnological products should be regulated. Comments have been made such as, "We do not need to worry about these things, because we have a good regulatory system in place." This is an argument regularly made in both Canada and the United States. However, in both these countries, there are strong political forces striving to minimize government involvement by reducing the funding for regulatory agencies and the testing of new products. These political forces are aiming to increase the speed by which products are approved for the market, both in the biomedical and agricultural sectors. In Canada, there is a new initiative called "Smart Regulation," which is questioning the requirements for extensive testing so products can be brought to the market faster and more efficiently. The anti-regulation movement is even stronger in the United States than Canada.

We need to exercise caution. A technology that can lead to the alleviation of much suffering and harm is also a technology that poses profound questions for us as an Anabaptist community, a Christian community, and a larger community in which we all live.

Note

1. Maurice Merleau-Ponty, *Humanism And Terror: An Essay On The Communist Problem* (Boston: Beacon Press, 1969).

CHAPTER TWENTY-NINE

Facing Biotechnology as an Alternative Community of Worship, Character, and Discernment

Joseph J. Kotva Jr.

Dr. Joseph J. Kotva Jr. is the executive director of the Anabaptist Center for Health-Care Ethics (ACHE).

As I review the conference presentations in this book, I am inclined to agree with the conviction voiced by Stanley Hauerwas that "the first social task of the church is to be the church."[1] Faced with the impressive and growing powers of biotechnology, I am reminded that we are lost in the world without God's gift of the church. The church is the principle place where we are equipped with the character, convictions, and relationships that enable us to both navigate through and witness to the world—including the world of biotechnology.

Several conference participants also discerned a reminder of the church's centrality. Indeed, the church's importance is the one "Anabaptist" emphasis signaled by multiple presenters. Conrad Brunk concludes his paper by noting the Anabaptist priority of moral community and "the idea that truth is found in the Spirit-led discernment of the community."[2] Randall Longnecker begins with a word of thanks that he belongs to a community of knowledge and wisdom.[3] Graydon Snyder describes the Anabaptist ideal that the authority "comes from the faith community and is led by the Holy Spirit and the study of the Scripture, as it makes contextual decisions."[4] Stanley Hauerwas warns that our distinct community is being seduced into thinking that we belong to some wider social "we" other than the church.[5] Finally, the conference organizer, Roman Miller, describes an evangelical Anabaptist ethic rooted in a Christocentric community.[6]

I want to continue this theme of the church's importance in the face of biotechnology by developing three interrelated ideas: First, the church is a community of worship and character formation. While this claim may not at first appear relevant to biotechnology, I suggest that our engagement with such technology depends on how well we have been formed in the church as Christians. Second, the church is a community of moral discernment. In this section, I highlight numerous developments related to biotechnology that require the church's gifts of discernment. Third, the church is meant to be an alternative model and contrast society. Here I suggest that maintaining alternative practices, ranging from communal discernment to adoption, will constitute an essential element of our witness and offer of good news to a world engrossed in the powers of biotechnology.

Community of Worship and Character

Awe and gratitude

If the church is to be about anything, it is to be about worship, about attending to God.[7] We gather to offer prayers of gratitude and to sing songs of praise. We gather under the assumption that if we are attentive, the words of Scripture and sermon can by the Holy Spirit become God's Words to us. We gather for worship.

This unremarkable claim that in the church we gather for worship has remarkable implications for how we engage biotechnology. Consider, for example, that gathered worship cultivates and refines the sensibilities of awe, wonder, and gratitude. We learn to appreciate the manifold works of God as we read many of the Psalms, sing many of the great hymns and choruses, witness new faith commitments sanctified in baptism, share together in the Lord's table, and listen to each other's praises during various "sharing times." Worship offers us an opportunity to experience the wonder and awe that accompanies an awareness of God's presence and God's work. In worship we learn to gratefully recognize God at work even when that work seems concealed from the world.

These sensibilities are relevant to how we engage in biotechnology. Rather than fear, distrust, arrogance, or overconfidence in human ingenuity, the appropriate response to many developments in biotechnology is a God-directed sense of wonder, awe, and gratitude. For example, these are the appropriate responses to the incredible elegance of DNA and its work of coding proteins, the development of a human embryo from a group of undifferentiated cells into a child, and the dedication to the relief of human suffering exhibited by many scientists.

As an example from the conference, wonder and gratitude are appropriate when Carole Cramer tells us that tobacco, of all things, may provide a safe and effective means of producing glucocerebrosidase for those with Gaucher Disease.[8] And when Leslie Biesecker told us that the Amish penchant for genealogy will now enable them to better care for their children, some of us should have responded "praise God!" Knowing when to respond with wonder, awe, and gratitude, and knowing to whom these dispositions are due, provides an important point of departure in our dealings with biotechnology.

Respect for creation

Relatedly, the context of worship provides us an opportunity to develop a sense of respect and reverence for creation. The Scriptures begin with an account of God's care for God's creation, where day after day God looks at the creation (including us) and calls it good. So too, the Psalms testify to God's care for God's creation. For instance, in Psalm 50, God says, "For every wild animal of the forest is mine, the cattle on a thousand hills. I know all the birds of the air, and all that moves in the field is mine."[9]

Jesus also assumes the value of creation and God's care for it. That assumption is why Jesus assures us of God's care for us by first pointing to God's care for the birds of the air and the flowers and grass of the field.[10] The same type of assumption is at work when the apostle Paul reminds us that we join the rest of creation eagerly waiting for God's full redemption.[11]

Besides the reading of the Scriptures, our hymns are a likely aspect of worship to move our hearts and minds toward a sense of reverence for God's creation. *Hymnal: A Worship Book* contains dozens of hymns regarding God's relationship to creation. "When the morning stars together," "All creatures of our God and King," "I sing the mighty power of God," "For the beauty of the earth," and "God of the fertile fields" are among those hymns that move us to regard the creation with respect.[12]

This worship-based sense of respect for creation will likely inform our dealing with biotechnology in various ways. Consider, for example, conference participant Stanley Hauerwas's comment about Dolly, "Why did we want to clone Dolly? These kinds of capacities must be subject to purposes beyond curiosity."[13] Hauerwas is correct that such efforts must be subject to reasons beyond curiosity. We need those reasons in part because without them such efforts will violate our respect for creation's integrity, violate the sense of reverence for what God has made.

We intervene in creation all the time, of course. But people well-shaped by a community of worship to respect God's creation will recognize before others do when such intervention requires justification. As examples, I suggest that such justification is required of the genetic altering and patenting of mice to develop cancer (the "Oncomouse")[14] or the cloning of cows engineered for faster cheese production[15] or efforts to get an embryo from stem cell-derived egg and sperm.[16] People well formed in respect-for-God's-creation will be among the first to recognize when such efforts require good reasons and they will not bless those efforts without better claims than sheer curiosity (and, I suspect, better claims than simple economic gain or research expediency).[17]

A worship-based sense of respect and reference for creation also positions us better to recognize and resist biotechnology that is driven by what Alan Verhey identifies as "the Baconian project":

> In Bacon's view knowledge is power over nature, and mastery over nature inevitably brings human well-being in its train. Both this account of knowledge and this confidence are shared by much of Western culture. The Baconian project sets humanity not only over nature but also against it. The natural order and natural processes have no dignity of their own; their value is reduced to their utility to humanity. And nature does not serve humanity "naturally." Nature threatens to rule and to ruin humanity. . . . Nature may be—and must be—mastered. . . . The Baconian project finds a natural expression in genetic enhancement. Nature has no moral standing. If nature or humanity can be 'enhanced,' it should be. The nature we are is the nature we suffer from.[18]

A worship-based respect for creation will enable us to identify and resist when a Baconian view of a strong dichotomy between humanity and nature and the corresponding need to technologically subjugate nature is prominent in biotechnological efforts.

Finally, this sense of respect for creation may prove an important component in moral "repugnance" at certain efforts in biotechnology. Leon Kass has argued against human cloning in part based on our response of repugnance at the idea. Kass assumes that most of us respond to the idea of human cloning with a sense of revulsion, that we literally shudder at the idea. He recognizes that revulsion is not an argument and that we sometimes later discover that our earlier revulsion was completely misplaced. Still, Kass argues that with cloning, like other "crucial cases . . . repugnance is the emotional expression of deep wisdom, beyond reason's power completely to articulate it."[19] Much like the horror that we experience regarding rape, farther-daughter incest, and the mutilation of a corpse, repugnance regarding cloning is a vital marker that something is deeply wrong with the contemplated practice.

There are important arguments to be made against human cloning, ranging from the likely physiological harm done to the cloned child to the commodification of the practice of procreation. Yet, for Kass, repugnance first alerts us that there is something seriously wrong with human cloning and convinces us that what is wrong goes beyond what we are able to articulate.

Kass is right to reject human cloning. He is also right to point to repugnance. Strong emotions are sometimes key moral indicators. Indeed, a significant moral role for strong emotions is a fairly common experience. For example, for those with well-formed characters, experiencing a strong emotional reaction of anger, whether to a news report or to something done to oneself or an acquaintance, is a likely indicator that an injustice has been perpetrated.

We do not dispassionately stand outside the situations of life determining that some injustice has been done. Although a bit oversimplified, it is more accurate to say that we get mad or angry amid life's situations and then, upon examination, determine that an injustice has been done or that the response of anger is misplaced.[20] Moreover, strong reactions of anger or other emotional states often convince us that the injustice or other moral value at stake is greater than we are currently able to articulate. Strong emotional responses often alert us to morally serious situations, and they sometimes convey a depth of seriousness beyond what we can express.

I highlight the importance of strong emotions and Kass's attention to repugnance because well-formed, worship-based reverence for God's creation is essential if our own sense of repugnance is to be trusted as a moral guide in matters of biotechnology. The fact is that strong emotional responses like repugnance will provide one level of moral guidance in these matters. The question is not whether such responses will guide our judgments but whether those responses derive from an appropriate reverence for creation born out of our corporate worship of God.

If we have learned together a deep sense of respect for God's good creation, then we will need to seriously evaluate and possibly reject new biotechnological developments that evoke a sense of repugnance. Conversely, if we are well formed in this way, lack of repugnance is one sign that a new development can be accepted, even embraced, as an appropriate form of intervention in creation.

Patience, humility, and hope

Belonging to a community of worship is also vital in the formation of the triplet virtues of patience, humility, and hope. For instance, consider the connection between prayer and patience. We pray and learn to pray amid the congregation, and we learn patience as we learn to pray well.

Prayer requires that we learn to quiet our hearts and wait; it requires a different sense of time's passage. Westerners are obsessed with speed, efficiency, and progress. We hurry everywhere and always, continually anticipating the next moment. Archbishop Anthony Bloom describes this sense of hurry as a continual effort "to live an inch ahead of ourselves."[21] But prayer requires something different: a certain suspension of time and a posture of attentive waiting. Bloom describes this posture as similar to the combination of stillness, repose, and intense alertness that goes with bird watching.[22]

To learn to pray is to learn to step out of the frenzy of activity that engulfs us so that we might attend to God, so that we might talk with (not at) God. As Michael Duffey notes, "Prayer is first of all the intention to create an opening, a space where we might wait for the stirrings of God."[23] Attending to God, talking with (not at) God, requires a different sense of time's passage: We must learn to wait. We must learn patience.

Of course, other aspects of worship also require patience—the sermon, for example. Even for those gifted with strong preachers, it requires patience to really listen for fifteen, twenty, thirty minutes. To carefully attend to the preacher's words in such a way that God might speak to us, that God might challenge and transform us, requires patience. The "sharing time" of many services is also an occasion for patience. To listen to others in a way that we might hear a word from God requires patience. So too, to lovingly and carefully listen to those brothers and sisters who share every week or whose sharing is unclear or whose sharing seems improper to the setting requires that we grow in patience.

Many aspects of worship inculcate humility. For instance, in adoration and praise our focus shifts from ourselves to God. In praising God we stop being preoccupied with ourselves and thereby move toward the virtue of humility. Whenever we "enter the rarefied air of selfless devotion,"[24] our gaze has shifted from self to God. One paradox of this shift is that we gain a more truthful sense of our place in the universe and consequentially move toward the virtue of humility. Such adoration and praise happens in prayer and song, but can also be occasioned by aspects of worship as diverse as a wall hanging or stained glass window, a Scripture reading or a story well told.

Prayers of confession and petition also teach humility. As we rightly learn prayers of confession, we learn to own our limitations, failures, and rebellion. As we learn to pray prayers of petition, we are reminded of our needs and our dependence on God and others. Thus, as we learn proper confession and petition, we grow in humility.

Christian humility is not a groveling, debasing sense of inferiority. Instead, humility involves owning a truthful account of one's place in the world. Such an account includes the reality that we are cherished children of God and that we are taught to ask for things—food, forgiveness, safety—because we are worthy of receiving good things from God. The truly humble person has "neither too high nor too low" a self image, but instead disciplines her "vision with the insight that God loves all creation."[25]

Sermons and "sharing" often play an invaluable role in developing this truthful sense of our place in the world. Sermons about sin and judgment as well as about God's valuing us and our contribution to the kingdom, play a role in forming humility. Sharing that highlights our corporate responsibility, for good and ill, plays a role in forming humility; as does sharing that affirms individual accomplishments and service.

The Christian virtue of hope is likewise inculcated in worship. Hope is a kind of confident yearning. Hope is more than ungrounded wishing or mere fantasy, which often ends in disillusionment and despair. By contrast, hope has reasons for what it believes and clings with tenacity to those expectations. Christian hope steadfastly looks forward to the manifestation of God's good future.

In worship, we learn such hope primarily by attending to stories of those who have hoped in God, of God's faithfulness, and of God's promises for the future. In Scripture, sermons, and song we are reminded of countless numbers who clung to their hope in God and whose hope proved justified, though often not in the way or time they anticipated. The stories of Abraham and Sarah, Moses, Isaiah, Peter, Paul, Mary, indeed, above all the story of Jesus himself, are testaments to hope in God's faithfulness. As we read, tell, and sing these stories, they become part of our own identity and history, and we thus begin to acquire hope.

Of course, the stories and songs of hope in God's fidelity are not limited to characters from Scripture. For myself, the hymn "When peace like a river" fortifies my hope. I cannot help but be moved when the congregation lifts its voice to sing,

> And Lord, haste the day when my faith shall be sight,
> The clouds be rolled back as a scroll;
> The trumpet shall sound, and the Lord shall descend,
> Even so, it is well with my soul.

The cultivation of hope is strengthened by knowing that Horatio G. Spafford penned these words after having lost all four daughters in a ship collision shortly after having also lost his fortune in the great Chicago Fire of 1871.[26] For others, pictures and stories of Anabaptist martyrs are a similar source of hope.

The New Testament's eschatological vision also plays a role in cultivating Christian hope. We learn, for example, to understand and cling to God's good future as we attend together to the image of Christ's separation of the sheep from the goats. We learn to envision and hold to God's good future as we read the eschatological words of assurance to the church of Philadelphia[27] or see with John "the holy city, the new Jerusalem, coming down out of heaven from God" where God deals among mortals, wiping away our tears, ending death and pain, and "making all things new."[28]

These virtues of patience, humility, and hope are essential if we are to avoid hasty judgments about or rushed appropriation or rejection of new technologies. Consider, for example, conference participant Carl Bowman's mention of the automobile while pointing out that technological changes often have unforeseen consequences.[29] The automobile is a perfect example of why patience and humility are important when we consider how to appropriate significant new technologies. While the car does enrich our lives and make travel more efficient, it also has had numerous, largely unforeseen, negative consequences: encouraging a sedentary lifestyle, contributing to air pollution and global warming, playing a major (often negative) role in world politics via oil, and supporting urban sprawl while also pulling at the geographical threads of community.

The example of the unanticipated changes linked to the automobile should give pause and suggests the need for patience when considering major new technologies. We need patience if we are to take the time to fully evaluate those technologies to the best of our abilities. Equal levels of patience are needed whenever we conclude that the best approach is a selective appropriation of a specific technology. It is easier to fully embrace or reject a new development than to patiently appropriate that technology in a partial and selective manner.

We likewise need humility to inform the virtue of patience. Humility reminds us that our initial judgments are often mistaken and that taking time often improves those judgments. Humility reminds us of our own partial, limited vision and the need to take the time to listen to others in the process of evaluation. A humble patience would allow us to later change course when we realize that our initial judgments were too positive or too negative.

Humility is essential if we are to respond to Bowman's caution about "Chronocentrism"—our tendency to privilege our own time, discoveries, and ideas.[30] This caution fits with Troy Duster's sociological observation that in fields such as medicine and law there is an approximately fifty year cycle of looking back and judging that "they were caught up in the times" but then judging that we have now transcended those times and are objective.[31] As developments in biotechnology continue, it will require humility to recognize not only the folly but also the wisdom of previous generations as they have dealt with analogous issues. And it will require humility to chasten our own judgments with the realization that future generations will view our current ideas and choices as "caught up in the times."

Relatedly, as conference participant Conrad Brunk points out, we tend to assume the propriety of our own actions and motivations over those who disagree with us. Thus there is a current tendency to view Europeans as protectionist, obstructionist, and immoral in dealing with U.S.-led developments in genetically modified crops.[32] Yet, as Brunk points out, the reality is more complicated than that. It will take humility and patience to give the benefit of the doubt to those with whom we disagree and to listen carefully to their arguments and interests.

The need for humility and patience is further underlined by Conrad Brunk's appeal to Hans Jonas's notion of a "heuristics of fear."[33] Pointing out that developments in biotechnology are already littered with unforeseen consequences, Brunk argues that our moral thinking about the future must exhibit caution, must work from a heuristics of fear. Brunk is right to point out the reality of unforeseen consequences and to encourage caution in our appropriation of biotechnological innovations.

However, Brunk is mistaken to appropriate the language of "fear." Christians are directed by a deep sense of hope in God, not by fear. Indeed, freedom from fear is one way the Bible talks about Christ's work of salvation.[34] And it is the combination of freedom from fear and hope in God that leaves us free from the need to resort to violence, either to protect ourselves or to make things come out right.

A Christian approach of caution regarding biotechnology is enabled and properly directed by the virtues of patience, humility, and hope. Such an approach will seek to use biotechnology to aid human healing out of a sense of hope in God's healing intentions for the world. Yet the approach will proceed humbly, keenly aware of our propensity toward folly, and will proceed patiently, because God is who finally brings healing and salvation.

Transition

If space allowed, I would discuss other worship informed virtues—such as justice, solidarity, and truthfulness—that are relevant in our evaluation and appropriation of biotechnology. And if space allowed, I would talk about other aspects of church community life—such as role models and exemplars, friendship, support and accountability—that are as important as worship in character formation.

Still, enough has been said to suggest that one way that the church influences (or fails to influence) our engagement with biotechnology is indirect: through the cultivation of Christian character. The capacity for awe and gratitude, a deep respect for creation, and the virtues of patience, humility, and hope are key qualities in enabling and directing how we engage the new powers of biotechnology. We are thus dependent on the church being the church.

A Community of Discernment

Various conference participants, including Roman Miller and Graydon Snyder, mention the importance of community discernment as we come to terms with biotechnology. This desire for community discernment is on target, and Snyder is correct when he says that authority for decision making in Anabaptist theology "comes from the faith community and is led by the Holy Spirit and the study of the Scripture, as it makes contextual decisions."[35]

Unfortunately, after noting the need for community-based, contextual decisions, Snyder cuts short the process by making various pronouncements about what Anabaptists believe concerning biotechnology.[36] We are yet to have the types of community conversations that would justify claims about what Anabaptists believe regarding many of these matters. Indeed, the significance of the conference presentations is that they help initiate those conversations.

John Howard Yoder's "Hermeneutics of Peoplehood" is perhaps the best description of the Anabaptist ideal regarding communal discernment.[37] Arguing from both Scripture and history, Yoder describes a process of "practical moral reasoning" that is centered in the local, believing community. This process recognizes our communal nature and need for counsel but also values each individual participant as having joined voluntarily and as needing to be heard. The process is best described as a conversation that works toward consensus and includes attention to "principles, elements of character and due process, and elements of utility."[38] This conversation depends on the presence of God's Spirit and various gifted participants—including "agents of direction" (who state "a vision of the place of the believing community in history"), "agents of memory" (who help us attend to Scripture and worship), "agents of linguistic self-consciousness" (including teachers and theologians), and "agents of order and due process" (who oversee and moderate the conversation).[39] This multifaceted conversation recognizes that moral insight depends on both the intellect and the affections, both of which are previously formed in community.

I would add to Yoder's description the need for both localized, contextual decision-making and churchwide discernment and pronouncements. While the bulk of our conversation should take place in congregations and conferences, the example of the Jerusalem Conference in Acts 15 reminds us that there is also a need for broader church discussions.

Our grappling with biotechnology desperately needs the type of conversation Yoder describes. Spirit-driven, open conversation that invites various gifts and perspectives and that moves toward consensus will serve us well as we discern how we should engage these new powers. I now turn to examples surrounding biotechnology that require such attention.

The rhetoric of health and the role of wealth

Most biotechnology is promoted as aiding in human health, healing, and general flourishing. These claims are often justified. However, we need ongoing communal discernment to detect when the rubric of health and healing is concealing vested interests that might be morally troubling—for example, discerning when the underlying driving force is the acquisition of wealth rather than the promotion of health.

The need to parse out the rubric of health from other driving forces, especially economic ones, is suggested by several conference participants. Conrad Brunk, for instance, notes that besides beneficence and the desire to alleviate suffering, biotechnology is driven by social values and forces such as the quest for knowledge, the attraction of the technically sweet, the imperatives within technology itself, and competitive global economics.[40] Lawrence Ressler worries that the powers of biotechnology will likely further concentrate power and wealth in the hands of a few big businesses. Ressler rightly points out that Scripture continually warns against the concentration of wealth and that recent scandals involving big business corruption "are not aberrations in history."[41] Laura Powers is equally candid in urging us not to underestimate how much of biotechnology is propelled by vested economic interests.[42]

Parsing the acquisition of wealth from the promotion of health is often difficult and will require communal wisdom. Consider, for example, conference participant John Gearhart's interesting paper on stem cell research. Gearhart offers several "proof-of-principles" examples that suggest significant long-term health benefits resulting from this research. Yet, in arguing for full funding of this research, Gearhart appeals to our economic interests, pointing out that the "commercial" arms of many foreign governments are investing heavily in this research and that we risk losing important "intellectual property" if we do not follow suit.[43] How should the community of faith weigh such arguments? We need the church community's assorted voices and gifts if we are to faithfully weigh our desire to promote healing, our respect for the human embryos from which the stem cells are derived, and the economic interests promoting stem cell research.

Another example of needing to parse out the economic driving factors is suggested by Randall Longnecker's mention of testing for cystic fibrosis (CF).[44] As Longnecker observes, the tests available in their office primarily identify the forms of the CF mutation that impact those of Northern European descent. The tests are not particularly effective at identifying the forms of CF most frequent among people of Asian descent, a population in which CF is much less common. My understanding is that the same type of testing discrepancy exists between available, effective tests for those of Northern European descent and the lack of such tests to identify the dominant CF mutations among certain Native American groups, among whom CF is relatively common.[45]

Economics plays a significant role in this testing discrepancy in two related ways. First, the folks with the most significant economic power (those from Northern Europe) fund research most likely to benefit themselves. Thus, since CF is relatively common among Caucasians, tests are developed to identify this disorder. And since CF has numerous mutations, tests are developed to identify those mutations most common among Caucasians.

Second, the tests are developed for the demographic groups most likely to produce economic gain. Too few folks of Asian descent are affected by CF for the tests to be financially profitable. Too few Native American communities have the financial resources for those tests to be profitable. In short, wealth, both existing relative wealth and the acquisition of new wealth, guides the dispersion of this genetic test. How does our faith community think through and respond to this disparity?

Still another example of our need to wrestle with the role of wealth concerns patents. The United States has always offered patent protection to stimulate innovation, growth, and competitiveness. Granting the patent holder exclusive control over an innovation encourages investment and risk-taking by granting protection from imitators and offering the possibility of enormous profits. Over its history the U.S. has issued over five million patents, and the economic incentive associated with patents has been a driving factor in technological development, including developments in biotechnology. Present U.S. law allows the patenting of "whatever people can engineer, including living material."[46]

This patent situation encourages research and investment in biotechnology and has resulted in many promising developments. However, this open-ended approach to patents in biotechnology occasions two types of morally objectionable scenarios. First, exclusive control over such a wide range of developments makes it likely that some promising developments in biotechnology will be available only to the wealthy. For example, under current patent law access to the ability to identify and attack a protein produced by a cancer mutation or to a new vector technology for delivering gene therapy or a genetic specific pharmaceutical application could be limited to those with the financial resources to meet the patent-holder's asking price.

Limited access to new developments based in part in patent law is a real possibility, as is driven home by conference participant Timothy Jost's observations regarding the pharmaceutical industry.[47] As Jost observes, we already face a situation where access to pharmaceuticals is rationed according to wealth, where the poor and minorities lack equal access. The pharmaceutical industry is enormously profitable and is a dominant player in developing biotechnology and acquiring the consequent patents. Given the current pharmaceutical example, that access to developments in biotechnology will be limited according to wealth seems likely in the foreseeable future. Thus the very patent system that helps to drive developments in biotechnology also limits access to those developments.

The second type of concern regarding patents is that the current law may actually create an incentive for research and development we would find morally objectionable. Hypothetically speaking, one could patent a method of gene transfer for creating an altered human embryo that is especially useful in cancer research or for transgenic embryos or even for creating brain-less "near-humans" to be used for harvesting organs.[48] The point of these hypotheticals is that the current open-ended patent system may provide a financial incentive for morally dubious biotechnological developments against which there are no laws and for which there would be a market. As long as the U.S. grants patents to anything that can be engineered, there are at least potential financial incentives for developments in biotechnology that we in the church are likely to find troubling.

As the examples of embryonic stem cell research, cystic fibrosis, and patents suggest, we will need a discerning community to parse out the role of wealth from the rubric of health. Sometimes health really is the dominant agenda. Sometimes we will conclude that the search for wealth and the promotion of health are perfectly compatible. But it will require our best wisdom to uncover when the drive for wealth is undermining health, promoting injustice, or driving us toward frightening realities previously only imagined in science fiction.

It will also require our best wisdom to determine how we should respond. Should we use tests that are available to us solely because of our color or wealth? What advice do we offer our doctors and scientists when their research is promising but the origin or direction of the funding is questionable? Should we lobby Congress for specific kinds of legislation? What kinds? Should we use our voice as stockholders in biotechnology firms or should we remove our funds when the drive for wealth seems to overrun the concern for health? These are a mere sampling of the questions that cry out for a discerning community.

Who we are and who we will become

Communal wisdom is also needed in making judgments about who we are now and who we likely will become by engaging in certain practices made possible by biotechnology. As I suggested in my presentation on parental anxiety, who we are now (for good and for ill) is likely to have an enormous impact on the types of choices we make regarding biotechnology. If we hope to make Christian choices as we engage this technology, we need each other's wisdom to identify and confront the unchristian aspects of our current selves. Put frankly, my only chance of making Christian choices is if my Christian brothers and sisters have the courage to lovingly point out my unchristian attitudes, beliefs, and practices regarding children, parenting, the poor, and so on. Without that supportive accountability, I will almost inevitably make choices that reflect weaknesses in who I am now.

Even this way of putting a concern for "who we are" is too individualistic because the question is not merely "Who am I now?" but also "Who are we now?" All of us are situated within communities whose language, worldview, and values we share. The choices we make reflect and reinforce or diverge and challenge those community values.

Parenting is again the good example. Decisions about when to have children and what children to have are made within a community ethos. Consider, for example, the greater social value placed on boys over girls in India and China. When this social value regarding children (part of who we are) is combined with the technology of amniocentesis, we have families routinely choosing to terminate unwanted females. This combination of "who we are" and biotechnology then influences "who we will become" by reinforcing the social preference for boys and the resulting skewed gender ratios.[49]

Who we are, individually and socially, is therefore a significant consideration as we approach biotechnology. And there are reasons for concern about who we are in the U.S. In terms of parenting, already three decades ago Christian ethicists were warning that "increasingly the concern is with making perfect children and making children perfect," replacing a tradition of uncalculated nurture, trust, and acceptance.[50] The ready availability of sperm banks where one can choose the appearance, social standing, and IQ of the donor, as well as the frequency with which parents program virtually every moment of their children's days, are current examples that give credence to that warning.

We are also a people with a frightening history of, and current propensity toward, eugenics. As the mention of Walter Rauschenbusch in conference participant Stanley Hauerwas's response implies, advocates of eugenics spanned the political and social spectrum during the first half of the twentieth century.[51] Some used eugenic arguments to advance nationalism, class and race discrimination, and immigration restrictions. But others saw eugenics as a way of breaking down class distinctions and helping to eliminate the causes of poverty.[52]

The eugenic movement included both "positive" efforts to produce more folks with wanted characteristics and "negative" efforts to eliminate less fit individuals by eliminating their ability to reproduce. On the positive side, folks with certain characteristics, such as high intelligence or social standing, were urged to marry folks with similar characteristics and were urged to have more children. On the negative side, tens of thousands of Americans were sterilized, usually against their will, and often while in prison or homes for the mentally ill.[53]

Much of the original inspiration for the Nazi eugenics movement came from the eugenics efforts in the U.S. and Britain. The eventual discrediting of an overt eugenics movement in the U.S. came from several directions, including better scientific understandings of the importance of environmental influences on how organisms develop, a papal condemnation of eugenics, and the recognition of the horrors carried out by the Nazis in the name of eugenics.[54]

While there are now few explicit proponents of eugenics, there are signs that our culture ("who we are") still tends toward positive and negative eugenics. It is my concern about current eugenic tendencies that makes me ambivalent about presentations such as conference participant Ruth Schwartz Cowan's case study of Cyprus.

I agree with Cowan that the testing program in Cyprus is a good example of using genetic screening for public health. Most U.S. population screenings of newborns are to be commended on the same grounds. However, if I read her rightly, Cowan's presentation includes a sub-theme that we are not headed toward the bottom of the slippery slope of eugenics since decisions about genetic testing are being determined "generally and culturally" rather than by a centralized authority.[55] This sub-theme is questionable.

It seems likely that an open, capitalist, consumer oriented market is just as capable of heading down the eugenics trail as is a centralized, tyrannical power. Our society spends tens of millions of dollars annually on cosmetic surgery; every newsstand includes dozens of magazines that focus on looking better; "Ultimate Makeover" and "The Swan" are centerpieces of primetime television. In such a setting, putting genetic technology in the hands of the consumer—that is, making choices "generally and culturally" about biotechnology— is a near sure recipe for eugenics.

Evidence for our current eugenic tendencies comes from many directions. For instance, despite an official policy of being "value neutral," there is anecdotal evidence that genetic counselors often depict the consequences of various genetic disorders in the bleakest terms, even though for most conditions a positive diagnosis reveals little about the severity of the disability's expression. Folks are routinely encouraged to terminate pregnancies that reveal a disorder and routinely encouraged to refrain from having children if they themselves carry a disorder.[56]

Relatedly, of women offered prenatal genetic testing, 50 percent accept, and of those, 90 percent will terminate the pregnancy upon the diagnosis of down syndrome (trisomy 21). Moreover, the majority will terminate pregnancies if ultrasound or other tests reveal abnormalities such as cleft palate or an extra digit on the hands or feet.[57]

Besides these more "negative" eugenic tendencies, we have evidence of our "positive" eugenic tendencies in our experience with hGH (human growth hormone). Previously retrieved from fresh cadavers, hGH was the first hormone we learned to genetically synthesize. This genetic synthesis addressed the limited availability and fears of safety that accompanied the cadaver-derived hormone. The primary therapeutic use of hGH is for children who cannot produce the hormone and will, among other symptoms, end up abnormally short. With the advent of synthesized hormone, two new groups immediately sought access to hGH: athletes and parents of medically normal but statistically short children. These groups were not seeking therapy but enhancement.[58]

In broader social terms, who we are includes some tendency toward eugenics. It will take the wisdom of Christian community to identify when we are succumbing to the same tendencies. It will take the grace of Christian community to instead make choices from a very different sense of who we are as God's children.

It will also take the wisdom of Christian community to discern the likely influence of biotechnology on who we will become. In thinking through options, we need to ask who we as individuals, community, and society will likely become in adopting those options. Will we become more or less just or generous or humble or welcoming or wise? There is, for instance, concern in the disability community that the routine prenatal screening to eliminate genetic disorders will slowly make our society less welcoming of people with disabilities and more punitive toward parents who choose to have children who have genetic disorders.[59]

In making choices about biotechnology or otherwise, we are in part making choices about our future identity and future way of proceeding in the world. In discussing parenting, Alan Verhey wonderfully captures this future-oriented dynamic of current choices:

> [R]eproductive choices must be considered and evaluated . . . as choices that establish ways of being parents as well as ways of becoming parents. A decision about the reason to become a parent or about the way to become a parent establishes a parental identity and helps determine subsequent parental choices. The woman who chooses to have a child using sperm donated by a Nobel Prize winner in chemistry, for example, is probably more likely than other mothers to enroll her child in the seven-day seminar entitled 'How to Multiply Your Baby's Intelligence'. . . . The choice about how and why to become a parent affects the sort of parent one subsequently will be; it already establishes a parental identity.[60]

What Verhey says of parenting is true in some form of all the questions we confront in biotechnology—in our choices we help to establish our future identity and a way of being. What Verhey's comment leaves unsaid is that we need the wisdom of Christian community if we are to make these choices well.

In thinking about who we are and who we will become, we need to recognize that Christians are called to strive toward perfection.[61] Some accounts of biotechnology also talk about moving toward perfection. But these are different accounts of perfection. There is no gene therapy or genetic enhancement to move us toward the Christ-like perfection of nonviolent love, endless generosity, genuine humility, mercy, joy, hope, and so on. Instead, it is amid the Christian community's mutual moral counsel that we are most likely to discern what choices will move us toward becoming the kind of people we are called by Christ to be.

Asking the right questions

In practical moral reasoning, it is unlikely that we will reach the right conclusions if we are not asking the right questions. One gift of Christian communal discernment is that we can help each other ask the right questions. There are multiple examples of this help in the conference presentations. For example, Stanley Hauerwas's response tries in various ways to ask whether we were even asking the right questions. Hauerwas argues that we were being rhetorically co-opted into accepting as our own the cultural values shaping developments in biotechnology. He illustrates this concern in various ways, including challenging the plural use of "creations" in the conference name, highlighting John Gearhart's rhetorical turn in suggesting that scientists must "listen to society," and disputing LeRoy Walters's assertion that Anabaptists believe in a strong separation between church and state. Both in the broader argument and in the specifics, Hauerwas's response attempts to help us ask the right questions by challenging the questions that we are asking.

Conrad Brunk challenges us to ask the right questions about the implicit consequentialist thinking that often surrounds discussions of biotechnology. In particular, Brunk points out our inability to actually calculate consequences by pointing to numerous unintended consequences.[62] And more poignant, he suggests that as Anabaptists we are vulnerable to consequentialist calculations because we so highly value the goods of health, healing, and food. Brunk notes "that the almost unconditional commitments" to these goods "may blind Anabaptists to the limits that are needed to respect the way in which Anabaptists pursue goods . . . [upon which] the whole nonresistance philosophy is based."[63] Brunk thereby challenges us to ask better questions by showing us how our commitment to some values may be causing us to ignore others.

Arlene Wiens implicitly invites us to ask different questions when she underlines our society's propensity to spend on high technology at the beginning and end of life while badly underfunding public health initiatives. The same invitation is visible when Wiens recalls the common nursing experience that our treatments often do more *to* patients than *for* them.[64]

Hauerwas, Brunk, and Wiens provide examples of helping us ask the right questions. Still, not all conference presentations may ask the right questions. For example, Carole Cramer outlines efforts to develop a mucosal vaccine for amoebic dysentery, a waterborne disease associated with poor sanitation.[65] Why focus, however, on helping people cope through vaccination with poor water rather than focus on the social/political/economic situation that forces folks to live with unsanitary water? This effort strikes me as looking for a technological solution to a political and economic problem.

Here again we need the community's wisdom to know if we are asking the right questions about amoebic dysentery. In this determination we need multiple voices, including church relief workers and water specialists who strive to improve sanitation in poor countries, political analysts who know the social and economic issues, and scientists who understand the pros and cons of developing this type of mucosal vaccine.

LeRoy Walters's paper on human embryonic stem cell research also makes me wonder whether we are asking the right questions. For instance, Walters refers to "the moral status of the five-day old human embryo" as "a central ethical question" and as "[p]robably the most central and debated ethical question surrounding human embryonic stem cell research."[66] I do not dispute that this is a significant question, but I wonder if the question is overvalued and whether this is an example of allowing the world to frame the question for us. Perhaps the central question regarding human embryonic stem cell research is whether this is a just use of society's wealth, a possibility suggested by Wiens's comments about public health. Or perhaps the central question is what kind of people we will become as we pursue this research and how it might change our understanding of practices such as parenting.

I do not claim to know the central issue here. I do claim that we need the church community's discernment in figuring out the right questions to ask regarding this research. Is the central question the status of the embryo, the justice of the financing, the character-shaping power of the research, some combination of these questions, or another set of questions altogether? I can see no way through these murky issues without the mutual moral wisdom of our sisters and brothers in the church.

A similar problem concerns Walters's apparent appeal to popular opinion in persuading us that we should support human embryonic stem cell research. Walters surveys various public policy options regarding this research and structures his presentation to show that the more affirming options have the greatest support among various states and nations. He takes a similar approach in surveying religious views.

It strikes me that Walters is asking and answering the wrong question, a question about public opinion. We can surely learn from others, from their reasoned arguments, and from an account of how their conclusions fit with their other convictions and worldview. But Walters does not provide this type of engagement in his survey. Instead, his policy and religious survey seems geared to convince us that we should support embryonic stem cell research because the majority does.

As Christians, we know that the wide, popular way is often the way to destruction.[67] As Anabaptists, we know what it is to hold convictions as true (such as nonviolence) that are rejected by the majority. It is debatable whether we should even ask about popular opinion, let alone allow it a central place in our moral discernment. I am not arguing against Walters' conviction that we should in some way affirm human embryonic stem cell research. I am of a mixed mind regarding this research and yearn for the community's moral discernment on this matter. What I question is whether Walters is offering us the right question. In this matter, as in so many others, we need the Spirit-led, Bible-reading, multi-gifted community of practical moral reason.

A Contrast Society

My comments have focused on how much we need the church as we face the new powers of biotechnology. I want to conclude by suggesting that a focus on how we live together as church while facing these new powers also has implications for witness and mission.

Yoder and Hauerwas on church as mission

John Howard Yoder and Stanley Hauerwas, an Anabaptist and a friend of Anabaptists respectively, repeatedly claim that the church is meant to be an alternative community or contrast society. While Yoder and Hauerwas are often accused of advocating a withdrawal from surrounding society, their shared emphasis on the church as a contrast society derives from deep commitments to mission and witness, what Yoder once called a "missionary ethic of incarnation."[68] The realization that the church is called to be different from the world, that it is by nature a "minority" (Yoder) or "alien" (Hauerwas) community, is essential to the church's mission to the world. Without this realization, the assumption that we are at home in the world and the desire to be relevant will push the church to concede both faithfulness and an identity particular enough to have anything worth saying to the world.[69] Said more positively, the church's willingness to remain faithful, to be different, and sometimes to stand in opposition to the world is what allows the church to offer good news to the world.

Thus the very center of the church's witness and mission to the world is the church's existence as a contrast model or alternative community.[70] According to Yoder and Hauerwas, when the church's life is faithful to the story of Jesus, it offers nothing less than a "foretaste" and the "first fruits" of the kingdom of God.[71] While the kingdom of God is certainly more than the church, it is in the shared life of the church that we get a hint or preview of God's kingdom come in full. Said differently, the pattern and ways of relating that we find in the church's shared life is a prefiguring or modeling of God's will for human socialness as a whole. Thus the church is to live in such a way that it "represents the kind of society that all of society ought to be" and will be in God's final loving triumph.[72]

The point is that the church's life *is itself* witness and offer to the world. The gathering and practices of the faith community constitute a public offer to the world.[73] When, for example, the church exhibits patience amid the rush and antagonisms of society, when it takes time to nurture friendships, when it serves the neighbor irrespective of how insignificant that neighbor appears to others, then the church's life is witness and mission, a gesture and offer to the world.[74] So too, when the church welcomes the stranger and exhibits the patience to care for widows and orphans, it is offering a contrast model.[75] Indeed, even the act of gathering to attend to God is (or ought to be) an offer to the world by demonstrating that we are one people.[76]

By displaying alternative ways of dealing with conflict, responding to enemies, and handling tragedy, the church offers its own life as an alternative to the world and as a foretaste of God's coming rule.[77] By exhibiting servanthood, truth telling, and hope, the church witnesses to the inbreaking power of God.[78] And when the church refuses to use violence and other illicit means in the name of a just clause, it rejects human presumptuousness and witnesses to the conviction that God in Christ, not us, finally controls history.[79]

This understanding of the church's life as witness and mission does not mean that wider society must accept the church model whole cloth for the church to serve the world by modeling an alternative. For example, Hauerwas observes that, "Schools, hospitals, factories, and social services were all originally social inventions created by Christian moral commitments that forced us to find reasonable responses." He goes on to suggest that current Mennonite practices regarding the law might help others to "find means to avoid the depersonalization of our legal system" and even help reform other relations (such as physician-patient) which are becoming largely adversarial.[80] Yoder similarly points to the church creating institutional models—such as schools, hospitals, voluntary service agencies, even Algerian reforestation—which were later adopted, adapted, and supported by wider society, universities, and governments.[81] Thus, the church models and pioneers practices which may be adopted by the larger society even when it does not come to share the community and convictions that first drive the church to develop those practices.

Living as contrast society in a age of biotechnology

If Yoder and Hauerwas are right, how we respond to biotechnology is not merely a matter of our own purity or ethics; it is also a matter of mission and witness. A few moments within the conference hint at how this witness might work.

Consider Kabiru Kinyanjui's comments about the need for community participation. Kinyanjui argues that current decision-making processes regarding biotechnology ignore different folks within the community and their possible contributions, but that for this technology to have a just impact on society, we need "researchers, politicians, professionals, physicians, parents, and children [to] work together making those kinds of decisions."[82]

These comments from Kinyanjui provide a perfect instance of where the church's life can itself be witness. If we strive, however imperfectly, to live as a community of mutual moral discernment, we will thereby witness to the world, offering the type of community participation that Kinyanjui recognizes as essential for the just appropriation of biotechnology.

Another example of the church's life as witness is suggested by Leslie Biesecker's mention of the Amish.[83] The desire to welcome and care for their children prompts these Amish communities to open their genealogies to outsiders, to participate in adult genetic screening and the use of ultrasound during pregnancy to determine which children should be born in a hospital, instead of at home. By contrast, prenatal diagnosis is not used because it does not fit with their understanding of what is required to welcome and care for their children.

This strikes me as a profound witness at three levels. First, the community selectively appropriates the new technology. They do not shun all of the new developments; neither do they adopt each new technology under the assumption that since it can be done, it should be done. Rather, the technology is accepted or rejected based on whether it fits with existing moral commitments.

Second, the language of choice, individual freedom, and autonomy is absent from Biesecker's description of this case. Instead of focusing on individual desires, we have an example of some type of communal decision making based around shared community values.

Third, there is a different attitude toward children here than is often evident in the wider culture. There is no hint in the Amish example of looking for perfect children, only a community looking to welcome all children who come their way. If the rest of the Anabaptist community can do as well at selective appropriation of biotechnology, community discernment, and the welcoming of children, we will be offering a witness to the world by those very activities.

As a concluding example, let me pick up on the Amish welcoming of children and Roman Miller's mention of adoption. Many concerns about biotechnology surround fears that society will become increasingly less tolerant and welcoming as the technology is used to eliminate disease and handicaps and to select or enhance characteristics. Since our society is already often intolerant, I take it that these fears are well founded. It seems to me that in such an environment the church's example as a community of welcome could be profound witness and alternative. One sign of such welcome is to privilege adoption, especially of those children who are otherwise unlikely to find adoptive families.

I am not an adoptive parent, but I was privileged to pastor for ten years a congregation with several families constituted by adoption. These families were an ever-present sign of welcome, and I saw them as a parable for our own relationship to God, which the apostle Paul describes as that of adopted children.[84] In an age of biotechnology, I can think of no better witness than for the church to readily give emotional and financial support to the practice of adoption.

Notes

1. E.g., Stanley Hauerwas, *In Good Company: The Church As Polis* (Notre Dame, Ind.: University of Notre Dame Press, 1995), 57.

2. See Conrad Brunk, "The Biotechnology Vision: Insight from Anabaptist Values," chapter 8 in this book.

3. See Randall Longnecker, "The Face of Overpowering Knowledge," chapter 20 in this book.

4. See Graydon Snyder, "Bioethics: How Will Anabaptists Respond?" chapter 23 in this book.

5. See Stanley Hauerwas, Anabaptist Eyes on Biotechnology," chapter 26 in this book.

6. See Roman J. Miller, "Viewing Bioethics Through Anabaptist Eyes," chapter 7 in this book.

7. For example, 1 Cor. 14:26; Eph. 5:19; Col. 3:16; cf. Acts 16:25.

8. See Carole Cramer, "Genetically Modified Plants and Organisms," chapter 4 in this book.

9. Ps. 50:10-11, *Contemporary English Version (CEV)*; cf. Ps. 140.

10. Matt. 6:26-30.

11. Rom. 8:19-23.

12. Rebecca Slough, managing ed, *Hymnal: A Worship Book* (Scottdale, Pa.: Mennonite Publishing House, 1992), 34, 48, 46, 89, 390.

13. See Stanley Hauerwas, "Anabaptist Eyes on Biotechnology," chapter 26 in this book.

14. E.g., "Supreme Court Rejects Patent on Genetically-Modified Mouse," *CBC.CA News*, Dec. 5, 2002, http://www.cbc.ca/stories/2002/12/05/scc_mouse021205.

15. Andrew Pollack, "Cloned Cows Are Engineered To Speed Up Cheese Making," *New York Times*, 27 January 2003, http://www.nytimes.com/2003/01/27/national/27MILK.html?tntemail1.

16. See John Gearhart "The New Genetics: Stem Cell Research and Cloning," chapter 1 in this book.

17. By contrast Nobel laureate Paul Berg has argued for a search for knowledge that has "no boundaries." See: Abigail McDaniel, "Recent Genetic Innovations Raise Troubling Ethical Questions," *The Stanford Daily*, 9 February 2004, http://daily.stanford.edu/tempo?page=content&id=13036&repository=0001_article.

18. Allen Verhey, *Reading the Bible in the Strange World of Medicine* (Grand Rapids: William B. Eerdmans Publishing Company, 2003), 152–53.

19. Leon R. Kass, "Why We Should Ban Human Cloning Now: Preventing a Brave New World," *The New Republic*, 21 May 2001, http://www.thenewrepublic.com/052101/kass052101.html.

20. Virtuous and vicious people alike take their anger to indicate injustice. The difference is that the former are more likely than the latter to be able to evaluate the appropriateness of their strong emotional response and that in the former that strong response is more often rightly placed.

21. Anthony Bloom, *Beginning to Pray* (Ramsey: Paulist Press, 1970), 82.

22. Bloom, *Beginning to Pray*, 91.

23. Michael K. Duffey, *Be Blessed in What You Do: The Unity of Christian Ethics and Spirituality* (New York: Paulist Press, 1988), 38.

24. Richard J. Foster, *Prayer: Finding the Heart's True Home* (San Francisco: Harper, 1992), 81.

25. Richard Bondi, *Leading God's People: Ethics for the Practice of Ministry* (Nashville: Abingdon Press, 1989), 143–44.

26. See: The Cyber Hymnal, "It is Well with My Soul," http://www.cyber-hymnal.org/htm/i/t/itiswell.htm.

27. Rev. 3:7-13.

28. Rev. 21:2-8.

29. See Carl D. Bowman, "Emerging Biotechnologies: A Historical Perspective," chapter 13 in this book.

30. Ibid.

31. Troy Duster, "Behavioral Genetics, Genetic Technology, and the Problem of Public Understanding," paper presented at Sequencing the Future: Ethical, Legal and Social Issues Arising from the Human Genome Project (California State University, Long Beach, 2001), http://ethics.acusd.edu/video/CSULB/Genome/3_duster.html.

32. See Conrad Brunk, "The Biotechnology Vision: Insight from Anabaptist Values," chapter 8 in this book.

33. Ibid.

34. E.g., Heb. 2:15; cf. 1 Peter 3:9-15.

35. See Graydon Snyder, "Bioethics: How Will Anabaptist Respond?" chapter 23 in this book.

36. Statements such as "Anabaptists approve the use of stem cells and fetal tissue unless the tissue comes from an implanted fetus" are particularly unfounded and probably inflammatory (Graydon Snyder, "Bioethics: How Will Anabaptists Respond?" See p. 222 in this book.). Snyder might be right about what we should conclude, but we are yet to have the conversations needed to substantiate such claims. The few documented Anabaptist-related conversations about biotechnology are referenced in: Joseph J. Kotva Jr, *The Anabaptist Tradition: Religious Beliefs and Healthcare Decisions*, Religious Traditions and Health Care Decisions Handbook Series (Park Ridge: Park Ridge Center, 2002).

37. John Howard Yoder, *The Priestly Kingdom: Social Ethics As Gospel* (Notre Dame: University of Notre Dame Press, 1984), 15–45.

38. Ibid, 36.

39. Ibid.

40. See Conrad Brunk, "The Biotechnology Vision: Insight from Anabaptist Values," chapter 8 in this book.

41. See Lawrence Ressler, "Menno Simons, Anabaptism, and the Promises of Biotechnology," chapter 19 in this book.

42. See Laura E. Powers, "Biotechnology through the Lens of Public Policy," chapter 15 in this book.

43. See John Gearhart, "The New Genetics: Stem Cell Research and Cloning," chapter 1 in this book.

44. See Randall Longnecker, "The Face of Overpowering Knowledge," chapter 20 in this book.

45. Duster, "Behavioral Genetics."

46. Stephen F. Sherry, "The Incentive of Patents," in *Genetic Ethics: Do the Ends Justify the Genes?* ed. John F. Kilner, Rebecca D. Pentz, and Frank E. Young (Grand Rapids: William B. Eerdmans Publishing Company, 1997), 113.

47. See Timothy S. Jost, "Biotechnology and Public Policy: An Anabaptist Response," chapter 22 in this book.

48. Cf. Sherry, "The Incentive of Patents," 118–19.

49. Cf. Glenn McGee, *The Perfect Baby: Parenthood in the New World of Cloning and Genetics*, 2nd. ed. (Lanham: Rowman and Littlefield, 2000), 16.

50. Allen Verhey, "The Death of Infant Doe: Jesus and the Neonates," in *On Moral Medicine: Theological Perspective in Medical Ethics*, ed. Stephen E. Lammers and Allen Verhey (Grand Rapids: William B. Eerdmans Publishing Company, 1987), 492.

51. See Stanley Hauerwas, "Anabaptist Eyes on Biotechnology," chapter 26 in this book.

52. McGee, *The Perfect Baby*, 10–11.

53. Arthur J. Dyck, "Eugenics and Historical and Ethical Perspective," in *Genetic Ethics: Do the Ends Justify the Genes?* ed. John F. Kilner, Rebecca D. Pentz, and Frank E. Young (Grand Rapids: Wm. B. Eerdmans, 1997), 27; McGee, *The Perfect Baby*, 15.

54. McGee, *The Perfect Baby*, 10; Dyck, "Eugenics and Historical and Ethical Perspective," 28–29; Pope Pius XI, "Casti Connubii: Encyclical of Pope Pius XI on Christian Marriage" (1930), #68-70, http://www.vatican.va/holy_father/pius_xi/encyclicals/documents/hf_p-xi_enc_31121930_casti-connubii_en.html.

55. See Ruth Schwartz Cowan, "Eugenics, Genetic Screening, and the Slippery Slope," chapter 11 in this book.

56. Dyck, "Eugenics and Historical and Ethical Perspective," 30–34; cf. Dorothy Wertz, "Drawing Lines: Notes for Policymakers," in *Prenatal Testing and Disability Rights*, ed. Erik Parens and Adrienne Asch (Washington, D.C.: Georgetown University Press, 2000), 278.

57. See Amy Laura Hall's comments during the panel presentation at: "Custom Kids? Genetic Testing of Embryos," The Genetics and Public Policy Center (Renaissance Washington Hotel, Washington, D.C., 8 January, 2004), http://www.dnapolicy.org/policy/pgdForum.html.

58. Thomas H. Murray, "The Ethics of Genetic Enhancement: How Far Would You Go to Improve Your Game?" paper presented at San Diego Science & Technology Council conference presentation, 8 September (2003), http://ethics.sandiego.edu/video/SDSTC/Murray/index.html.

59. DPI Europe, "Disabled People Speak on the New Genetics," http://www.dpieurope.org/htm/bioethics/dpsngfullreport.htm.

60. Verhey, *Reading the Bible in the Strange World of Medicine*, 168–69.

61. Matt. 5:48; cf. 5:20, 19:21; 1 Cor. 9:24-27; Phil. 2:16, 3:11-17; Gal. 2:2; Heb. 12:1-3

62. See Conrad Brunk, "The Biotechnology Vision: Insight from Anabaptist Values, " chapter 8 in this book.

63. Ibid.

64. See Arlene Wiens, "Biotechnology through a Nursing Ethics Lens," chapter 16 in this book.

65. See Carole Cramer, "Genetically Modified Plants and Organisms," chapter 4 in this book.

66. See LeRoy Walters, "Ethical Issues in Biotechnology: Human Embryonic Stem Cell Research and the Anabaptist Vision," chapter 9 in this book.

67. Matthew 7:13-14

68. Yoder, *The Priestly Kingdom*, 44.

69. John Howard Yoder, *For the Nations: Essays Public & Evangelical* (Grand Rapids: William B. Eerdmans Publishing Company, 1997), 48-49, cf., 51-55; Hauerwas, *In Good Company*, 53-56; Arne Rasmusson, *The Church as Polis: From Political Theology to Theological Politics as Exemplified by Jürgen Moltmann and Stanley Hauerwas*, Revised (Notre Dame, Ind.: University of Notre Dame Press, 1994), 210-11.

70. E.g., Stanley Hauerwas, *A Community of Character: Toward a Constructive Christian Social Ethic* (Notre Dame, Ind.: University of Notre Dame Press, 1981), 50, 84.

71. Stanley Hauerwas, *The Peaceable Kingdom: A Primer in Christian Ethics* (Notre Dame, Ind.: University of Notre Dame Press, 1983), 60-62; Stanley Hauerwas, *Against the Nations: War and Survival in a Liberal Society* (Minneapolis: Winston Press, 1985), 119; Hauerwas, *In Good Company*, 157; Philip LeMasters, *The Import of Eschatology In John Howard Yoder's Critique of Constantinianism* (Lewiston, N.Y.: Edwin Mellen Press, 1992), 33-34, 68-69; Yoder, *For the Nations*, 228; John Howard Yoder, *The Royal Priesthood: Essays Ecclesiological and Ecumenical* (Grand Rapids: William B. Eerdmans Publishing Company, 1994), 146; John Howard Yoder, *The Christian Witness to the State* (Newton: Faith and Life Process, 1964), 10; Yoder, *The Priestly Kingdom*, 92.

72. Yoder, *The Priestly Kingdom*, 93; see also Hauerwas, *In Good Company*, n.12, p. 250.

73. Yoder, *For the Nations*, 27-28; Hauerwas, *The Peaceable Kingdom*, 99-100.

74. Stanley Hauerwas, *Christian Existence Today: Essays on Church, World, and Living in Between* (Durham, N.C.: Labyrinth Press, 1988), 105-06.

75. Hauerwas, *The Peaceable Kingdom*, 144; Hauerwas, *Community of Character*, 10-11.

76. Hauerwas, *In Good Company*, 157; Hauerwas, *The Peaceable King-*

dom, 100, cf., 108.

77. Rasmusson, *The Church as Polis*, 314.

78. Yoder, *For the Nations*, 233-34.

79. John Howard Yoder, *The Politics of Jesus*, second ed. (Grand Rapids: William B. Eerdmans Publishing Company, 1994), 228-47, cf; Hauerwas, *Community of Character*, 11; Stanley Hauerwas, *Dispatches from the Front: Theological Engagements with the Secular* (Durham: Duke University Press, 1994), 116-35; Hauerwas, *The Peaceable Kingdom*, 136-41.

80. Hauerwas, *Christian Existence Today*, 81-82.

81. John Howard Yoder, *The Original Revolution: Essays on Christian Pacifism* (Scottdale, Pa.: Herald Press, 1977), 157-58.

82. See Kabiru Kinyanjui, "Crosscultural Approach to Biotechnology," chapter 12 in this book.

83. See Leslie Biesecker, "Human Genetic Therapies and Manipulations," chapter 3 in this book.

84. Rom. 8:15, 23; Gal. 4:5; Eph. 1:5.

CHAPTER THIRTY

All Considered: Shared Themes and Growing Edges

James C. Peterson

Dr. James C. Peterson is the R. A. Hope Professor of Theology and Ethics and director of the Ph.D. program at McMaster Divinity College at McMaster University.

Conrad Brunk writes that he saw as much variety of views through Anabaptist eyes at the conference from which this book emerged as he has in secular meetings with no claim of a common community. As the book demonstrates, the conference included a rich variety of perspectives and insights. That was not disillusioning; the purpose of the conference was to engage and inform the discussion, not end it. It may also be a better goal to seek harmony than unison. Harmony is not anarchic freedom but coordinated differences that enrich the whole. Have harmonious themes already developed at this early stage of discussion? The Anabaptist tradition hopes and looks for them as a result of listening together for the direction of one Lord.

While there are no formal poll results to report, reflecting on what was said at the conference and written afterward by conference participants, some themes of substantial consensus do seem to be developing. These are briefly summarized below and followed as well by a description of some of the differences. This description of common and contested themes is unavoidably an interpretation. Part of the ongoing discussion would rightfully be how to further refine this summary as well as how to best develop the many remaining growing edges.[1]

Shared Themes

The center

Each day of the conference began with hymns of praise and thanks to God the creator. That was a fitting context for the deliberations. The Anabaptist tradition has always sought to honor God at the center of all that is, including the daily practices of God's people. The attempt of the conference was not for human beings alone to plan their lives but rather to recognize God's direction. For Anabaptists, God's character and will are particularly revealed in Jesus Christ. Menno Simons often began his writings with the text of 1 Corinthians 3:11: "For no one can lay any foundation other than the one that has been laid; that foundation is Jesus Christ." The conference participants often turned to the example, teaching, and ongoing life of Jesus Christ.

Jesus is lauded not only for ideas but also for life practice. Anabaptists seek to be not just solitary believers in Jesus Christ but followers of him together. The result is not just a list of avoidances but ways to be, to live, to contribute. Neighbor love cannot be equated with simple utilitarian maximization of some good, but it does include an orientation and living choice to serve and help our neighbors to the best of our ability. The lauded commitments and actions of Mennonite Central Committee would be an example.

There was also an evident commitment to actively listen to one another. Anabaptists have long perceived that God chooses to reveal his ways and will through his people. That requires his people actively to seek to hear the breadth of voices of those who follow Christ. The design of the conference and the actions of the participants exemplified that commitment.

Calling

While one should listen broadly within the faith community, there was an expectation that the Anabaptist perspective and life would likely be distinct from the broader culture and even much of Christendom. Anabaptists have often been a persecuted minority. Indeed part of their tradition of service is to be different, to embody an alternative way of life. While there were a few references to public policy, most of the discussion focused on what Christians should do, not what governments should legislate. Most participants seemed more interested in leading by example, trying to offer a working, visible, alternative, than in forging requirements for the wider society.

The first and often all-consuming responsibility of the Christian community is to live out a called and distinct life, not to assure that society turns out right.

Part of that call is our care for the physical world that God has entrusted to us. It remains God's creation. We are responsible for how we treat it. For much of its history Anabaptists have farmed the land and so feel acutely the sense of stewardship of that resource and the benefit of being able to use fewer pesticides or to increase yields. Humans have always shaped nature from the slingshot as an arm extender to leavened bread.[2] The world can be shaped to better feed the hungry, to relieve suffering, to heal. We should do all that we can to meet the needs of the people of the world, particularly those in greatest need. Of course, these worthy goals are not our only concern and how they are obtained matters as well.

Means

Granted the common warning today that particular facts are always presented from a perspective, getting the facts as straight as possible was a priority at the conference. Care was taken to ground the conference in an accurate understanding of current and near capabilities as described by leaders in their fields.

It was widely advocated that we can show due respect for God's creation while safely shaping plants and animals to better serve. Creation has been entrusted to us as a garden, not as a wilderness.

As to our own physical form, there was a clear recognition that genes are limited in their import. They shape only part of our physical form and the physical is only part of what matters in life. Genetic intervention cannot offer utopia and should not be allowed to distract us from what is most important, yet rightfully used it can be of genuine service.

How genetic intervention is used will affect our attitudes toward God, creation, and one another. We would do well to approach these challenges with Christian virtues such as patience, humility, and hope that build not fear, rather respectful caution and a servant's heart. To live in that way we will need to listen carefully to one another as our one Lord works in each and in all of us.

Growing Edges

While the above themes were widely affirmed, there were ideas that were briefly raised without time to address them or that revealed that we were far from consensus. The following describes some of the discussion at those points that calls for our further attention. Most prominent were ones that could be grouped around questions of the parent/child relationship or the provision of genetic intervention.

Parents and children

Human genetic intervention is likely to be most effective early in development when the recipients either cannot speak for themselves with mature competence or are utterly silent. Many decisions may fall then to parents. The concern was raised that intervening genetically in one's children may cause parents to see their children as artifacts of their own making. That would certainly be an ill turn; yet when a child is born now with a cleft palate and parents authorize surgery so their child will be able to better eat and speak, they are not automatically desensitized to their child as an entrusted gift. They intervene in their child's physical form precisely because they love him and further, are responsible to do what they can to help him.

Physical intervention of itself need not cause one to think of the recipient as a thing or product. Full acceptance of a child need not subvert care. A mother may regularly scrutinize her daughter's fair skin for cancerous moles to remove them before they risk the child's life. Such scrutiny and intervention would not show or trigger any less acceptance of her daughter, rather lovingly protecting and caring for her. Would genetic interventions have a different effect?

Does rejecting the status quo by deliberately intervening inevitably lead down a slippery slope to eugenics? We will need to clarify if our concern is with a conceptual slippery slope or a social one. Both see initial steps as acceptable of themselves, but then leading to horrible ones. The first sees no logical reason to stop between the first steps and the later horrors. The second is concerned that despite good reasons to stop, once the first step is taken, society will descend to the worst abuses whether there are good reasons to stop or not. To apply a slippery slope argument in this case, we also will need to define what it is about eugenics that is to be avoided, in that "eugenics" literally means a healthy birth, not of itself a bad thing. Is the eugenics concern with eugenics itself or how it has been used in the past as an excuse for racist coercion and even murder? Must eugenics by its very nature always lend itself to such abuse?

Would intervention in our children violate their dignity? Dignity has often been cited, especially in the European discussion, but has functioned like a Rorschach test that seems to refer to whatever the speaker sees. The first step in hearing this concern would be to explain more clearly what dignity actually means.

Again because many genetic interventions are proposed for early in development, the status of the human embryo was either directly addressed by most speakers or attempts were offered to frame discussion away from that question. Trying to discern the status of the human embryo is a discussion as old as at least Aristotle, yet as new as embryos in vitro. It is hard to avoid in that whether one is dealing with a fellow human being or not would seem to be quite relevant to appropriate treatment. If five-day-old embryos are protected as fellow human beings, many people lose a promising chance at saving their lives. If embryos are taken apart for their stem cells to work toward life saving measures, the lives of the embryos are lost.

If we protect human embryos, some Anabaptists see fellow human beings (the embryos) being saved and other Anabaptists see the lives of people (afflicted with Parkinsons, Alzheimers, etc) being lost. If we use human embryos, some Anabaptists see fellow human beings (those afflicted with disease) being saved and others see people (the embryos) being lost. For either course, there are some Anabaptists who see fellow human beings saved and some who see the lives of people being lost. It is not surprising that feelings run high with lives at stake.

Further caution was expressed that even if embryos are not yet fellow human beings, sacrificing them would encourage a harmful attitude of disrespect for human life. Others were concerned that forbidding early embryo use for research that might save many lives encourages a harmful attitude of callous indifference to our neighbors in need.

Providing human genetic intervention

Concerning the provision of human genetic intervention, we may have a parallel with the guest who had two complaints about the food catered on her vacation: "Number one, the food was terrible. Number two, the portions were too small." Equitable access is not an issue until one has a clear good to distribute. If human genetic intervention becomes in some cases an accepted good, both safe and efficacious, how will it be made available to those who already struggle with access to food or medical care?

It may be that genetic intervention will begin with affluent parents using their discretionary income to pursue advantages for their children, just as they do now, for example, when providing an expensive private education.[3] In essence, many affluent families may volunteer their children for the last level of standard testing for any new pharmaceutical or other medical intervention, broader population use. Once techniques are relatively perfected, government may have the economic incentive to offer intervention widely to maintain a competitive economy with other countries or as a newly possible contribution to the long-standing goal of equality of opportunity. The greatest challenge concerning provision may become not access, rather balancing child and parent rights in regard to opting out. We see that conflict today in regard to some government required vaccinations. Provision beyond national boundaries will also be complicated as with other goods today.

Onward

Again this conference was intended as a start to the conversation, not its end. Much has been accomplished and there is much more to do. We need each other both to see what we have yet missed and to help each other live rightly according to what we now see we should.

Notes

1. For further reflection on some of the points raised at this conference one might begin with books such as *God and the Embryo*, ed. Brent Waters (Georgetown University Press, Washington, D.C., 2004), or James C. Peterson, *Genetic Turning Points: The Ethics of Human Genetic Intervention* (Grand Rapids: William B. Eerdmans Publishing Company, 2001).

2. These examples are from Carl D. Bowman's presentation.

3. Joseph Kotva suggested that this may be an example of already overprivileging one's children.

The Index

The Editors

Editor **Dr. Roman J. Miller** is the Daniel B. Suter Endowed Professor of Biology at Eastern Mennonite University where he teaches courses in physiology, development biology, philosophy of science and bioethics. His diverse research interests include the role of phytoestrogens in the development of mammalian reproductive tissues and the interaction of Anabaptist thought in bioethics. He is also the editor of *Perspectives on Science and Christian Faith*, the quarterly journal of the American Scientific Affiliation and serves the church as an Overseer for a cluster of five Mennonite congregations.

Editor **Dr. Beryl H. Brubaker** is provost at Eastern Mennonite University. She received her doctor of science in nursing from the University of Alabama at Birmingham. She co-edited Bioethics and the Beginning of Life with Roman Miller in 1990 to publish presentations of a 1987 forum at Eastern Mennonite.

Editor **Dr. James C. Peterson** is the R.A. Hope Professor of Theology and Ethics and director of the Ph.D. program at McMaster Divinity College at McMaster University, one of Canada's leading research universities. He is also an ordained pastor in the American Baptist Churches, holds a PhD in ethics from the University of Virginia, and has been a research fellow in molecular and clinical genetics at the University of Iowa. His recent publications include *Genetic Turning Points: The Ethics of Human Genetic Intervention* and a chapter in *God and the Embryo*.

At the time of his work on this book, Assistant Editor **Timothy H. Shenk** was a sophomore honors student at Eastern Mennonite University pursuing a major in history with minors in biology, psychology, and socioeconomic development. Tim was born and raised in Virginia. He attended Eastern Mennonite High School, where he was editor of the school newspaper and served in various other leadership roles. Hobbies include reading, web development, soccer, singing, and enjoying the outdoors.

At the time of her work on this book, Assistant Editor **Amy K. Stutzman** was a senior at Eastern Mennonite University pursuing a major in English with a minor in journalism. While at EMU, she has enjoyed writing for the school newspaper the *Weather Vane*. Born and raised in Birmingham, Alabama, she attended Parkway Christian Academy, where she was active in the choir and various other organizations. In her free time, she enjoys watching movies, reading, and spending time with friends.

Roman J. Miller   *Beryl H. Brubaker*   *James C. Peterson*

Timothy H. Shenk,   *Amy K. Stutzman*